CW00953938

Monarchy and Lordships
in the Latin
Kingdom of Jerusalem

Monarchy and Lordships in the Latin Kingdom of Jerusalem 1099–1291

STEVEN TIBBLE

CLARENDON PRESS · OXFORD
1989

Oxford University Press, Walton Street, Oxford OX2 6DP
Oxford New York Toronto
Delhi Bombay Calcutta Madras Karachi
Petaling Jaya Singapore Hong Kong Tokyo
Nairobi Dar es Salaam Cape Town
Melbourne Auckland
and associated companies in
Berlin Ibadan

Oxford is a trade mark of Oxford University Press

Published in the United States
by Oxford University Press, New York

British Library Cataloguing in Publication Data
Tibble, Steven
Monarchy and lordships in the Latin Kingdom of Jerusalem,
1099–1291.
1. (Kingdom) Jerusalem. Politics, history
I. Title   320.9569
ISBN 0–19–822731–0

Library of Congress Cataloging in Publication Data
Tibble, Steven.
Monarchy and lordships in the Latin kingdom of Jerusalem.
1099–1291/Steven Tibble.
p. cm.
Includes bibliographical references.
1. Jerusalem—History—Latin Kingdom, 1099–1244. 2. Jerusalem—
Politics and government. 3. Balance of power. 4. Monarchy—
Jerusalem. 5. Jerusalem–Nobility. I. Title.
D183.T53 1989
956.94'4203–dc20   89–23093
ISBN 0–19–822731–0

Typeset by Cambrian Typesetters, Frimley, Surrey
Printed and bound in Great Britain by
Bookcraft Ltd, Midsomer Norton, Bath

To
Jonathan Riley-Smith

Acknowledgements

I WOULD like to express my gratitude to all those who made it easier to write this book: my parents, and brothers Barry and Andrew, for their encouragement; Dr Chris Marshall and Dr Peter Pattinson for their support, both academic and otherwise; Alan Cruickshank for his help with the maps; the staff of the Institute of Historical Research for their patience; and the late Otto Smail for his help with research in Palestine.

I would also like to thank Valin Pollen International, particularly Angus Maitland and Dale Fishburn, who gave me a sabbatical from the world of advertising and PR in order to complete this study.

Most of all, however, I would like to thank Professor Jonathan Rilcy-Smith for his objectivity, constructive comments, and above all for his unfailing enthusiasm. I could not have hoped for a better mentor.

S. T.

Contents

Maps

MAP 1 is derived from J. S. C. Riley-Smith, *The Feudal Nobility and the Kingdom of Jerusalem 1174–1277* (London, 1973). All the other maps are derived from J. Prawer and M. Benvenisti, 'Crusader Palestine', sheet 12/IX of the *Atlas of Israel* (Jerusalem, 1960) and J. S. C. Riley-Smith, *The Knights of St John in Jerusalem and Cyprus, c.1050–1310* (London, 1969).

Tables

Abbreviations

AOL	*Archives de l'orient latin*
B.-B.	*Le Cartulaire du Chapitre du Saint-Sépulcre de Jérusalem*, ed. G. Bresc-Bautier
Cart. du St-Sépulcre	*Cartulaire de l'église du Saint-Sépulcre de Jérusalem*, ed. E. de Rozière
Cart. gén. Hosp.	*Cartulaire général de l'ordre des Hospitaliers de Saint-Jean de Jérusalem (1100–1310)*, ed. J. Delaville Le Roulx
Chartes de Josaphat, ed. Delaborde	*Chartes de la Terre Sainte provenant de l'abbaye de Notre Dame de Josaphat*, ed. H. F. Delaborde
Chartes de Josaphat, ed. Kohler	*Chartes de l'abbaye de Notre-Dame de la vallée de Josaphat en Terre Sainte (1108–1291): Analyse et extraits*, ed. C. Kohler, ROL 7
Cod. dip. geros.	*Codice diplomatico del sacro militare ordine gerosolimitano oggi di Malta*, ed. S. Paoli
EHR	*English Historical Review*
Eracles	*L'Estoire de Eracles empereur et la conqueste de la Terre d'Outremer*, RHC Oc. 1–2
Ernoul	Ernoul, *La Continuation de Guillaume de Tyr (1184–1197)*, ed. M. R. Morgan
Ernoul, ed. Mas-Latrie	Ernoul, *Chronique d'Ernoul et de Bernard le Tresorier*, ed. L. de Mas-Latrie
Hist. dipl. Fred. II	*Historia diplomatica Frederici secundi*, ed. J. L. de Huillard-Breholles

Qalanisi, ed. Gibb	Ibn al-Qalanisi, *Dhail tarikh Dimashq*, extr. tr. H. A. R. Gibb
QFIAB	*Quellen und Forschungen aus italienischen Archiven und Bibliotheken*
Reg. Hier.	*Regesta regni Hierosolymitani 1097–1291*, comp. R. Rohricht
Reg. Hier. Add.	*Regesta regni Hierosolymitani Additamentum 1097–1291*, comp. R. Rohricht
RHC arm.	*Recueil des Historiens des Croisades: Documents arméniens*
RHC lois	*Recueil des Historiens des Croisades: Lois*
RHC oc.	*Recueil des Historiens des Croisades: Historiens occidentaux*
RHC or.	*Recueil des Historiens des Croisades: Historiens orientaux*
RHDFE	*Revue historique de droit français et étranger*
ROL	*Revue de l'orient latin*
Survey of Western Palestine	C. R. Conder and H. H. Kitchener, *Survey of Western Palestine*
Tab. ord. Theut.	*Tabulae ordinis Theutonici*, ed. E. Strehlke
Tafel–Thomas	*Urkunden zur alteren Handels- und Staatsgeschichte der Republik Venedig mit besonderer Beziehung auf Byzanz und die Levante*, ed. G. L. F. Tafel and G. M. Thomas
ZDPV	*Zeitschrift des deutschen Palastina-Vereins*

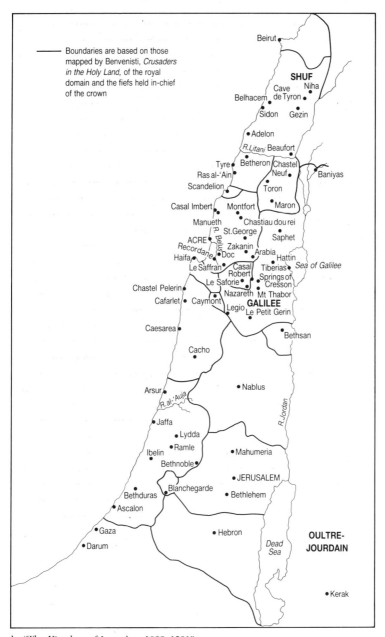

Beirut

SHUF

Cave
Niha
Belhacem de Tyron
Sidon Gezin

Adelon
R.Litani Beaufort
Tyre Betheron Chastel
Ras al-'Ain Neuf
Scandelion Baniyas
Toron
Casal Imbert Montfort Maron
Manueth Chastiau dou rei
St.George
ACRE Zakanin Saphet
Recordane Doc Arabia
Haifa Hattin
Le Saffran Casal Tiberias Sea of Galilee
Robert Springs of
Le Saforie Cresson
Chastel Pelerin Nazareth Mt Thabor
Cafarlet Caymont **GALILEE**
Legio Le Petit Gerin
Caesarea
Bethsan
Cacho
Arsur Nablus
R.al-'Auja
Jaffa
Lydda
Ibelin Ramle Mahumeria
Bethnoble
JERUSALEM
Bethduras Blanchegarde Bethlehem
Ascalon
Gaza Hebron **OULTRE-**
Darum Dead **JOURDAIN**
Sea

Kerak

Boundaries are based on those
mapped by Benvenisti, *Crusaders
in the Holy Land*, of the royal
domain and the fiefs held in-chief
of the crown

R. Belus

R.Jordan

1. "The Kingdom of Jerusalem 1099–1291"

1
Introduction

THE RELATIONSHIP between the monarchy and nobility of the Latin Kingdom of Jerusalem is a subject which has attracted the attention of many historians. Broadly, three views of the relationship between the kings and their lords have been propounded. The first school of thought, of which J. L. La Monte was the last proponent, argued that the Latin Kingdom represented a state of 'pure feudalism' where the king was *primus inter pares* and a vigorous nobility exercised effective control over an emaciated monarchy.[1]

The next generation of historians of the Latin East, of whom Professors Jean Richard and Joshua Prawer are notable, tended to take a rather different view, emphasizing the power of the monarchy and the dynamic nature of feudal society in the kingdom.[2] Still later, Professor Jonathan Riley-Smith, in his examination of the constitutional history of the Latin Kingdom, has put forward the view that the power of the nobility has been underestimated, though his views by no means go as far as those of La Monte.[3]

Useful work has also been carried out on individual lordships of the Latin Kingdom: the most prolific historians in this field have been Professor John La Monte, who was writing in the 1930s, and more recently Professor Hans Mayer. These studies, though raising many important points of detail, have tended to concentrate on the genealogy of seigneurial families, rather than the lordships themselves.[4]

Given the eminence of the historians who have already looked at the relationship between the monarchy and the nobility a fresh

[1] La Monte, *Feudal Monarchy in the Latin Kingdom of Jerusalem, 1100–1291* (see e.g. pp. 88–9).

[2] Richard, *Le Royaume latin de Jérusalem*, pp. 61–79; Prawer and Benvenisti, *Crusader Institutions*, pp. 3–45; Cahen, 'La Féodalité et les institutions politiques de l'Orient latin', in *Oriente et occidente nel medio evo*.

[3] Riley-Smith, *The Feudal Nobility and the Kingdom of Jerusalem, 1174–1277*.

[4] See the bibliography for monographs by La Monte and Mayer.

examination of the subject may appear rather presumptuous. My justification lies in the selection of source materials upon which I have placed most reliance. Previous work on the subject, whatever the final conclusions reached, has primarily been based on the legal texts of the period (generally composed by members of the nobility). I have concentrated my efforts on the surviving charter evidence, supplemented wherever possible by chronicles from the twelfth and thirteenth centuries: I have tended to give little weight to the views of jurists unless these are confirmed by other sources. Also my attention has been focused on those fiefs which were, for most of their history, in the hands of the nobility or generally regarded as seigneuries. Areas which were primarily royal domain land have only been mentioned in passing: the dower lands around Nablus, for instance, have not been dealt with in detail.

It has long been accepted that the legal texts written by the nobility inevitably reflect the attitudes and aspirations of their class and that for this reason the constitutional importance of the lords presented in such texts is exaggerated. Where the lawyers were ostensibly reporting facts, however, the information they present is generally taken at face value: the most important examples of this are John of Ibelin's list of the rights and military quotas of the seigneuries. But these are at the same time both an invaluable source for the period and a positive hindrance to the study of the feudal structure of the Latin Kingdom. By presenting us with a snapshot of the seigneurial system at a specific moment, John has encouraged historians to place less emphasis on the investigation of the fluid nature of the relationship between the king and his leading vassals, and the seigneurial framework within which they all had to operate. Moreover, the lists, as they now survive, are incomplete and often inaccurate. So these ostensibly invaluable lists have, in practice, retarded the study of the nobility by misleading historians on points of detail and, much more importantly, by discouraging potentially fruitful lines of enquiry: although historians have used charter evidence on an *ad hoc* basis, the implicit assumption has tended to be that the feudal map presented by John of Ibelin is substantially correct and little attempt has been made to look actively for lordships or royal policies where the lists give no reason to indicate that any should exist.

As with John of Ibelin, several other sources have had to be used with caution because of their distance from contemporary Palestine, both in terms of geography and time: the 'Lignages d'Outremer' in particular have to be viewed with circumspection.

For more information one must turn to the surviving charter evidence. At first glance these charters are singularly inappropriate for any examination of the monarchy or the nobility as secular records of this kind (with the partial exception of the deeds of the Seigneury of Joscelyn de Courtenay) have been lost. The charters that have come down to us are almost entirely those issued by or to religious institutions and Italian merchant communities and as such present negative evidence, for in many cases they show what properties a given lord could not have owned, or those which he had owned in the past but had now disposed of.

Against their undoubted shortcomings, however, two points need to be made. Firstly, by their sheer number the surviving charters provide a host of specific details which, analysed in the light of other sources, can give us important evidence about secular, as well as religious, society. Secondly, although the evidence provided by them is, by its very nature, 'negative' in terms of much of what it says directly about secular society, the weight of negative evidence is sometimes so great that one can draw very positive conclusions from it. So much evidence exists from religious charters about the Lordship of Caesarea, for instance (see chapter 4), that one can derive a relatively clear picture of land ownership in the seigneury: the weight of evidence telling us what resources within the lordship were *not* available to the lords of Caesarea is such that one has a reasonably accurate view of what the lords *did* have available to them. The cartularies of the Hospitallers, the Teutonic Knights, St Lazarus, the Holy Sepulchre, and the monastery of Our Lady of Josaphat are particularly useful, as will be seen by the frequent reference to them throughout.

Pursuing this line of inquiry has led to a conclusion that I had not expected to find when starting the study: that the relative power of the seigneuries has been substantially overstated, even by Professors Prawer and Richard, and that the monarchy had far more control over the baronage and feudal structure of the kingdom, particularly in the twelfth century, than has hitherto been recognized: a degree of control, moreover, that was sometimes exercised so consistently as to constitute a genuine expression of *policy*.

2

Royal Manipulation of the Feudal Structure

IN any discussion of the balance of power between the monarchy and the nobility of the Latin Kingdom, a primary consideration must be the extent to which the feudal framework was both unchanging in time and rigid in structure. John of Ibelin presents us with a list of the lordships, their rights and obligations. Because of the natural appeal of accepting this list as a key point of reference, historians have tended to assume implicitly, with minor exceptions, that it was a broadly accurate representation of the number and extent of the lordships of the Latin Kingdom, particularly in the twelfth century.

The fluidity or rigidity of the feudal structure lies at the heart of the balance of power between the monarchy and nobility. If we accept that the framework was more or less rigid then we will also have to accept that the king was faced with a series of tenants-in-chief of great power, entrenched in their positions of authority and status. If, on the other hand, we find that the feudal structure was fluid and, moreover, that this fluidity was susceptible to the control of the king, the balance of power in the internal politics of the kingdom clearly swings in favour of the monarchy.

A close examination of the evidence shows that the seigneurial pattern of the Latin Kingdom was indeed far more fluid than has hitherto been imagined and that this fluidity of structure was controlled, either potentially or in practice, by the kings, who could manipulate the feudal structure by a series of mechanisms which were used in an *ad hoc* manner to counter real or perceived threats, protect the wider interests of the kingdom as a whole, or enhance their power. Moreover, as we shall see, there is overwhelming evidence that some royal actions were carried out so consistently, both with regard to different lordships and during different reigns, that they might legitimately be described as acts of royal policy: the Kings of Jerusalem and their central advisers can be seen to have developed an unchanging attitude towards several key aspects of the feudal system in which they operated and developed consistent (though not always successful) responses to those conditions.

The key to the fluidity of the feudal structure lies in four main mechanisms: the reversion of lordships to the royal domain; the ability to create lordships; the retention of lands in the royal domain; and the exercise of deliberate limitations on the extent of existing seigneuries. Though the function and effects of these mechanisms inevitably overlapped, it is perhaps worthwhile to examine each in turn.

The reversion of lordships to the monarchy was in many instances the main opportunity for royal manipulation, by whatever means, to be initiated. The process whereby an existing lordship returned to the control of the royal domain for a period of time was extremely important in shaping the feudal structure of the kingdom, and not just because of the temporary boost it gave to the king's revenues: another significant aspect lay in the power vacuum which such a reversion represented—a vacuum which was filled by the monarchy and could be turned to the king's advantage, even if he did not always choose to do so.

The reversion itself could take place in three main ways. The most common, particularly in the first half of the twelfth century, was when a seigneurial family died out: the high mortality rate of the nobility, coupled with the fact that seigneurial families were not as yet well established, meant that reversion by this means occurred frequently. Again, reversion might be accomplished when the king stepped in forcibly to take possession of a fief owned by a rebellious vassal. As we shall see, there is evidence that this happened several times in the twelfth century (much more often than has hitherto been supposed). Finally, reversion might be accomplished by another overt method: the repossession of the fief by sale or exchange, sometimes even on a semi-involuntary basis on the part of the lord concerned.

It was from the political and structural exploitation of this reversion, rather than just the material gains it produced, that the monarchy derived its most important benefits. While the lordship was in the hands of the king he could change its form, its military potential, and ultimately the degree of power which any future lord of the seigneury would be able to wield. Even if the king chose not to carry out such dramatic changes, he could, at the very least, ensure that the new tenant was a man believed to be reliable and loyal to the monarchy. In short, after any reversion, a lordship was reorganized in a way which would be acceptable to the king.

Ironically, it was the king's power to create new lordships which provided him with one of his most important tools in controlling and manipulating the nobility. The opportunity to create a new lordship occurred in two main circumstances: either when newly captured lands came into the possession of the crown or when an existing seigneury reverted to the royal domain.

Royal policy towards the creation of lordships—and there are strong indications that there was indeed a consistent policy—was naturally enough a response to the feudal framework within which the Kings of Jerusalem found themselves operating. Royal policy in this respect operated in three distinct phases. The first phase, at the beginning of the twelfth century, was one in which the biggest seigneuries of the kingdom were created: the Principality of Galilee, Oultrejourdain, the County of Jaffa, and the 'super-lordship' of Sidon and Caesarea. The looser structure at the beginning of the kingdom's history (a legacy of the sometimes ambiguous relationships of the participants in the first crusade), and the chronic shortage of manpower may partially account for this phenomenon. In a period of unprecedented expansion, when Frankish fervour and confidence was at its height, it may also have been felt that there was plenty of land for everyone and that further additions to the kingdom would follow quickly. Even in this phase, however, embryonic doubts about the wisdom of having such powerful vassals seem to have surfaced: the refusal to give Haifa to Tancred (thereby denying the Principality of Galilee an outlet to the sea) would seem to fall into this category. The second phase saw active steps being taken to reverse the effects of the first. Although the realization that the kingdom was not susceptible to indefinite growth, and an awareness of the inhibitions that very large seigneuries could impose on the monarchy, must have occurred gradually, this transition seems to have taken place relatively quickly. We find that royal actions become increasingly orientated towards the diminution of the larger seigneuries and the creation, often at their expense, of smaller lordships. This process, which we examine in detail below, seems to have been successful in imposing a greater level of royal control over the kingdom: smaller seigneuries presented no threat to the monarchy and could, in some cases, even be made dependent on an administrative centre of the royal domain rather than being accorded the full status of a major lordship.

In terms of the effect of this change of policy on external affairs, however, the royal policy of containing and diminishing the larger lordships was only partially successful. In areas where military pressures were less significant (such as the southern borders or the interior of the kingdom) the creation of smaller lordships does not seem to have had an adverse effect on the ability of the kingdom to defend itself. In areas of high intensity threat, however, smaller lordships seem to have been under-resourced for the military tasks they had to face. We find an increasing recognition on the part of the monarchy that larger seigneurial units should be set in place on the eastern borders, a recognition which marks the third phase of royal policy towards the creation of lordships. Despite the partial failure of the royal policy of creating small lordships at the expense of larger ones (at least in a military context) it is clear that the monarchy could, and did, use the creation of the seigneuries as an extremely effective way of limiting the power of the most threatening element of the nobility in its dealings with the crown.

The retention of lands in the royal domain was another means of exercising control, the effect of which was to ensure that a higher proportion of the kingdom's resources was under direct royal control at any given time. Historians, partially as a result of over-reliance on John of Ibelin, have tended to pre-date the existence of many lordships, placing their creation much earlier than the evidence would suggest. There has also been a tendency to ignore the fact that several lordships were, in fact, part of the royal domain for much of the kingdom's history. The royal ability to retain for long periods of time lands which are generally thought to have been independent lordships is indicative of another way in which the king could pull the balance of power still further in his favour.

Finally, the exercise of deliberate limitations on the extent of the seigneuries was another way in which to increase royal resources at the expense of potentially troublesome vassals. As with estimations of temporal existence, historians have tended to overestimate the geographical extent of many seigneuries. As we shall discuss, in several important cases lands thought to have been part of an independent lordship were, in fact, retained in the royal domain for long periods of time.

Similarly, there was also a clear tendency to 'deny' lands to a lordship which one would otherwise expect to control them. These lands could either be given to another (less threatening) lordship, be formed into a lordship in their own right, or be retained in the royal domain.

It is apparent that the feudal structure retained a much higher degree of fluidity than has hitherto been assumed, and that that fluidity was largely within the control of the monarchy. The following examination of each lordship (in the order in which they were created) shows how royal policy towards the nobility was translated into detailed action.

THE LORDSHIPS OF HEBRON AND BETHGIBELIN

The Lordship of Hebron, and the detachment from it of the Lordship of Bethgibelin, provides an example of one way in which the king could manipulate the feudal structure by the creation of new lordships at the expense of existing ones. The instability of the family lines of the early Lords of Hebron also highlights the way in which frequent reversion to the crown, particularly in the first half of the twelfth century, caused the seigneurial fabric of the Latin Kingdom to be much more fluid than has generally been supposed.

Historians have not been able to agree about the lordship's early history.[1] Gerard of Avesnes, who has sometimes been called the first lord, does not appear to have been Lord of Hebron, but rather to have been given a castle near it by Godfrey de Bouillon (Thecua, Carmel, and Samoe are the most obvious possibilities).[2] The lordship had certainly been created by 1100,

---

[1] Benvenisti, *The Crusaders in the Holy Land*, p. 161; Richard, *Le Royaume latin*, p. 84; Prawer, *Crusader Institutions*, p. 23; Du Cange, 'Les Familles d'outre-mer', pp. 423–5. For recent work on Hebron see Mayer, 'Die Herrschaftsbildung in Hebron', pp. 64–81.

[2] Albert of Aix, pp. 507–8, 510, 516; see also Riley-Smith, 'The Motives of the Earliest Crusaders', p. 726.

however, by which time we find Galdemar Carpenel as lord.[3]

The death of Galdemar without heirs in 1101 provided the first opportunity for the king to take the Lordship of Hebron back into his hands. Many other such opportunities arose: all the early lords (Galdemar Carpenel 1100–1, Roger of Haifa 1101–2?, Hugh I of St Abraham *c.*1104, Walter Mahomet *c.*1108– *c.*1115/18, Baldwin of St Abraham *c.*1120–36, and Hugh II of St Abraham *c.*1136–49) were apparently unrelated and the death of each would have provided the king with the chance of restructuring the administration of the territory before enfeoffing it (if he chose to do so) to a new lord. There is evidence that such restructuring, always in the king's favour, did indeed take place. We have seen, for instance, that Godfrey de Bouillon gave one of the nearby castles to Gerard of Avesnes before the Lordship of Hebron was founded. There is nothing to indicate that the castles of Thecua, Samoe, or Carmel were ever held by the Lords of Hebron, and it is possible that they were retained in royal hands.

There is also evidence that the foundation of the Lordship of Bethgibelin was instigated by King Fulk rather than by Hugh II of St Abraham. A document of 1136 tell us

Proinde ego Fulco . . . confirmo domum cujusdam loci, nomine Bethgibelin, quem Hugo de S. Abraham rogatu nostro . . . ecclesie sancti Joannis Hospitalis quod est in Iherusalem . . . in manu domini Raimundi ipsorum magistri, libere cum subscriptis casalibus et eorum pertinentiis in perpetuum donavit. Que ab antiquis his fuisse et esse nuncupata nominibus posteritas tradit: videlicet Beithsur, et aliud Beithsur, de Irnachar, de Irrasin, Charroubete, Deirelcobebe, Meimes, Hale, Bothme, Helhtawahin.

In addition, Fulk himself gave the Order four nearby casalia (villages): Fectata, Sahalin, Zeita, and Courcoza. The new Lordship of Bethgibelin was thus set up at the direct request of the king ('rogatu nostro').[4] By instigating this administrative change Fulk was fulfilling two aims at once: he was introducing the Military Orders into the area in order to keep up pressure on the Egyptian garrison of Ascalon, while at the same time, by

[3] For Galdemar's lordship see Riley-Smith, 'The Motives of the Earliest Crusaders', pp. 728–9; Albert of Aix, pp. 523, 526, 549; *Cart. gén. Hosp.*, No. 20; *Reg. Hier.*, No. 57; *Cart. gén. Hosp.*, No. 225; *Reg. Hier.*, No. 293.

[4] *Cart. gén. Hosp.*, No. 116; *Reg. Hier.*, No. 164.

detaching a castle and a sizeable tract of land, he was able to reduce the power of one of the larger lay seigneuries.

So it can be seen that the monarchy exercised significant control over the Lordship of Hebron, over and above the authority implicit in the relationship between a king and his lords. This pattern of the use of (or potential to use) effective control mechanisms is one which we shall see repeated throughout the histories of the seigneuries of the Latin Kingdom.

THE PRINCIPALITY OF GALILEE

Perhaps not surprisingly, given its size and importance, the Principality of Galilee received royal attention from the first days of the kingdom. We find an early example of the deliberate territorial limitation of a seigneury in the refusal to grant Haifa to Tancred and, once again, the instability of the family lines of the first princes ensured that the fief reverted to royal control at frequent intervals.

Recent work has changed views of the early history of the Principality of Galilee. It has been demonstrated that Tancred captured Bethsan in the second half of August 1099, but that he did not take Tiberias, which was occupied by Godfrey de Bouillon probably in early September. Tancred was initially given merely the castellany of Tiberias. It was only when he encountered difficulties in imposing Frankish rule over the region east of the sea of Galilee and had to call for Godfrey's assistance that it was apparently decided that Tancred was under-resourced for the task he had to face and was granted Tiberias in fief, together with the as yet uncaptured town of Haifa.[5]

The policy of the rulers of Jerusalem in limiting the powers of the Princes of Galilee began with Godfrey de Bouillon. Godfrey seems to have thought better of his earlier generosity towards Tancred, and instead promised Haifa to Galdemar Carpenel.

[5] Riley-Smith, 'The Motives of the Earliest Crusaders', pp. 726–7; Ralph of Caen, pp. 703–4; Albert of Aix, pp. 517–18; William of Tyre, pp. 437–8. In 1110 King Baldwin I confirmed that Godrey de Bouillon had previously given the Hospitallers Casal Hessilia. This property, though it cannot be exactly located, seems to have been in the Principality of Galilee (either Kh. el-'asalije, south-south-east of Safed, or 'assile, north-west of Safed): see *Cart. gén. Hosp.*, No. 20; *Reg. Hier.*, No. 57. The grant was also confirmed by Baldwin III in 1154: *Cart. gén. Hosp.*, No. 225; *Reg. Hier.*, No. 293. The gift was almost certainly made in the period when Tancred was merely Castellan of Tiberias and adds further weight to Riley-Smith's view of the early history of the principality.

Haifa was not captured until after Godfrey's death and Baldwin I, no doubt agreeing with his predecessor's aim of trying to contain or reduce the principality (and block any outlet it might have to the sea) settled the matter in favour of Galdemar.[6]

Royal authority over the fledgling principality was manifest in other ways as well. Under pressure from Baldwin I, Tancred resigned the principality, and took over the regency of Antioch on condition that he would be allowed to resume the principality after an interval of at least fifteen months.[7]

That Baldwin agreed to this condition implies that the Princes of Galilee immediately following Tancred were *not* given the fief as a hereditary possession. Hugh de St Omer, for instance (Tancred's immediate successor), left two young daughters as heirs. King Baldwin I gave the principality to the unrelated Gervaise de Bazoches. Though military considerations were doubtless better served by this arrangement, it may also reflect the principality's status as a non-hereditary fief as long as Tancred wanted to regain it.

It is interesting to note that it was not until 1120 that a seigneurial family emerged in Galilee. The first four princes (Tancred, Hugh de St Omer, Gervaise de Bazoches, and Joscelyn de Courtenay) were all unrelated: the principality seems to have reverted to the royal domain on the death of each prince and the king was thus able to ensure that only trusted appointees were given the fief. Royal control was even closer during the period 1109 to December 1112. Tancred was given back the principality in 1109 but does not seem to have returned to Galilee: the king probably exercised effective control over it in this period and it is he whom we find concluding a treaty with the Muslims about the Terre de Sueth in 1109.[8]

Clearly the principality, potentially one of the most trouble-some seigneuries from the king's point of view, was subject to substantial and effective control by the monarchy in its formative years. As we shall discuss further, the process of manipulating (and weakening) the principality did not stop here but continued throughout the twelfth century.

---

[6] Albert of Aix, pp. 521–4, 531, 532, 537–8.   [7] ROL 9 (1902), 404–8.
[8] Albert of Aix, pp. 667–8; Qalanisi, ed. Gibb, p. 92; Abou'l-Mehacen, p. 491; Abou'l-Modaffer, p. 541.

THE LORDSHIPS OF TORON, BANIAS, AND CHASTEL NEUF

The inextricably linked histories of the Lordships of Toron, Banias, and Chastel Neuf provide striking examples of the effectiveness of royal policy in manipulating the larger lordships by the foundation of new seigneuries and also demonstrate that, whatever the political gains for the king, this process worked against the wider interests of the kingdom, leaving lordships too scantily resourced to be able to fulfil their military commitments. This is all the more striking because it has never been remarked on by historians of the Latin East and, indeed, the relationship of the three lordships to each other has never been examined in detail.

Hugh de St Omer, Prince of Galilee, built Toron to put pressure on the Muslim garrison of Tyre.[9] The effectiveness of this and the promptness of Frankish civil settlement, was demonstrated by the response of Tyre's garrison. Shortly after the death of Hugh a sortie was launched against Toron and the fauberg destroyed (though one must assume that it was still a relatively rudimentary settlement at this stage).[10]

It is possible that the small castle of Qalat Doubal, later to become part of the Lordship of Toron, was also built about this time.[11] According to the *Survey of Western Palestine* the fortification, built on a steep and narrow spur to the east of Toron, was early crusader work and it was suggested that it too had been built by Hugh de St Omer.[12] Hugh also seems to have built Chastel Neuf (Hunin).[13]

At some point after the death of Hugh de St Omer, Toron was detached from the Principality of Galilee and made into an independent lordship. It is not clear whether this took place immediately after the death of Hugh, whether Toron remained in the Principality of Galilee for a while, or whether it temporarily became part of the royal domain. Deschamps and

[9] William of Tyre, pp. 502–3.
[10] Qalanisi, ed. Gibb, p. 75; Abou'l-Modaffer, p. 530.
[11] Prawer–Benvenisti Map, ref. 196/287.
[12] *Survey of Western Palestine*, i. 123.
[13] Benvenisti, *The Crusaders in the Holy Land*, p. 302. Jean Richard thought that Chastel Neuf was only created in 1179: in this he is perhaps confusing Chastel Neuf with 'Castellum Novum' (i.e. Montfort), which changed hands around that time, or with the rebuilding of Chastel Neuf after its recapture by the Franks: see *Le Royaume latin*, p. 83.

2. Toron, Banias, and Chastel Neuf

Richard felt that the Seigneury of Toron was created shortly after Hugh's death. Benvenisti felt that this did not take place until 1115. I would tentatively suggest that the earlier date is more likely: the death of Hugh without heirs would have provided the king with the ideal opportunity to reduce the power of the Principality of Galilee. It would also have made military sense to put the fortress of Toron, and possibly that of Qalat Doubal, under the control of someone who could devote his full attention to the active prosecution of the war against Tyre and the defence of the eastern borders.[14]

The Lordship of Banias was also created in this period: the Assassins gave Banias to Baldwin II in 1128.[15] William of Tyre

[14] Deschamps, *La Défense*, ii. 118, and Richard, 'Le Royaume latin', pp. 82–3; Benvenisti, 'The Crusaders in the Holy Land', p. 302.

[15] Ibn al-Athir, 'Kamil', 1. 384–5; William of Tyre, p. 656–7; Abou'l Feda, p. 18.

tells us that Baldwin immediately gave it to a certain Renier Brus. From this it has generally been assumed that Banias was an independent lordship created in 1128. Certain evidence argues against this, however. We know that a Muslim attack on the city was carried out in 1132 in direct retaliation for the Lord of Beirut's alleged maltreatment of Arab merchants.[16] If there was no connection between the Lordships of Beirut and Banias this action would make no sense. A charter of Humphrey II of Toron is even more conclusive. Humphrey had gained the Lordship of Banias by marrying the daughter and heiress of Renier Brus. When he tried to dispose of half of Banias to the Hospitallers it was specified that he held the town from the Lord of Beirut.[17] It thus seems likely that although, as William of Tyre says, Renier Brus was given Banias, it was as a sub-fief to be held from the Lord of Beirut.

It is perhaps also significant to note to whom Baldwin II did *not* give the new fief. Judged purely by geographical criteria, Banias would belong most obviously to the Lordship of Toron. It was not made part of the lordship, however, and was not even given to Humphrey I of Toron as a sub-fief. Once again, we can see in this the king seeking to create smaller fiefs, rather than enlarge existing ones.

At some point between 1140 and 1157 Renier Brus died and the Lordship of Banias passed into the hands of his son-in-law Humphrey II, Lord of Toron.[18]

In 1157 Humphrey II entered into negotiations for the grant of half of Banias and Chastel Neuf to the Hospitallers. Record of this unusual and puzzling arrangement is contained in William of Tyre and a single surviving charter. William of Tyre is frank in telling us that Humphrey was forced into trying to make the

---

[16] Qalanisi, ed. Gibb, p. 216.

[17] *Cart. gén. Hosp.*, No. 258; *Reg. Hier.*, No. 325.

[18] I believe, though cannot prove conclusively, that this transfer probably took place towards the earlier part of this period. Humphrey II was a resourceful, stubborn, and gallant knight, respected by Muslims and Franks alike: it is unlikely that in 1157 he would have entered into unpalatable negotiations for the alienation of a large part of the lands of Banias and Chastel Neuf without first having ensured that there was no other way in which they could be safeguarded. In other words, it seems likely that it was only after years of incessant military activity around Banias (a razzia in 1151 and a siege in 1153) that Humphrey II was forced to the conclusion that his resources alone were insufficient for its defence. We last hear of Renier Brus in 1140 (William of Tyre, p. 690). The weight of probability thus seems to place Humphrey's assumption of the Lordship of Banias in the 1140s rather than the 1150s.

arrangement because of the expense of defending Banias. He says that the arrangement was to be that the Hospitallers would own half the city of Banias and its outlying dependencies, pay half the expenses, and be responsible for the defence of half the town. William also relates that the Hospitallers agreed to these terms and had already assumed responsibility for their part of the town *before* assembling a convoy for the reinforcement of the garrison. A Muslim force destroyed the convoy, however, and the Hospitallers reneged on their agreement, returning the town to Humphrey. The destruction of the convoy, precipitating Hospitaller withdrawal from the agreement, occurred on 26 April 1157. In the siege of Banias that followed (May–June 1157) the defence of the town was undertaken by Humphrey II and there is no mention of any Hospitaller involvement. The Order must therefore have given up responsibility for the part of the town which they had taken over, prior to the despatch of the convoy, almost immediately after the disastrous engagement of 26 April.

The agreement to the original transfer of property to the Hospitallers has survived in a royal document which is puzzlingly dated as 4 October 1157:

. . . concedo et confirmo donum quod Humfredus de Torono, constabularius meus . . . fecit. . . . medietatem castelli Paneadensis, et medietatem castelli Novi, et domos domine Alberehe de Torono, et duas vineas in territorio Toroni, quas Guido de Scandalione Hospitali tradidit, et in Torono hospitale cum suis omnibus pertinentiis . . . Donum autem illud, quod de medietate castelli Paneadensis Humfredus constabularius Hospitali fecit, concessione Gualterii Berytensis, de cujus feodo movet . . .[19]

Later authorities have produced markedly different views of the transaction; such differences of opinion generally being caused by differing attempts to explain the incongruous dating of the charter of 4 October 1157. Paul Deschamps came up with the interesting suggestion that the return of the 'urbem' (in William of Tyre's words) to Humphrey was only part of the arrangement.

[19] William of Tyre, pp. 826–8; see also Qalanisi, ed. Gibb, pp. 330–2. Interestingly, Qalanisi thought that the convoy, though primarily Hospitaller, contained some Templars. He also said that the force consisted of 700 horses and an infantry contingent; though almost certainly an exaggeration, there can be no doubt that a substantial military force was involved. The fact that it was felt necessary to provide such a guard for a convoy to Banias shows just how precarious the Frankish presence there must have been, and how untenable it had become. *Cart. gén. Hosp.*, No. 258; *Reg. Hier.*, No. 325.

He posited that the Hospitallers had returned the town of Banias as being indefensible, but retained their gifts and responsibilities at the castle of Banias, which he thought one could equate with the castle of Subeibe.[20] Riley-Smith, on the other hand, has argued that the charter of 4 October 1157 was either issued late, or was merely issued formally so that the agreement could be annulled, and pointed out the close parallels between this process and the discrepancies in the dating of charters relating to the acquisition of Arsur by the Hospitallers in similar circumstances.[21]

Riley-Smith is almost certainly correct in his analysis and the parallels with Arsur are indeed striking. Recent scholarship has shown that Subeibe was *not* the castle of Banias, and William of Tyre is explicit in stating that the Hospitallers withdrew from the agreement they had made with Humphrey.[22] Moreover, there is no later reference to the Hospitallers in relation to Banias: three letters referring to the loss of Banias in 1164, and the chronicle of William of Tyre, all fail to mention the Order. The grant of the right to Banias to Joscelyn de Courtenay in 1186, also specifically said that Joscelyn should hold it (should it be recovered) on the same conditions as it had been held by Humphrey of Toron, with, again, no mention of the Hospitallers.[23]

Deschamp's hypothesis, though clever, thus seems implausible. Several further points need to be made, however, which previously have not been commented upon. Firstly, Chastel Neuf has generally been assumed to have been part of the Lordship of Toron. Chastel Neuf and Banias are linked more closely together in this document, however, than are Chastel Neuf and Toron. We know from the charter that the Hospitallers were given half of Banias and half of Chastel Neuf. William of Tyre, however, is specific in saying that the Brothers were to receive half of Banias and half of its outlying dependencies: Chastel Neuf thus seems to have been part of the dependencies of the Lordship of Banias, rather than Toron.

This would also explain references in John of Ibelin, where Chastel Neuf is more closely related to Banias and Assebebe than

[20] Deschamps, *La Défense*, ii. 156 n. 3.
[21] Riley-Smith, 'The Knights of St John', p. 72 n. 3.
[22] See e.g. Benvenisti, pp. 147–57.
[23] *Tab. ord. Theut.*, No. 21; *Reg. Hier.*, No. 653.

to Toron.[24] It is also significant that of the subsidiary 'gifts' made to the Hospitallers, only one (a hospital at Toron) was possibly a personal possession of Humphrey and even this was of a non-economic nature. It is also the case that there is no evidence linking Chastel Neuf to the Lordship of Toron prior to Humphrey II's acquisition of the fief of Renier Brus. As we shall see, there was a real distinction between the resources made available for negotiations with the Hospitallers for the defence of Banias, and those which Humphrey II was determined to retain.

We have already seen that the fief of Reiner Brus was held from the Lord of Beirut; that Humphrey II acquired the fief by marriage to the heiress of Banias, Renier's daughter; and that all the evidence points towards Chastel Neuf having been part of the fief of Renier Brus. The grants made to the Hospitallers (primarily half of Banias and half of Chastel Neuf) were made 'concessione Gualterii Berytensis, de cujus feodo movet . . . .'. Thus Humphrey II must have held Banias and Chastel Neuf from Walter of Beirut. There is no question, however, in this or any other document, of Humphrey holding either Toron or any other of his possessions as a rear-fief of the Seigneury of Beirut. With this it becomes clear that there were two major seigneurial distinctions inherent in the treaty.

Firstly, there was a distinction between the inheritance of Humphrey I, as it passed to Humphrey II, and that of Renier Brus, as it passed to Humphrey II by marriage. It was the Lordship of Banias (i.e. the inheritance of Renier Brus) that was under military pressure and becoming almost untenable. Humphrey II, by this document, made it plain that he was prepared to alienate half the fief to the Hospitallers, rather than see the seigneurial centre fall into Muslim hands. In doing so, however, he was *not* prepared to offer the Hospitallers any lands in his own patrimony, the Lordship of Toron. Humphrey II had strong administrative and political reasons (as well as the obvious emotional motivation) for not involving the Lordship of Toron in the affairs of the Lordship of Banias: Banias was held as a rear-fief of Beirut—it was clearly undesirable to alienate fiefs held directly from the king in order to retain those held only as sub-fiefs. This provides a striking example of the legal, administrative, and emotional forces that caused different fiefs, even when held in

[24] John of Ibelin, pp. 421, 423.

the hands of the same family or individual, to be treated as separate units.

Secondly, there was a distinction between the properties mentioned in the document as being given to the Hospitallers in return for their aid in defence of Banias, and those which clearly were not. In addition to the two castles of Renier Brus, we are told that the Order would receive the houses of 'domine Alberehe de Torono', two vineyards in the territory of Toron, 'quas Guido de Scandaleone Hospitali tradidit' and a hospital in Toron, with everything pertaining to it.

What seems to have happened is that the Order took advantage of the agreement drawn up with Humphrey II to secure a confirmation of their properties in the Lordship of Banias *and* the Lordship of Toron: the gift of vineyards to the hospital by Guy de Scandaleon seems unrelated to the agreement directly concerning the defence of Banias, and one would not normally have expected a hospital in Toron to have been in the possession of its lay lord. One suspects that the houses formerly belonging to 'Alberehe de Torono' were also a previous acquisition by the Brothers.

With these distinctions in mind, one has clues to the earlier history of the region. We have seen that Chastel Neuf was probably built by Hugh de St Omer in *c*.1105–7 and that it was later part of the fief of Renier Brus. It thus seems that on the death of Hugh de St Omer the king took the opportunity to create *two* new lordships from the northern territories of the Principality of Galilee: the separate seigneuries of Chastel Neuf and Toron (Banias was still in Muslim hands). Chastel Neuf may initially have been part of a fief of which another seigneurial centre was at Assebebe, tentatively sited by Prawer and Benvenisti to the north of Banias and Subeibe.[25] John of Ibelin says that: 'La seignorie de l'Assebebe a court et coins et justise. Et a l'Assebebe a court de borgesie et justise. Et a Chastiau Neuf a court de borgesie et justise.'[26] John thus keeps Assebebe and Chastel Neuf separate from other seigneuries in his list, including those of Toron and Banias.

This would have meant that a relatively unknown seigneury was responsible for a large part of the eastern border of the Latin Kingdom in the early twelfth century. The lack of evidence

[25] See Richard, 'Les Listes des seigneuries'.   [26] John of Ibelin, p. 421.

surviving about the seigneury is entirely consistent with other eastern border seigneuries in the north of the kingdom: the Schuf–Gezin and Ahmud. Assebebe itself must have fallen into Muslim hands in the twelfth century (though I can find no chronicle confirmation of this) as John of Ibelin also tells us: 'De . . . l'Assebebe . . . quel servise il deivent ne sai ge mie la certainete, por ce que il ne furent grant piece a en mains de Crestiens.'[27]

It would thus seem that those portions of the Seigneury of Assebebe still in Christian hands came into the possession of Renier Brus (i.e. Chastel Neuf and its dependencies). This transfer probably took place before 1148, by which point I have suggested that it was most likely that Humphrey II had acquired the fief of Renier Brus. As Chastel Neuf, like the rest of the fief of Renier Brus, is known to have been a sub-fief of Beirut, it is possible that the original Lordship of Assebebe had been as well.

Finding out by a process of elimination what comprised the Lordship of Renier Brus tells us more about what comprised the Lordship of Toron. The castle of Qalat Doubal is sited to the east of the castle of Toron. Although there is no unambiguous documentary evidence for the castle, it was not included in the agreement of 1157 as being part of the fief of Renier Brus, so one might reasonably assume that it was in the Lordship of Toron. This hypothesis is consistent with the opinions of the *Survey of Western Palestine*.

I would posit that the Kings of Jerusalem originally had a specific policy of creating a series of small lordships at the expense of the very large ones (such as the County of Jaffa and Ascalon, and the Principality of Galilee) for obvious political reasons; as military pressures grew, however, other considerations had to take precedence and a transformation of the seigneurial structure resulted. The Seigneury of Assebebe came into the hands of Renier Brus, who, with the resources of the Lordship of Banias behind him, might have been expected to be better able to cope with the pressures imposed by border life (there is no way of knowing whether Renier was given the entire fief of Assebebe, or whether he was only given the remnants of the lordship, centred at Chastel Neuf, after Assebebe itself had already fallen).

Banias in turn, however, proved to be too weak a unit to

---

[27] Ibid. 423.

survive on its own: it was continually harassed by the Muslims and twice captured by them. We next find the de Toron family in possession of the fiefs of Renier Brus, but even this new fief (by which unitary ownership and leadership was assured for the seigneuries of Toron, Banias, and what remained of the Lordship of Assebebe), defended by the extremely capable Humphrey II of Toron, proved insufficient for its own defensive needs. Humphrey was forced to try to bring in external aid (the Hospitallers) and when this failed, the fall of Banias was inevitable. In 1180, with the ineffectual (and very young) Humphrey IV of Toron in charge of the seigneury, the entire border sector held by the lordship was in peril, and the king had to step in to assume either direct control through his officers or secondary control through his close relatives.[28]

Royal policy on the north-eastern borders thus seems to have been, in large measure, a failure. Though there were political motives for wanting a series of relatively small lordships, these new entities proved under-resourced for the task they had to face. As we shall see, other small border lordships seem to have come under the control of their larger seigneurial neighbours: the Schuf–Gezin appears to have gone to Sidon, while Ahmud went to Beirut. Similarly, the Lordships of Assebebe and Banias were merged, first with each other, and then with Toron. The very completeness of the failure of these early lordships has resulted in our lack of knowledge about them: as the lists of John of Ibelin show, once their practical existence ceased, near contemporaries were unable to recall even such important details about them as the knights' service they had once owed the crown.

In their place we find the defence of the eastern borders increasingly being taken over by the larger coastal fiefs, which grew to accommodate these defensive responsibilities: the revenues of trade were thereby combined with the military demands of defence. Thus, Beirut took over Ahmud, and Sidon the Schuf–Gezin. (The granting of the overlordship of Banias to the Lordship of Beirut may have been an intermediate stage in this development: if so, the experiment does not seem to have been successful.) The process of assimilation by larger lordships may also account, at least in part, for the form which the

---

[28] William of Tyre, pp. 1012–13; see also chapter 3, section 5, The Lordship of Toron.

Seigneury of Joscelyn de Courtenay eventually took: by 1187 it was an extensive wedge of land extending from the coast to the eastern border. Moreover, after the collapse of the Seigneury of Joscelyn, Toron was eventually combined with Tyre, thus creating another wedge of land from coast to border. Although one cannot prove that there was an explicit royal policy underlying these changes in seigneurial structure, there is a mass of circumstantial evidence for such a policy.

In the absence of any help from the Hospitallers, Humphrey II had to rely on his own resources, and a quick defensive response from royal forces, to defend his fiefs. Banias was besieged from May to June 1157 and the town and its defences destroyed: only the citadel survived the attack.[29] Baldwin III relieved the town and set about repairing the damage. On the return march, however, the royal forces were defeated and Banias once again was besieged. The rebuilding work was undone, but once more the approach of a royal army forced the Muslims to withdraw.[30] The lordship could not long survive intact, given the pressure exerted on it. In 1164 Banias fell, this time never to be recovered.[31]

A further blow came in 1167, when Chastel Neuf fell. The garrison retired from the castle, leaving Nur-ad-Din a free hand in destroying the fortifications.[32] The lack of resources available to Humphrey II and the increasingly untenable nature of border fortresses in the area is attested to by the feeling amongst the garrison that resistance was futile, and the fact that Humphrey II felt unable to rebuild the castle (until 1178).[33] Humphrey died in 1179, engaged, appropriately enough, in an attack on Muslim forces around Banias.[34]

The early history of the Lordships of Toron, Banias, and Chastel Neuf shows that the Kings of Jerusalem could, and did, take advantage of the reversion of the larger seigneuries to royal control. Moreover, royal actions with respect to the creation of

[29] Qalanisi, ed. Gibb, pp. 334–5; Abu-Shamah, iv. 87; William of Tyre, pp. 826–30.
[30] William of Tyre, pp. 832–3; Qalanisi, ed. Gibb, p. 336.
[31] William of Tyre, pp. 876–7; William of Newborough, i. 156; 'Annales de Terre Sainte', p. 432; Ibn al-Athir, 'Kamil', i. 540–2.
[32] Ibn al-Athir, 'Kamil', i. 551.
[33] For the rebuilding of Chastel Neuf, see Deschamps, *La Défense*, ii. 130.
[34] William of Tyre, p. 999; Ibn al-Athir, 'Kamil', i. 635; see also *al-Maqrizi*, tr. Blochet, ROL 8 (1900–1), 530–1.

smaller lordships out of the larger ones were so consistent that one might reasonably describe them as a policy, albeit undeclared as such. It is also clear that, while the monarchy could derive political benefits from reducing the power of the larger seigneuries, external developments eventually outweighed those benefits: in the face of increased military pressure, royal policy towards the small, eastern border lordships had to be reversed. These small units, though politically desirable in a domestic context, were under-resourced to meet the military tasks thrust upon them.

THE ORIGINS OF THE LORDSHIP OF CAESAREA

The Lordship of Caesarea, as so many seigneuries, has been assumed to have been created at an earlier stage than the evidence would suggest. The town of Caesarea was captured on 1 May 1101 by Baldwin I, one of the first major ports to be captured after the first crusade. It appears that the town was given to the Archbishop of Caesarea to defend: as at Ramla–Lydda, however, this arrangement was short-lived.[35] It has generally been assumed that the lordship was created for Arpin of Bourges almost immediately after the capture of the town. Albert of Aachen, however, merely tells us that: 'Post haec Joppen Rex in magna gloria secessit, Arpinum de Boduordis civitate, principem magnificum, ad custodiendos muros et portam civitatis relinquens.' This looks like the usual appointment of a governor or castellan to look after the captured town, and there is nothing to indicate that Caesarea left the royal domain at this time.[36]

The retention of Caesarea in the royal domain even after the appointment of Arpin is shown by Fulcher of Chartres when he says: 'The king, when he heard this, collected his men from Jerusalem, Tiberias, Caesarea and Haifa' (referring to the period June–August 1101).[37] Ekkehard of Aura also lists the king's possessions as including Caesarea.[38]

Caesarea was only created as a lordship in c. 1110, when it was given to Eustace I Grenier (the same year in which Eustace received Sidon.[39]

[35] *ROL* 9 (1902), 429–32; Fulcher of Chartres, pp. 400–4; Albert of Aix, pp. 543–4; William of Tyre, pp. 471–2.

[36] Albert of Aix, p. 544; Prawer, *Crusader Institutions*, p. 24.

[37] Fulcher of Chartres, p. 408.   [38] Ekkehard of Aura, p. 33.

[39] La Monte, 'The Lords of Caesarea', p. 145; 'The Lords of Sidon', pp. 185–6.

THE ORIGINS OF THE LORDSHIP OF SIDON

With the Lordship of Sidon one finds the situation whereby large feudal units could be deliberately created for the use of a trusted ally of the Crown. Significantly, when the continued unitary possession of the fiefs (Caesarea and Sidon) in the hands of a trusted companion could no longer be assured, they were split between two heirs, possibly at the instigation, and certainly with the blessing, of the Crown.

Sidon was captured in December 1110 by Baldwin I with the naval assistance of King Sigurd of Norway. The city was given to Eustace I Grenier, one of the king's most trusted followers.[40] At some time around 1110 Eustace had also been given the Lordship of Caesarea. In entrusting the two seigneuries to Eustace, King Baldwin was creating a very substantial power-base for his supporter. It is noteworthy that after Eustace's death (*c.*1123) the two lordships were never again held by one man: such a large power-base was an asset when in the hands of a trusted follower, but could have been a liability in the hands of anyone else.

THE LORDSHIP OF BEIRUT

Beirut was captured by the Franks in 1110. After the capture of the town Baldwin I spent a fortnight there reorganizing his forces and, presumably, determining the future administration of the new acquisition. The Seigneury of Beirut was created and entrusted to Fulk de Guines (one of the four sons who accompanied Count Baldwin de Guines on the first crusade).[41] This arrangement does not seem to have lasted long, however, for in 1125 we find the apparently unrelated Walter Brisebarre I in possession of the fief.[42]

The Lordship of Beirut provides a striking example of the way

---

[40] William of Tyre, pp. 517–19; Albert of Aix, p. 679; Ibn al-Athir, 'Kamil', i. 276; Qalanisi, ed. Gibb, p. 107; Fulcher of Chartres, p. 548, also specifically mentioned that the rural inhabitants of the area agreed to stay and continue to cultivate the land under Frankish rule.

[41] Fulcher of Chartres, pp. 534–6; William of Tyre, pp. 515–16; Albert of Aix, pp. 675–6; Abou'l-Mehacen, p. 539; 'Historia Nicaena vel Antiochena', p. 181; Moeller, 'Les Flamands du Ternois au royaume latin de Jérusalem', pp. 191–2; Lambert of Ardres, p. 574.

[42] Tafel–Thomas, i. 90–4, no. 41; *Reg. Hier.*, No. 105.

in which historians have tended to overestimate the physical, as well as temporal, extent of the secular lordships. Where the status or ownership of a tract of land is not known the tendency has been to place it within the boundaries of the nearest known seigneury. While this process is understandable, and in some cases unavoidable, it can sometimes produce major errors. By assuming too much from the feudal administrative structure outlined by John of Ibelin, historians have been encouraged to avoid a thorough examination of other evidence.

The dangers inherent in this are apparent in the case of Beirut, and a very false picture of the extent of the seigneury has been built up by making assumptions that are either not supported or directly contradicted by charter evidence. Nickerson described the boundaries of the lordship as being 'in the north the Nahr al-Qalb, or Dog River, which also separated the principality [*sic*] of Jerusalem from the county of Tripoli; in the south, the Damour River; in the east, the crest of the Lebanon mountains'.[43] In this she agreed with the opinions of Rey.[44] Similarly, the Prawer–Benvenisti map places the boundaries of the seigneury far to the east of Mount Glavianus, and even further east than the Toron Ahmud. Benvenisti, in his administrative map of the kingdom, also conforms to this view.[45] In short, all authorities see the Seigneury of Beirut as a large territorial bloc of considerable inland extent. There is, however, little evidence to support this view.

The case of Mont Glavian is one aspect of this. In October 1125 King Baldwin II built the castle of Mont Glavian, or Mont Glaiven, in the hills around Beirut, about six miles from the town itself. 'Hoc in anno, mense Octobri, aedificavit rex castellum unum in montanis Beryti . . . Hunc montem Glavianum vocant a digladiando, quia ibi rei digladiabantur qui apud Berytum damnandi iudicabantur. Abest autem ab urbe ipsa vi miliariis.' William of Tyre also tells us that 'rex super urbem Beritensem in montanis castrum unum, cui Mons Glavianus nomen, fundavit'.[46]

It has generally been assumed that this new castle was in the

[43] Nickerson, 'The Seigneury of Beirut', p. 148.
[44] Rey, 'Les Colonies', pp. 521–4.
[45] Benvenisti, *The Crusaders in the Holy Land*, 2nd edition, p. 410.
[46] Fulcher of Chartres, pp. 771–2; William of Tyre, pp. 605–6.

Lordship of Beirut, possibly because of the references to the mountains and city of Beirut. Nickerson, for instance, felt that: 'Baldwin [II] showed, indeed, a certain solicitude for his protégé in building the new fortress of Mont Glainen, or Mont Glavianus . . .' and described the castle as being one of the subdivisions of the seigneury.[47]

It is interesting to note, however, that the most common phrase describing an administrative relationship, 'in territorio', is missing and that there is no mention of a Lord of Beirut. As Beirut was the site close to the new castle that was best known to readers of Fulcher of Chartres and William of Tyre, it is perhaps not surprising to see that it is mentioned in a descriptive context. Moreover, the exact site of Mont Glavian is now unknown, but the most likely position, shown on the Prawer–Benvenisti map, is closer to the casalia of the Lordship of the Schuf (such as Boussah and Boocosta) than to Beirut.

Evidence also exists from the thirteenth century that the Lordship of Beirut was territorially small and was recognized as such. Henry of Cyprus gave Balian, Lord of Beirut, a substantial fief in the royal domain at Acre, including the small castle of Casal Imbert: '. . . je Henri . . . otrei et conferm en pardurable fie a tei Johan d'Ibelin, segnor de Baruth, et à tes heirs en creissement de ton fie de Baruth le don et le fie, que je donai a Balian d'Ybelin, ton père, segnor de Baruth jadis, et à ses heirs en creissiment dou fie de Baruth . . .'.[48] The last phrase clearly implies that the new territory was to be given as an actual increase in size to the fief of Beirut, rather than as just another additional fief in the lord's hands.

A series of documents in the 1260s also shows that the eastern marches of what is considered to have been the Lordship of Beirut were in fact an independent or semi-independent lordship, the Seigneury of the Toron Ahmud.[49] The idea that the Lordship of Beirut had only a very limited hinterland is also demonstrated in the details of a treaty drawn up between Isabella, Lady of Beirut, and Baybars in 1269. The Lady of Beirut was said to possess seventeen properties, including Beirut itself. Of these sites ten can now be located with some degree of certainty. A look

[47] Nickerson, 'The Seigneury of Beirut', pp. 148–9.
[48] *Tab. ord. Theut.*, No. 105; *Reg. Hier.*, No. 1208.
[49] See this chapter, under The Lordship of Toron Ahmud.

at a map of the area shows that all these properties were either on the coast or very close to it. This would tend to confirm indications that the Lordship of Beirut was a coastal strip rather than a large territorial bloc.[50]

Moreover, an examination of the properties that were within the boundaries of what has been generally accepted as the Lordship of Beirut provides surprising evidence. Only nine crusader sites have been accurately identified in the area between the Damor river and the 'Flum de Baruth' on the Prawer–Benvenisti map. These properties are:

casal Delbon: said in 1257 to be in the Lordship of Schuf;[51]
casal Damor: this property, sited well to the north of the River Damor, is said in 1262 not only to belong to the Lord of Sidon, but to be part of the Lordship of Sidon;[52]
casal Behnayl: said in 1257 to be in the Lordship of Schuf;[53]
Toron Ahmud: an independent or semi-independent lordship;
en Naeme: a fortification, part of the Lordship of Beirut in 1269 (al Na'ima);
casal Kaffarhammie: said in 1257 to be in the Lordship of Schuf;[54]
casal Elmunzura: said in 1257 to be in the Lordship of Schuf;[55]
casal Boocosta: said in 1257 to be in the Lordship of Schuf;[56]
casal Boussah: this casal, sited very close to Beirut itself, was said in 1257 to be in the Lordship of Schuf.[57]

Thus, only one of these properties was in the Lordship of Beirut. As we have seen, the treaty with Baybars of 1269 paints a relatively detailed picture of a lordship consisting of a thin coastal strip and extensive trading interests. One is left with the impression of a very urbanized lordship, with only small amounts of agricultural land dependent on it. Beirut must have been a seigneury in which the vast majority of the lord's revenues were

---

[50] Holt, 'Baybars's Treaty with the Lady of Beirut in 667/1269'. Names and positions on Dussaud's maps of Syria (Map 3) are as follows: Junia (Djouni) B1; al-'Adhab (Ba'abda?) B2; Sinn al-Fil (Sinn el-Fil) B2; al-Shuwayf (Shouweifat) B2; al-Rah (from the wording of the treaty it appears al-Rah must be near Shouweifat); Antalyas (Antelyas) B1; al-Hadida (Hadire?) B1; al-Bashariyya (Boshriye) B1; al-Naima (Na'ame) A2; Beirut (Beirut) A1.

[51] *Reg. Hier.*, No. 1253.   [52] Ibid. 1318.   [53] Ibid. 1253.
[54] Ibid.   [55] Ibid. 1256.   [56] Ibid.
[57] Ibid. 1253.

generated by urban trade. Similarity of interests may at least partly account for the rapport achieved by the lords of Beirut with the European merchant communities.

Far from creating a territorially substantial lordship, the kings of Jerusalem merely gave the lords of Beirut the town itself and a few casalia. The hinterland was either retained directly in royal hands (e.g. Mont Glavian) or formed into independent or semi-independent lordships (i.e. the Schuf and Toron Ahmud). The territorial weakness of the Seigneury of Beirut may explain why it seems to have been given to Banias as a rear-fief. It is significant, however, that this territorial 'increase' was given in the form of a separate rear-fief which was not geographically contiguous with the Lordship of Beirut, thus ensuring that a full territorial consolidation (which would have been potentially threatening to the monarchy) could not take place.

THE LORDSHIP OF NAZARETH

The Lordship of Nazareth, like that of Toron, was detached from the Principality of Galilee and provides another example of the practice whereby the king took advantage of the temporary reversion of a major seigneury to the royal domain to weaken it by detaching a portion of its lands and making a separate lordship.

Links between the religious Seigneury of Nazareth and the Principality of Galilee are attested to from the earliest days of the kingdom's history. Tancred originally re-established the church at Nazareth. William of Tyre tells us that he was generous in endowing the church with lands, though he goes on to say that many of these were illegally taken back by later princes of Galilee.[58] The clear implication is that the Seigneury of Nazareth was originally a full and integral part of the Principality of Galilee and that later princes continued to have a close relationship with the Lordship.

A charter of 1121, issued by the Bishop of Nazareth, indicates that the Lordship of Nazareth was already in existence. After citing various witnesses to the act, specifically said to be clerical, the bishop turned to the laity: amongst the latter were 'Martino Nazareno interprete', 'Roberto de Aquila', and 'Rogerio Argeloth,

[58] William of Tyre, pp. 436–8.

episcopi pincerna'.[59] The bishop clearly had an administrative structure as elaborate as those in lay fiefs at a relatively early stage. 'Martino Nazareno interprete' (i.e. the bishop's dragoman) may have been the 'Martinus vicecomes' (probably Viscount of Nazareth) whom we find witnessing a charter for the Bishop of Nazareth in 1115, where we also find the vassal 'Robertus de Aquila' once again.[60]

It is therefore certain that the territory of Nazareth was detached from the Principality of Galilee by 1121 at the latest. The principality reverted to royal control several times during this period, and it seems likely that, as in other cases around Tiberias, the king took the opportunity to decrease its power before creating a new lordship.[61]

THE LORDSHIP OF OULTREJOURDAIN

The original establishment of what was to become the Lordship of Oultrejourdain, one of the largest twelfth-century seigneuries, was a royal enterprise, with the lands initially being part of the royal domain. It was Baldwin I who took all the initiative in its foundation: on 28 November 1100 he led an expedition of over 600 men, including 140 knights, which, finding the capture of Ascalon too daunting a prospect, turned to the south-east, ranging as far as the southern tip of the Dead Sea.

In February–April 1107 Baldwin returned to the area with 500 soldiers where he found 3,000 Damascene soldiers building a castle to control the local caravan routes. The Saracens were obliged to retreat after destroying their fortifications.[62] While Baldwin did not feel strong enough to attempt to annex and fortify the area at this time, this expedition marks the first point at which Muslim control of the land and the caravans that used it was brought into question. Forcing the Muslims to relinquish close military control of the area (by obliging them to dismantle their fortifications) was merely the first step in imposing royal control over the region.

Baldwin I maintained pressure on Oultrejourdain by his return

[59] *Chartes de Josaphat*, ed. Delaborde, No. 9; *Reg. Hier.*, No. 97.
[60] *Chartes de Josaphat*, ed. Kohler, No. 6; *Reg. Hier. Add.*, No. 81*a*.
[61] See end of chapter 5.
[62] Fulcher of Chartres, pp. 376–84; Albert of Aix, pp. 535–6, 644; Qalanisi, ed. Gibb, pp. 81–2.

in 1112–13 with another expedition (said to have consisted of approximately 300 men, though if the figure of 200 knights in the party is to be believed, there must surely have been more than 300 men in the expedition as a whole). The force captured a substantial Damascene caravan, a success which must have emphasized the economic advantages to be derived from the complete control of the region.[63]

By 1115 Baldwin felt strong enough to subjugate the Oultrejourdain to permanent Frankish control. In that year work was started on the first Latin fortification in the region, the castle of Montreal. William of Tyre makes clear the motivation underlying the castle's foundation: it was felt that the garrison of Montreal would be able to protect the lands around it, which were already tributary to the king, from the incursions of the Saracens.[64] Clearly, even before 1115, royal influence in the region had been strong enough to enforce at least an element of revenue collection.

Direct royal administration of this profitable area was clearly what Baldwin I intended: there seems to have been no question at this point of establishing a Seigneury of Oultrejourdain. There were financial benefits from the caravan traffic, and William of Tyre tells us that the land was very fertile and produced abundant supplies of grain, wine, and oil.[65] Albert of Aix explicitly tells us that the king built Montreal to dominate the commercial routes in the area.[66]

An inscription found above a door in the castle, dated 1118, sheds further light on royal administration:

UGO VICE . . . QVI . . . MCXVII[67]

This seems to indicate that the castle was initially commanded by a certain Viscount Hugh (otherwise unknown). It seems likely that he was the local judge for Latin settlers, but also combined this function with the castellany of Montreal, as did the royal Viscount of Jerusalem at this time.

The generally accepted view amongst historians of the Latin East has been that royal administration of Oultrejourdain was

---

[63] Albert of Aix, p. 693; Qalanisi, ed. Gibb, pp. 130–1.
[64] William of Tyre, pp. 534–6; Fulcher of Chartres, pp. 592–3.
[65] William of Tyre, pp. 534–6.   [66] Albert of Aix, pp. 702–3.
[67] Deschamps, *La Défense*, ii. 43 n. 1.

extremely short-lived, that Romain de Puy was made first lord of the region and that the transfer of power took place by 1118 at the latest.[68] This view is not only surprising (for why would the king willingly deprive himself of the direct enjoyment of substantial revenues so soon after his efforts had attained them?) but also extremely speculative.

The hypothesis that Oultrejourdain had left the royal domain by 1118 rests upon two sentences in William of Tyre: 'Romanus de Podio, dominus regionis illius que est trans Jordanem', and '. . . quidam nobilis homo, Paganus nomine, qui prius fuerat regius pincerna, postmodum habuit Terram trans Jordanem, postquam Romanus de Podio et filius eius Radulfus, meritis suis exigentibus, ab ea facti sunt exheredes et alieni'.[69]

It has always been argued that Romain de Puy was made Lord of Oultrejourdain before 1118 and that he was dispossessed before 1126 for organizing an internal revolt, at which date we find Pagan the Butler signing himself as lord. We also know that Romain de Puy played a major part, together with Hugh of Le Puiset, in a revolt against King Fulk in 1134. Naturally, this incongruity has caused problems for those who argue that Romain was Lord of Oultrejourdain, for how could Romain be given the opportunity to revolt twice and be dispossessed twice?

Hans Mayer has discussed the issue in some detail.[70] He argues that after rebelling against King Baldwin II (by 1126), Romain, far from being exiled, was given lands in the royal domain around Samaria, and that it was from the power-base of these lands that he was able to revolt again in 1134. He concludes by saying that: 'The fact that a dispossessed lord had strong reasons to oppose the monarchy has never so far been considered a possible factor in this revolt [i.e. the revolt of 1134], although the discontent of men out of favor has certainly always been a strong incentive to rebellion.'[71]

The only reference connecting Romain with Oultrejourdain that does not come from William of Tyre is to be found in a

[68] *ROL* 4 (1896), 19–24; Prawer, *Crusader Institutions*, pp. 27, 438; Deschamps, *La Défense*, ii. 45; Mas-Latrie, 'Les Seigneurs du Crac de Montreal', pp. 479–80; Mayer, 'Studies in the History of Queen Melisende', pp. 105–6; Grousset, 'Histoire des croisades', i. 281.

[69] William of Tyre, pp. 651, 703.

[70] Mayer, 'Studies in the History of Queen Melisende', particularly pp. 104–8.

[71] Ibid., 105–6.

pancart of the monastery of Josaphat, dated 1130. In this document King Baldwin II confirmed that Pisellus, Viscount of Jerusalem, had given the monks '. . . casale nomine Meschium et terras que sunt juxta viam que ducit ad flumen Jordanem et ultra flumen, in territorio Belcha, casale unum nomine Bessura cum omnibus appendiciis suis, concedente domino rege Balduino [i.e. King Baldwin I]'. At the end of the pancart, however, Bessura was mentioned again and we are told that 'Romanus vero de Podio et Richildis uxor sua et heredes eorum concesserunt eidem ecclesie supradicte in terra Belcha casalia Bessura et La cum omnibus pertinentiis eorum.'[72]

The scribe obviously had two different documents in front of him and, as Baldwin II makes clear in the charter, the gifts to the monks were to be covered in chronological order. It is apparent that the gift of Pisellus was made during the reign of Baldwin I (i.e. before April 1118) while the concession of Romain was granted in the reign of Baldwin II (between 1118 and 1130). Both Bessura and La were casalia in the north of what was later accepted to be the 'Lordship of Oultrejourdain'. This charter demonstrates that Romain owned extensive estates in the area: he had been asked by the brothers of Josaphat to provide a confirmation that they had been given two casalia in his fief, namely Bessura (which had previously been given to them by Viscount Pisellus) and La (given by an unknown donor). It is noteworthy, however, that Romain is *not* referred to as 'Lord of Oultrejourdain'.

Against Mayer's hypothesis, which is the most detailed and sophisticated exposition of the traditional view of the status of Romain de Puy and Oultrejourdain, can be set very strong arguments. What we know of Romain's landed possessions, for instance, does not indicate that he was a man who held extensive estates outside the royal domain proper. Indeed, all the surviving evidence points towards both Viscount Pisellus and Romain having had a large proportion of their fiefs in royal domain land. Pisellus owned casal Meschium and lands to the west of the Jordan (i.e. not in Oultrejourdain). We also know that Pisellus owned casal Cadichinos, a village located in the royal domain between Bethlehem and Jerusalem.[73] Romain is shown, in a

[72] *Chartes de Josaphat*, ed. Delaborde, No. 18; *Reg. Hier.*, No. 134.
[73] Ibid. 983.

document of 1110 (when Ramla was still in the royal domain), to have owned lands in Ramla. Similarly, in 1128 he is attested to have an interest in the casalia of Cafermelic(h) and Betheflori, both sited in the royal domain around Nablus.[74] Both men thus appear, despite their known holdings to the east of the Jordan, to have held extensive fiefs in the royal domain: in the case of Viscount Pisellus at least, these holdings seem to have constituted the bulk of his fief.

The early history of Oultrejourdain would also tend to argue against its existence as a seigneury by 1118 at the latest. We have seen that Baldwin I took a great interest in the region, and particularly in its first Frankish castle, which he significantly named Montreal (or Mons Regalis). He probably also left a viscount in charge of the castle.[75]

Baldwin had built Montreal with the express intention of gaining control of lucrative caravan routes and ensuring continued payment of tribute from the surrounding casalia. The theory that Romain de Puy was made Lord of Oultrejourdain and then dispossessed by 1126 at the latest implies that this important territory, in which the king seemed to take a personal interest, was given away almost immediately: the king's motivation for doing so remains obscure and unexplained.

It is also the case that if Romain was Lord of Oultrejourdain, he must have been in open revolt against the king twice: firstly before 1126 (by which time Pagan the Butler is known to have been lord), and again in 1134. This hypothesis is unconvincing. The revolt of Oultrejourdain in 1126, if it took place, would have been the first internal revolt in the Latin Kingdom and would, in view of the substantial size of the territories involved, have been a major political event. It is all the more surprising, therefore, that the revolt is not mentioned by any chronicler (the remark of William of Tyre refers to the revolt of 1134, which we know to have taken place). That Romain was put in a position where he was *able* to revolt twice is also scarcely credible: we know that he still held extensive fiefs in the royal domain around Nablus in 1128, two years after the posited revolt had taken place.[76] A rebel

---

[74] *Cart. gén. Hosp.*, No. 20; *Reg. Hier.*, No. 57. Confirmed in *Cart. gen. Hosp.*, No. 225 of 1154; *Reg. Hier.*, No. 293; *Cart. du St-Sépulcre*, No. 44 (B.-B., No. 30); *Reg. Hier.*, No. 121.

[75] See above and n. 64.

[76] *Cart. du St-Sépulcre*, No. 44 (B.-B., No. 30); *Reg. Hier.*, No. 121.

could normally expect death, or at best exile, if he failed in his enterprise. That Romain should have been rewarded for his action with fiefs in the royal domain stretches credulity.

The way in which the Lords of Oultrejourdain styled themselves also provides significant evidence. We are fortunate in having eight surviving references to Romain de Puy in charters. Throughout his life, whether before, during, or after the period in which he is supposed to have been Lord of Oultrejourdain, he was referred to simply as 'Romanus de Podio'. Similarly, Romain witnessed documents in 1112, 1115, 1128, and 1133: in each of these documents he appears as 'Romanus de Podio'.[77]

By way of comparison, each of the other accepted Lords of Oultrejourdain can be found to have referred to themselves (often from a much smaller sample of surviving documents) as such. We find, for instance:

Paganus, dominus regionis trans Jordanem sitae;[78]
Mauricius, Montis Regalis dominus;[79]
Philippus de Monte Regali;[80]
Milo, dominus Montis Regalis,[81]
Rainaldus, quondam Antiochiae princeps, nunc vero Hebron-[s]ensis et Montis Regalis dominus.[82]

Even William of Tyre's reference to Romain as 'dominus regionis illius que est trans Jordanem' is ambiguous: it does not necessarily imply, for instance, that he was lord of all the trans-Jordanian territories that later became the Seigneury of Oultrejourdain.[83]

Mayer's hypothesis also ignores a crucial charter of July 1161. In this document King Baldwin III gave Philip de Milly the Lordship of Oultrejourdain and went on to detail the main elements which comprised the fief. The major part of these were described as being: '. . . qua Paganus, pincerna regius in vita sua hec omnia . . . tenuit et habuit.[84] The reference to Pagan has never been remarked upon, but it does seem rather odd. When the charter was issued there had already been (according to

---

[77] *Reg. Hier. Add.*, No. 68a; *Reg. Hier.*, Nos. 79, 91, 105, 121, 147.
[78] Ibid. 250.   [79] Ibid. 279.   [80] Ibid. 412.
[81] Ibid. 496.   [82] Ibid. 551.   [83] William of Tyre, p. 651.
[84] *Tab. ord. Theut.*, No. 3; *Reg. Hier.*, No. 366.

accepted theory) four Lords of Oultrejourdain, with Philip de Milly becoming the fifth. Why would Pagan, the second lord, be singled out for special mention? I would suggest that Baldwin III, in making his brief outline of Oultrejourdain, was in fact describing the lordship as it was when first constituted, and that the reference to Pagan was as the archetypical lord of the region. In other words, Baldwin was exhibiting the medieval respect for tradition by referring to the lordship under its *first* lord, Pagan the Butler. This view is strengthened by the fact that Baldwin then went on to make new grants of land and service to the lordship: in other words, juxtaposing modern additions with the archetypical central core of Oultrejourdain. Similarly, although later Lords of Oultrejourdain, such as Reynald de Chatillon, sometimes made reference to their predecessors by name, there is never any mention of Romain de Puy.

I would argue that accepted views of Oultrejourdain from 1118 to 1126 are extremely unconvincing and rest on the flimsiest of evidence. In their place one can propose a much simpler sequence of events. Romain was lord of a *portion* of the territory that later became the Seigneury of Oultrejourdain: in view of his overlordship of Bessura and La, the 'terra Belcha' would seem to be the most likely position for his fief. It is interesting to note that the 'terra Belcha' retained its identity as an administrative unit even in the 1160s, lending credence to the hypothesis that it had at one point constituted a separate fief. A document of January 1166 confirmed that Philip de Milly had given the Templars '. . . dimidium tocius illius quod habuit in Belcha . . .'.[85] This hypothesis makes William of Tyre's assertion that Romain was a lord of 'regionis illius quae est trans Jordanem' consistent with the evidence showing that he could not have been lord of the entire Oultrejourdain.

It is clear that Romain was involved in a revolt against royal authority, but only *one* (in 1134). Until now the 'revolt of 1126' has been posited as explaining William's statement that Romain had his fiefs confiscated because of his revolt (though note that William mentions only one revolt). If Romain was not Lord of Oultrejourdain, however, the need to invent a 'revolt of 1126' disappears: he revolted, together with the Count of Jaffa, in 1134

[85] *Chartes de Josaphat*, ed. Delaborde, No. 18; *Reg. Hier.*, No. 134; *ROL* II (1905–8), 183–5.

and was then dispossessed of his lands throughout the kingdom, including those in the 'terra Belcha'. With the 'lordship' of Romain de Puy disposed of, one sees that the Oultrejourdain was kept in the royal domain until *c.*1126, at which time it was given to a trusted official of the royal household, Pagan the Butler.

In the Lordship of Oultrejourdain one thus finds, once again, the tendency to understate royal influence in its early history and to pre-date the existence of the Lordship itself.

THE LORDSHIP OF BETHSAN

Much the same is true in the Lordship of Bethsan. In the late summer of 1099 Tancred and a group of eighty followers occupied the undefended town of Bethsan. He did not, however, as has generally been supposed, take Galilee: the occupation of Bethsan was perhaps a deliberate attempt to be independent of Godfrey de Bouillon, who occupied Tiberias (probably in early September).[86] Bethsan was thus never part of the Principality of Galilee.

Once again, historians have tended to try to place John of Ibelin's feudal structure much further back in the history of the Kingdom than the evidence would justify. La Monte, for instance, in his study of the Lords of Bethsan, says that it 'is probable that this unnamed Bethune (who has generally been called Adam) was granted the fief of Bethsan by Hugh de St Omer at the same time Hugh was himself granted Tiberias by King Baldwin' (i.e. March 1101).[87] There is absolutely no evidence to support this contention, however, and on the contrary, as Bethsan was never part of the Principality of Galilee, Hugh could not have given it to anyone.

Surviving evidence is inconclusive, but may indicate that King Baldwin I took advantage of Tancred's departure in 1101 to retain Bethsan in the royal domain. In 1106–7, for instance, it is the king, rather than a Lord of Bethsan, whom we find confirming that the monks of Mount Thabor owned Tubania, a casal which later evidence shows to have been within the territorial boundaries of the Seigneury of Bethsan, since in 1152 Hugh of Bethsan was

---

[86] Albert of Aix, p. 517. For a re-examination of the taking of Bethsan see Riley-Smith, 'The Motives of the Earliest Crusaders', pp. 726–7.

[87] La Monte and Downs, 'The Lords of Bethsan', p. 59.

given the two casalia of Tubania and Geluth (both sited to the north-west of Bethsan).[88]

Similarly, in 1110, it was the king who confirmed that the Hospitallers owned '. . . tertium [villein] quoque quem dedit Hugo in Bethan'. There is nothing to indicate that this Hugh was Lord of Bethsan: the gift may have been made by Hugh of Le Puiset or Hugh de St Omer (both of whom held fiefs nearby) or, indeed, by another Hugh altogether.[89]

It is only in 1128 that we find evidence for a Lord of Bethsan. In that year the fortified site of Calansue was given to the Hospitallers by Geoffrey de Flujeac.[90] When Baldwin II confirmed the gift in 1129 he made a point of mentioning that it had been made with 'Johannes de Bethsan', John of Bethsan presumably being Geoffrey's immediate overlord.[91] It is not certain that John of Bethsan was Lord of Bethsan, but as a document of 1149 says that John, Lord of Bethsan, had previously sold casal Assera to the Hospitallers, this seems extremely likely.[92] It thus appears that Bethsan was retained in the royal domain for far longer than has previously been supposed, and that it was not until the 1120s that the fief was allowed to leave direct royal control.

Moreover, even after the creation of the lordship, control of its destiny returned to royal hands. At some point in the mid-twelfth century the seigneurial family of Bethsan died out: the fief presumably reverted to the king, who then gave it to a certain Gremont of Tiberias.[93] Gremont's son, Adam, died at an early age leaving only minors, so once again the fief (by wardship in this case) reverted to the crown. Baldwin IV gave (or more likely sold) the wardship to Hugh de Gibelet.[94]

The king clearly had the opportunity, even if he did not choose to exercise it, to exert the highest level of influence over the ownership of the lordship and to decide whether or not to return it to the royal domain.

---

[88] *Cart. gén. Hosp.*, No. 2831; *Reg. Hier.*, No. 51; *Cart. gén. Hosp.*, No. 11; *Reg. Hier.*, No. 277.

[89] *Cart. gén. Hosp.*, No. 20; *Reg. Hier.*, No. 57.

[90] *Cart. gén. Hosp.*, No. 83; *Reg. Hier. Add.*, No. 121a.

[91] *Cart. gén. Hosp.*, No. 84; *Reg. Hier.*, No. 130.

[92] *Cart. gén. Hosp.*, No. 180; *Reg. Hier.*, No. 256.

[93] See La Monte and Downs, 'The Lords of Bethsan', pp. 60–3.

[94] See a document of November 1179, *Tab. ord. Theut.*, No. 12; *Reg. Hier.*, No. 588.

THE COUNTY OF JAFFA AND ASCALON

The County of Jaffa and Ascalon provides a major example of the way in which royal control could be extended to a troublesome, or potentially troublesome, seigneury. Firstly, the fief was retained in the royal domain for the first decade after its capture by the Franks. Secondly, once Count Hugh of Jaffa had demonstrated the extent of the threat he could pose to royal power (instigating the revolt of 1134) steps were taken to ensure that the lordship was either held directly in the royal domain or was given to a close relative of the king.

The importance of Jaffa was reflected in the early interest taken in it by the monarchs of the kingdom: in January 1100 Godfrey de Bouillon organized the refortification of the town.[95] The early significance of Jaffa was also recognized by the Church, as demonstrated by the demands of Patriarch Daimbert, who claimed Jerusalem and also the city of Jaffa with everything pertaining to it.[96] Despite the demands of the Church, however, it is clear that the city was part of the royal domain for several years in the first decade of the twelfth century.

In 1110, for instance, Baldwin confirmed to the Hospitallers that he had previously given them 'one good oven in Jaffa, and also lands and houses in diverse places in the same city'.[97] Similarly, in 1130 Baldwin II confirmed that Baldwin I had previously given the monastery of Josaphat two carrucates of land in the territory of Jaffa.[98]

It is only in 1110 that one finds a Count of Jaffa, Hugh I (Hugh II of Le Puiset).[99] The revolt of Hugh II in 1134 brought an early end to the fortunes of the La Puiset family. The eventual conclusion of the affair was that Hugh was banished for three years and that 'all his debts and whatever he had borrowed anywhere were to be paid from the revenues of his possessions'. As Mayer has pointed out, this statement clearly implies that the king was able to enjoy the revenues of the County in Hugh's

[95] Albert of Aix, p. 515. For recent work on the County of Jaffa and Ascalon, see Mayer, 'The Origins of the County of Jaffa'; id., 'Ibelin versus Ibelin'; id., 'The Double County of Jaffa and Ascalon'; id., 'John of Jaffa, his Opponents and his Fiefs'; Edbury, 'John of Ibelin's Title to the County of Jaffa and Ascalon'.

[96] William of Tyre, p. 441–2.

[97] *Cart. gén. Hosp.*, No. 20; *Reg. Hier.*, No. 57.

[98] *Chartes de Josaphat*, ed. Delaborde, No. 18; *Reg. Hier.*, No. 134.

[99] *Cart. gén. Hosp.*, No. 20; *Reg. Hier.*, No. 57.

absence.[100] An examination of Hugh's landed transactions do not indicate that he was in major financial difficulties (he was, for instance, generous to the Church) and suggests that the 'debts and whatever monies he had borrowed' were a pretext for, and legitimization of, the confiscation of the County by King Fulk.[101] Count Hugh died in exile, and the initial three-year period of royal control was extended: it was not until after 1221 that the County was allowed to leave the royal domain or the hands of the king's close relatives.

Jaffa remained in the royal domain from 1134 until 1151, when it was given by King Baldwin III to his brother Amalric.[102] In 1153 Ascalon was captured and also given to Amalric, but only after the king had derived considerable profit from the area and flooded it with royal appointees.[103] When Amalric ascended the throne (in 1163) the County reverted to the royal domain: it was only allowed to leave direct royal control in 1176, when it was given to the king's sister, Sibylle, and her husband, William de Montferrat.[104]

The next Count (Guy de Lusignan, 1180–6) also received the County only through his marriage to Sibylle. Upon Guy's accession to the throne in 1186 the County once again reverted to the royal domain. The pattern of only relinquishing direct control of the County to close relatives was followed by Guy: his brothers each became Count in turn. The sudden death of King Henry in September 1197 led to the election of Aimery as King of Jerusalem, and the County of Jaffa and Ascalon being once more incorporated into the royal domain.[105] Royal control of the County was only relinquished in the thirteenth century.

In the case of the County of Jaffa and Ascalon royal ability to control troublesome fiefs was amply demonstrated. During the period 1100–1221 the County was only out of effective royal control for a 24-year span (1110–34). Moreover, after 1134

---

[100] William of Tyre, pp. 653–4; Mayer, 'Studies in the History of Queen Melisende', p. 102.

[101] For Hugh's landed transactions, see: *Chartes de Josaphat*, ed. Kohler, No. 9; *Reg. Hier. Add.*, No. 102a; *Cart. gén. Hosp.*, No. 74; *Reg. Hier.*, No. 112; *Cart. gén. Hosp.*, No. 97; *Reg. Hier.*, No. 147.

[102] In 1151 we find Amalric appearing as 'Amalricus, comes Iope' for the first time: *Cart. du St-Sépulcre*, No. 49 (B.-B., No. 35); *Reg. Hier.*, No. 268.

[103] William of Tyre, pp. 803–5.   [104] William of Tyre, pp. 977–8.

[105] *Eracles*, p. 220; Ernoul, pp. 192–3; Amadi, *Chroniques*, i. 90–1; Ibn al-Athir, 'Kamil', ii. 86.

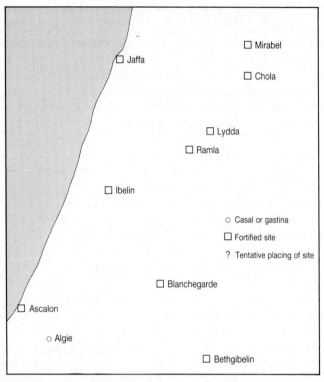

3. Jaffa, Ascalon, Mirabel, Ramla, Blanchegarde, and Ibelin

effective steps were taken to ensure that the County, if and when it was given in fief to a member of the nobility, was permanently weakened and its military potential severely curtailed.

THE LORDSHIP OF RAMLA

The Lordship of Ramla provides yet another example of the tendency of historians to pre-date the existence of seigneuries listed by John of Ibelin. Although various authorities disagree on minor details it is generally accepted that the original Lordship of Ramla and Lydda was a religious one, which was actively concerned with the colonization of Ramla and which existed until the period *c*.1110–*c*.1120. It is also assumed that between 1110 and 1120 Ramla was divided from Lydda, formed into a secular seigneury, and given to Baldwin, Lord of Ramla.

The evidence does not support these contentions. The bishop's Seigneury of Ramla–Lydda seems to have been extremely short-lived and military considerations forced King Baldwin I to dismantle it almost immediately. The castle of Ramla and its surrounding lands first became part of the royal domain and were later (by 1126) subsumed in the County of Jaffa. It is not until 1136 that we hear of a secular *Lordship* of Ramla being created, and even then it seems to have been a creation that (as we shall see) worked very much to the advantage of the king.

The existence of a bishop's lordship at Ramla–Lydda until the period *c.* 1110–*c.* 1120 has been generally accepted. Prawer goes even further and suggests that the Church played the prime motivating role in the colonization of Ramla.[106] This highly successful colonization was, Prawer feels, created by means of an agreement which the Hospitallers later called the 'consuetudinem Lithde, quam alio nomine vocamus Ramas'. Since the bishop was lord of both places, and supervised the colonization which lay between the two, it was a short step to call the 'custom of Ramle' the 'custom of Lydda'.[107]

The evidence does not support these assertions, however. The 'custom of Ramle' has not survived, and we have to rely on the statements of the chroniclers. The *Gesta Francorum* tell us that the princes of the first crusade gathered to choose a bishop at Ramla and gave him tithes, money, and animals, so that he might live in comfort with his followers ('qui cum eo essent'). William of Tyre says that the princes gave Ramla and Lydda to Bishop Robert 'cum adjacentibus suburbanis' and also that 'our men' ('nostri') constructed a fortress complete with walls and moat at Ramla, as they considered it would be difficult to occupy the space encompassed by the original walls with so few people. From Albert of Aix we learn that after a stay of three days at Ramla the crusaders anointed a bishop and left behind settlers to

---

[106] Prawer, *Crusader Institutions*, p. 123: 'probably between 1115 and 1120, Ramle already belonged to a seignor called Baldwin, who took part in the Council of Nablus'. Mayer, 'Carving up Crusaders', p. 117: 'The succession of the Lords of Ramla must be: (a) Baldwin I ca. 1110–1138 . . .'; see also Prawer, *Crusader Institutions*, pp. 114–15. For the most recent work on Ramla, see Mayer, 'The Origins of the Lordships of Ramla and Lydda'.

[107] *Cart. gén. Hosp.*, No. 399; *Reg. Hier.*, No. 457; Prawer, *Crusader Institutions*, p. 124.

'till the soil, organise justice and bring in the fruits of the field and the orchard'.[108]

The fate of the ecclesiastical Lordship of Ramla–Lydda is made clear by Fulcher of Chartres, however, who tells us that by 1101 King Baldwin I was already responsible for the garrison of Ramla: 'non enim tunc habemus plusquam CCCos milites et tantum de peditibus, qui Hierusalem et Ioppen, Ramulam, Caypham etiam castrum custodiebant'.[109] Later, in 1102, Fulcher confirms this when he tells us that there was a garrison of 15 knights in Ramla, placed there by the king, with Syrian farmers living outside. The Saracens, Fulcher tells us, who had often attacked these farmers, wanted to destroy them once and for all, and to raze the fortress which hindered their free passage over the plain. Besides which, they wanted to capture the bishop and his subordinates ('cum clientela sua') who occupied the church of St George.[110]

It is clear from the chronicles that it was the princes of the first crusade who established the seigneury, and that it was these laymen who left settlers behind. On the first occasion in which we hear anything about the inhabitants of Ramla after the initial placement, we are told that a royal garrison is in charge and actively defending the local peasantry. The bishop and 'clientela sua' are to be found only in the church of St George (i.e. not in Ramla at all, but in Lydda). The ecclesiastical lordship, piously established before a central monarchy existed, can be seen to have been dismantled by the king as soon as possible (i.e. by 1101) and became part of the royal domain: the early Lordship of Ramla–Lydda probably existed for a matter of months rather than years.

The idea that the secular Lordship of Ramla was formed in the period *c.*1110–*c.*1120 also rests on extremely flimsy evidence. We know only that a certain Baldwin owned property in and around Ramla and that an individual known as Baldwin of Ramla witnessed some charters in this period. This by no mean proves that he was Lord of Ramla.

In September 1109 or 1110 King Baldwin I confirmed that a

---

[108] *Gesta Francorum*, p. 87; William of Tyre, pp. 373–4. I interpret this to mean the *immediate* territory of the towns, rather than what later became the lordship; William of Tyre, p. 472; Albert of Aix, p. 461.

[109] Fulcher of Chartres, p. 389.   [110] Ibid., pp. 425–7.

certain Baldwin had previously given the Hospitallers villeins, lands, and houses in the city of Ramla. Similarly, in 1115 he confirmed that a certain Baldwin had given 'terram duobus aratris sufficientem' in the territory of Ramla to the monastery of Josaphat: this charter was witnessed by, amongst others, Baldwin of Ramla.[111]

We also know that Baldwin of Ramla owned extensive properties in what were certainly royal domain lands. In 1123 the Patriarch of Jerusalem confirmed that the monastery of Josaphat had previously been given 'terciam etiam partem decime Balduini Ramathensis de tribus casalibus quorum nomina sunt hec: Gemmail, Assir, Beithbezim . . .'. Of the three properties, only two can now be identified: Gemmail (or Gemail) was sited in the royal domain around Nablus, as was Beithbezim (or Bethbezim). In this context, it is perhaps not unwarranted to suggest that Assir may be identified with the village of Azeire, also in the royal domain of Nablus.[112]

One can see that Baldwin was a substantial property owner in and around Ramla and Nablus, but never referred to himself, or was called by others, Lord of Ramla. This is consistent with chroniclers' assertions that Ramla was under royal control in the early twelfth century. Rather than to suggest that a lordship existed at this time, it seems more likely that Baldwin was a senior vassal in the royal domain, who was given responsibilities for the administration of the royal domain at Ramla (perhaps as castellan, though this is never explicitly stated).

The fief of Ramla appears to have become part of the County of Jaffa in the mid-1120s. In January 1126, for instance, we find the Count of Jaffa confirming the possessions of the Hospitallers held in the territory of Ramla. In 1129 there is evidence that the Count of Jaffa had previously conceded the gift of two casalia in the territory of Lydda to the Hospitallers. Moreover, in a later confirmation of the same transaction (issued by Baldwin III in

---

[111] *Cart. gén. Hosp.*, No. 20; *Reg. Hier.*, No. 57. This was confirmed by King Baldwin III in 1154; *Cart. gén. Hosp.*, No. 225; *Reg. Hier.*, No. 293; *Chartes de Josaphat*, ed. Delaborde, No. 6; *Reg. Hier.*, No. 80.

[112] *Chartes de Josaphat*, ed. Delaborde, No. 12; *Reg. Hier.*, No. 101. This grant was confirmed in 1129 by a later Patriarch: *Chartes de Josaphat*, ed. Kohler, No. 17; *Reg. Hier. Add.*, No. 129a; Prawer–Benvenisti Map, ref. 164/181 for Beithbezim; ibid. 175/184 for Azeire; ibid. 169/170 for Gemmail.

1154) it is unambiguously stated that Count Hugh of Jaffa was Hugh of Ramla's lord at that time.[113]

It is not until 1136, however, that we hear of a Lord or secular Lordship of Ramla: Baldwin II of Ramla was present at the grant of the new castle of Bethgibelin to the Hospitallers, by which time he was already referred to as a lord ('de baronibus . . . Balduinus Ramathensis . . .').[114] It is significant that we first hear of a Lord of Ramla shortly after the revolt of Count Hugh of Jaffa and that Baldwin II of Ramla was present at the creation of a new part of the defences designed to isolate Ascalon. After Hugh's revolt in 1134 King Fulk created three new fortifications in the area: Bethgibelin, Ibelin, and Blanchegarde. Of these, the latter two were entities created out of lands belonging to the County of Jaffa.

In the aftermath of the revolt King Fulk deliberately set about reducing the power of the County by, amongst other things, giving more independence to its leading vassals. That Ramla was part of this process seems almost certain. Before the revolt of 1134 no one called himself, or was referred to as, Lord of Ramla. Afterwards we find Baldwin as 'de baronibus' in 1136 and appearing as 'Balduinus, Ramensis dominus' in Jerusalem in February 1138.[115] Moreover, in 1160 Hugh of Ibelin referred to Baldwin II of Ramla as 'Balduini, avi mei, Ramathensis Latinorum domini primi'.[116]

All this evidence points towards the creation of the Lordship of Ramla in the period 1134–6: for the lordship to have been created so soon after the revolt (and to have been the first of the four new entities) suggests that Baldwin, although a vassal of the County of Jaffa, remained loyal to King Fulk during the uprising, or at least changed sides at an opportune moment. The fact that a large part of the lands of the Ramla family seems to have been held directly from the king in the royal domain around Nablus may help to explain this loyalty.

Further evidence for the creation of the lordship about this time is given by the first appearance of administrative offers. It is

[113] _Cart. gén. Hosp._, No. 77; _Reg. Hier._, No. 113; _Cart. gén. Hosp._, No. 84; _Reg. Hier._, No. 130; _Cart. gén. Hosp._, No. 225; _Reg. Hier._, No. 293.

[114] _Cart. gén. Hosp._, No. 116; _Reg. Hier._, No. 164.

[115] _Cart. gén. Hosp._, No. 116; _Reg. Hier._, No. 164; _Cart. du St-Sépulcre_, No. 33 (B.-B., No. 34); _Reg. Hier._, No. 174.

[116] _Cart. du St-Sépulcre_, No. 65 (B.-B., No. 53); _Reg. Hier._, No. 360.

not until 1138–9 that we find a charter of the Bishop of Ramla witnessed by a certain 'Petrus vicecomes',[117] and in a document dated *c*.1159 we find it confirmed that 'Petrus de Ramla' had previously owned two *petias* of vineyards in the valley of St Mary.[118]

Thus, instead of the accepted view of the lordship being created in the period *c*.1110–*c*.1120, and being preceded by an ecclesiastical lordship, we can see that the territory of Ramla was only briefly allowed to leave royal control, from *c*.1126–34 when it was under the control of the Count of Jaffa. The lordship itself was not created until *c*.1136, and even then was only given to a trusted vassal. Moreover, it is worth noting that as the County of Jaffa was in royal hands in 1134, Ramla would have been a rear-fief of the royal domain at Jaffa rather than a fully independent seigneury.[119]

THE LORDSHIP OF MIRABEL

The existence of the Lordship of Mirabel also seems to have been pre-dated. It has been suggested that the castle of Mirabel was already the centre of a lordship in 1122, the seigneur of which was Balian the Elder, founder of the Ibelin family. This fief, it is claimed, was given to him by the Count of Jaffa, in whose domains it was before it became an independent seigneury: on Balian's death, it has been suggested, Mirabel passed to his widow, who married Manasses of Hierges.[120]

This theory is based on a series of misapprehensions and is indicative of the tendency of historians of the Latin East to assume that the feudal map of the Kingdom took the form presented to us by John of Ibelin at a much earlier date than was actually the case. The main evidence for this hypothesis is a charter of 1122 which has since been demonstrated to be a forgery.[121] When this is discounted all the evidence points towards the creation of lordships at a time when there was *no* Count of Jaffa (as with other sub-fiefs of the County such as

---

[117] *Chartes de Josaphat*, ed. Delaborde, No. 20; *Reg. Hier.*, No. 190.

[118] *Cart. de St-Sépulcre*, No. 129 (B.-B., No. 121); *Reg. Hier.*, No. 340.

[119] See this chapter, under The County of Jaffa and Ascalon.

[120] Benvenisti, *The Crusaders in the Holy Land*, pp. 194–5.

[121] *Cart. gén. Hosp.*, No. 59; *Reg. Hier.*, No. 100. For discussion of the authenticity of *Reg. Hier.*, No. 100, see Mayer, 'Carving up Crusaders'.

Ibelin, Blanchegarde, and Ramla). Indeed, it is difficult to see what could have motivated the Count to diminish his power by creating lordships within his own domains.

It is clear, however, that the fief *was* created and was given to the Ibelins. Fulk arrived in the Latin Kingdom in 1129 and died in November 1143. As Balian had proved himself loyal to the king during the revolt of his overlord, Count Hugh of Jaffa, in 1134 (and as the creation of sub-lordships in the County of Jaffa by the king after the revolt seems to have been a matter of deliberate policy) it is overwhelmingly likely that Mirabel was given to Balian between 1134 and 1143.

This hypothesis is substantiated by charter evidence. In January 1158 we find Hugh of Ibelin renouncing the legal dispute which had been taking place between his father and the Hospitallers over lands in Mirabel.[122] Similarly, in 1163 Hugh's brother, Baldwin of Mirabel, confirmed the donation of property in the Lordship of Mirabel that had previously been made by his father Balian the Elder and his mother Heloise.[123]

In this context it seems extremely likely that Balian the Elder was the first Lord of Mirabel and that the lordship was established by King Fulk, at the expense of the County of Jaffa, between 1134 and 1143.

THE LORDSHIP OF IBELIN

Balian the Elder, founder of the fortunes of the Ibelin family and Constable of Jaffa, remained loyal to the king during the revolt of Count Hugh le Puiset and was rewarded shortly afterwards by being given the castle and Lordship of Ibelin.[124] The castle of Ibelin itself was built in the reign of King Fulk, though the exact date is unknown.[125] Even then Ibelin was not made into an entirely independent lordship, but remained dependent on the County of Jaffa, which was itself part of the royal domain at that time.[126]

[122] *Cart. gén. Hosp.*, No. 263; *Reg. Hier.*, No. 330.
[123] *Cart. gén. Hosp.*, No. 327; *Reg. Hier. Add.*, No. 384*a*.
[124] William of Tyre, pp. 706–7.
[125] James of Vitry, ed. Bongars, p. 1071.
[126] See e.g. John of Ibelin, p. 417; *Cart. du St-Sépulcre*, No. 56 (B.-B., No. 41); *Reg. Hier.*, No. 299; *Cart. du St-Sépulcre*, No. 59 (B.-B., No. 46); *Reg. Hier.*, No. 300; *Cart. du St-Sépulcre*, No. 62 (B.-B., No. 50); *Reg. Hier.*, No. 301; AOL 2B, pp. 134–5, No. 15; *Reg. Hier.*, No. 303; AOL 2B, pp. 133–3, No. 14; *Reg. Hier.*, No. 308; *Cart. du St-Sépulcre*, No. 60 (B.-B., No. 47); *Reg. Hier.*, No. 332.

THE LORDSHIP OF BLANCHEGARDE

Blanchegarde, as with so many of the administrative units that later became lordships, was originally created as a sub-unit of the royal domain. In 1142 King Fulk erected the castle of Blanchegarde as part of the defensive network used to contain the Egyptian garrison of Ascalon. William of Tyre relates the construction of Blanchegarde in some detail and leaves us in no doubt that the castle was, upon completion, entrusted to royal castellans rather than made into a seigneury: 'Castrum ergo perfectum et omnibus partibus suis absolutum dominus rex in suam suscepit custodiam, et tam victu quam armis sufficienter munitum viris prudentibus et rei militaris habentibus experientiam, quorum nota est fides et probata devotio, servandum commisit.'[127]

Administration of Blanchegarde by royal castellans continued until the 1160s, and we are fortunate in having some evidence as to their identity. In April 1165 we find a certain 'Arnulfus, castellanus de Blancagarda' witnessing a charter in Jerusalem.[128] A pancart of 1185 also makes reference to a 'Holmundus Gilleberto castellano' who had previously sold the monastery of St Samuel two carrucates of land near Blanchegarde.[129] As Arnulf was Castellan of Blanchegarde when it was given to Walter of Beirut, 'Holmundus' must have been an earlier castellan.

Although Blanchegarde was administered by castellans from 1142 to 1166 it had not always been a part of the royal domain. Rather, the land on which the castle was built and the surrounding territory which later came to constitute the Seigneury of Blanchegarde was taken from the County of Jaffa. From the suppression of the revolt of Count Hugh (in 1134) until the grant of Jaffa to the king's brother Amalric (in 1151) the County of Jaffa was itself part of the royal domain: thus, from the time when Blanchegarde was built (1142) until 1151 the true administrative position of Blanchegarde is unclear. It was a small unit of royal domain within a larger area which was itself in the royal domain.

That the territory of Blanchegarde had been 'carved out' of the County of Jaffa is only apparent when one looks at the period

---

[127] William of Tyre, pp. 707–9.
[128] *Cart. gén. Hosp.*, No. 344; *Reg. Hier.*, No. 413.
[129] 'Sankt-Samuel', p. 68.

1151–63, when Amalric was Count of Jaffa. In April 1158 (the earliest charter reference to Blanchegarde) we find that the monastery of St Mary of the Latins owned a casal in the territory of Blanchegarde, and that its ownership of this property had been confirmed by Count Amalric, rather than the king.[130]

When Amalric became king in 1163 one would expect the castellan of Blanchegarde, who was Castellan Arnulf at that time, to have once again become a royal officer rather than an officer of the County of Jaffa and Ascalon (as Jaffa and Ascalon reverted to the royal domain upon Amalric's accession). It is therefore gratifying to find 'Arnulfus, castellanus de Blancagarda' in Jerusalem in April 1165, witnessing, together with other leading vassals of the royal domain of Jaffa and Ascalon, such as Roard of Jaffa and William Rufus, Viscount of Ascalon, a royal charter that dealt with casalia in the County.[131]

The foundation of Blanchegarde, therefore, was a *disestablishment*, rather than an establishment. It was carved out of the County of Jaffa and was only allowed to leave direct royal control to be given into the hands of the king's brother, Amalric.

The Lordship of Blanchegarde was instituted as an administrative unit independent of the County of Jaffa and Ascalon in 1166, when the impoverished Lord Walter of Beirut was forced to give up his lordship in exchange for Blanchegarde and a sum of money, in order to pay his debts: 'Et il vost laissier sa mere; si fina a la reyne Ysabiau en tel maniere, qu'il lor dona Baruth, et il li donerent la Blanche Garde en eschange et besanz aussi de quei il paia sa dette et delivera sa mère.'[132]

Although the 'Lignages' are wrong in ascribing these events to Queen Isabel's reign, the exchange is confirmed by charter evidence. In March 1164 we find Walter in Beirut giving lands to the house of St Lazarus and referring to himself as 'Gualterius Brisebarram, Berrithi dominus Dei gratia'.[133] By 1174 we find Walter making another gift to the Brothers of St Lazarus, but this time in his capacity as Lord of Blanchegarde: in a document of

---

[130] *Reg. Hier.*, No. 331. Possession of this casal was also confirmed in a papal charter of 8 March 1173, in which the monastery of St Mary of the Latins was described as having 'casale unum in territorio Blancegarde, quod privilegio comitis Amarrici vobis est confirmatum . . .', 'Papst-Kaiser', p. 57.

[131] *Cart. gén. Hosp.*, No. 344; *Reg. Hier.*, No. 413.

[132] 'Les Lignages', p. 458.

[133] AOL 2B, p. 139, No. 21; *Reg. Hier.*, No. 395.

February in that year King Amalric conceded to St Lazarus a grant of 40 besants to be collected annually from the port of Acre, a payment which had previously been made to Walter. Quite apart from providing an insight into Walter's revenues, this document also makes explicit the circumstances of Walter's lordship when Amalric refers to him as 'Galteri de Berito, Albe Custodie domino, quam ego ei pro Berito in cumcambio dedi'.[134] The exchange of Beirut can be fixed at 1166 as in the following year the king briefly gave the vacant lordship to Andronicus Comnenus.[135]

The acquisition of Beirut provided a substantial addition to the royal domain in return for an immediate capital outlay and a small castellany that had largely been militarily redundant since the fall of Ascalon in 1153 (a castellany that had, moreover, been carved out of one of the greater lordships). The king had little to lose and much to gain.

Moreover, although John of Ibelin tells us that Blanchegarde had rights of 'cours, coins et justise', the king was careful to ensure that even this relatively small lordship did not have too much independence: the military service owed for Blanchegarde was to be owed directly to the royal domain at Acre.[136] Blanchegarde, although a lordship, was thus retained as a rear-fief of the royal domain, rather than being given full status as a tenant-in-chief.

In Blanchegarde we thus find a striking example of the way in which the monarchy was able, if it chose, to manipulate the feudal map of the kingdom to suit its own ends: in this case increasing the royal domain at the expense of its more powerful vassals.

FULK AND THE RESPONSE TO THE REVOLT OF 1134

The royal response to the revolt of 1134 provides a remarkable, but hitherto unremarked upon, insight into the way in which the monarch could formulate and execute a consistent and conscious policy towards his greater vassals.

We have seen that the reign of King Fulk saw a major expansion in the number of seigneuries in the south of the

---

[134] *AOL* 2B, pp. 145–8, No. 28; *Reg. Hier.*, No. 512.
[135] William of Tyre, pp. 913–14.   [136] John of Ibelin, pp. 420, 425.

kingdom. Historians of the Latin East have traditionally seen this build-up, and the castle construction that accompanied it, as a direct response to the threat of attack from the Egyptian garrison at Ascalon. More recently, Mayer has suggested that King Fulk's quarrel with Count Hugh II of Jaffa was part of a deliberate attempt to increase the size of the royal domain. He suggests that after goading Hugh into revolt, Fulk 'reached his true goal of acquiring for the Crown the county of Jaffa'. [137]

Both of these hypotheses have elements of truth in them, but fail to connect the two incidents (i.e. the revolt of 1134 and the castle-building of the following decade) and place them in their full historical context. We have seen that several major structural changes in the seigneurial map of southern Palestine were effected by King Fulk in the aftermath of the revolt of 1134:

Jaffa itself was acquired for the royal domain;
the Hospitaller Lordship of Bethgibelin was created out of the Seigneury of Hebron;
the Lordship of Ibelin was carved out of the County of Jaffa;
the fief of Ramla, previously dependent on the County, was made into a separate lordship;
Mirabel, also previously dependent on the County of Jaffa, was formed into a separate seigneury;
the castle of Blanchegarde was built in lands belonging to the County and made into an administrative unit (a castellany) of the royal domain.

Such a major series of events, occurring so close together in terms of geography and time, cannot be coincidental. Existing hypotheses do not fit the facts, however. If defence had been the only objective of the exercise, this could have been achieved without creating a series of sub-lordships and castellanies both within and without the County of Jaffa. Simiarly, if the king's motivation behind the exile of Hugh II of Jaffa had merely been to increase the size of the royal domain, he would not have created lordships out of the County of Jaffa (which was, of course, part of the royal domain after 1134).

Rather, I would suggest that Fulk tried, successfully, to combine two objectives: firstly, he wanted to ensure that the County of Jaffa would never again be powerful enough to present

[137] Mayer, 'Studies in the History of Queen Melisende', pp. 95–111.

a major threat to the monarchy, and secondly, he wanted to obviate the threat of forays from Ascalon. He combined the two in an extremely efficient expression of deliberate royal policy. The County was severely weakened by the removal of Blanchegarde, Ramla, Ibelin, and Mirabel, and the opportunity was also taken to weaken the nearby Lordship of Hebron by removing Bethgibelin from its control. This determination to prevent a resurgence of power in the County was a policy which was consistently upheld by later Kings of Jerusalem: hence the large elements of royal domain retained in Ascalon after its capture in 1153[138] and the caution which ensured that the County itself was either part of the royal domain or in the hands of a close relative throughout the rest of the twelfth century.

Perhaps the most tangible way of measuring the loss of power of the County is by looking at records for military service. John of Ibelin tells us that the County, without Ascalon, owed the service of 75 knights.[139] By the time King Fulk had finished creating new lordships and castellanies only 25 knights would have been owed directly by the Count of Jaffa: of the original 75, 40 were jointly owed by Ramla and Mirabel, and 10 by Ibelin. The 8 (or possibly 9) knights owed for Blanchegarde, which was also previously part of the County, were transferred directly to the royal domain.[140] Thus, from a total of 83 or 84 knights in 1133, the County had been reduced to 25: the Count's capacity for independent military action had been severely curtailed. Though a later source, John of Ibelin shows the proportion of knights' service that was lost to the Counts of Jaffa and Ascalon.

In short, King Fulk's motivation for confiscating the County was more far-reaching than mere financial gain (though that undoubtedly played a part). After 1134 Fulk was determined to take advantage of the situation to ensure that the kingdom's defences against Ascalon were dramatically enhanced and that the power of the Counts of Jaffa would be broken forever: in both of these aims he succeeded admirably.

THE LORDSHIP OF DERA

The almost unknown Lordship of Dera provides a small but interesting insight into royal policy on the eastern borders of the

---

[138] See chapter 3, section 3, under The County of Jaffa and Ascalon.
[139] John of Ibelin, p. 422.   [140] Ibid. 425.

kingdom, particularly in view of the cases of the Lordships of Toron, Banias, and Assebebe.[141]

In 1118 King Baldwin II led an attack on the Cave de Sueth, which was surrendered to him, and went on to capture Dera,[142] which William of Tyre called, with reference to an event in 1147, 'civitas Bernardi de Stampis'.[143] Although we know nothing else of Bernard d'Étampes, a Tripolitan charter of 1143, which has not been remarked on previously, makes reference to a certain 'Bernardus Derat' who had given the Holy Sepulchre a peasant and a carrucate of land in casal Aer (in the County of Tripoli).[144] It looks as if, instead of giving the newly captured lands to the Principality of Galilee, as one might have expected given its location, Dera was given in fief to a Tripolitan knight and presumably held directly from the crown: another example of royal policy attempting to contain or reduce the larger fiefs.

THE LORDSHIP OF SCANDALEON

Scandaleon was built in 1116 by Baldwin I as a way of blocking the landward approaches towards Tyre.[145] The first Lord of Scandaleon does not appear until 1148 however, when 'Guidonis, Scandaleonis domini' witnessed a charter.[146] It thus appears that Scandaleon remained in the royal domain for several decades before direct royal control was relinquished.

Even after the Lordship of Scandaleon was created, however, it was not given the full status accorded to most other seigneuries. In common with Haifa and Blanchegarde, it was only given the status of a rear-fief of the royal domain at Acre.[147]

THE LORDSHIP OF ARSUR

Arsur, though later to be established as a seigneury, remained in the royal domain for most of the twelfth century. Arsur was captured by the Franks in 1101. King Baldwin left a royal

---

[141] See chapter 2, under The Lordships of Toron, Banias, and Chastel Neuf.
[142] Ibn al-Athir, 'Kamil', i. 315.   [143] William of Tyre, p. 728.
[144] *Cart. du St-Sépulcre*, No. 97 (B.-B., No. 85); *Reg. Hier.*, No. 218.
[145] William of Tyre, p. 543; Fulcher of Chartres, pp. 605–6. For the most recent work on Scandaleon, see Favreau, 'Die Kreuzfahrerherrschaft Scandalion (Iskanderune)'.
[146] AOL 2B, p. 127, No. 6; *Reg. Hier.*, No. 251.
[147] John of Ibelin, p. 425.

garrison in the town and then went on to besiege Caesarea.[148] From that time until 1163 (when we first find a reference to an individual who seems to be an independent Lord of Arsur) the town remained in royal hands, probably as a castellany. The circumstances under which the town left royal control and became a lay lordship are now completely unknown, but in 1163 a certain 'Johannes de Arsur' appears for the first time.[149] He later appears as 'dominus Johannes de Azoto' on a charter of the Prince of Galilee, making plain his status as lord.[150]

THE LORDSHIP OF THE SCHUF

The Schuf (the eastern hinterland between Sidon and Beirut) was always a troublesome area for the Franks. From the earliest times, the Muslims had taken active steps to ensure that possession of the region would be contested on an active basis.

The Maronite historian, Tannus ash-Shadyaq, tells us that Emir Ma'n al-Ayyubi received orders from Tughtigin in 1120 to move with his clan to the mountains of Lebanon which overlook the coast. Ma'n and his followers settled in Bahaelin in the Schuf and allied himself with the Tanukhid Emir Buhtur. Together they carried out raids against the Franks and formed a focus for local resistance: people came to his territory from areas under Frankish occupation.[151]

The Lordship of the Schuf, like the County of Jaffa, provides another example of the way in which the monarchy could respond to a threat posed by one of its tenants-in-chief: using rebellion as an opportunity not only to oust the offending individual but also to break the power of his fief to sustain a threatening level of military activity against the monarchy in the future.

The Seigneury of the Schuf is also significant as another lordship which has never been identified as such by historians of the Latin Kingdom. Where it has been remarked on, it has always been assumed merely to be a tract of land on the eastern

---

[148] Albert of Aix, pp. 542–3; William of Tyre, p. 468–9; Fulcher of Chartres, pp. 393–400.
[149] *Les Archives*, ed. Delaville, p. 99; *Reg. Hier.*, No. 379.
[150] *Cart. gén. Hosp.*, No. 398; *Reg. Hier.*, No. 448.
[151] Salibi, 'Maronite Historians', p. 188.

borders of the Lordship of Sidon. Because Julian, Lord of Sidon, sold the Schuf to the Teutonic Order, however, detailed evidence concerning the lordship exists for the period 1256–61.[152]

On 4 January 1257 (or 1256) Julian gave the Order 'toute ma terre dou Souf . . . et toute la seigniorie et toute la justise . . .'[153] Julian, Lord of Sidon, was clearly Lord of Schuf as only he was able to sell 'toute la seigniorie et toute la justise'. John of Schuf had earlier sold his fief in the Schuf to the Teutonic Knights, but had only been able to sell properties, rather than rights. On the same day that he gave the Teutonic Knights the Seigneury of the Schuf, Julian also gave the Order the fortress of Cave de Tyron: 'ma forteresse, la quele est apelee Cave de Tyron, et totes ses raisons, que je et mes heirs avons et avoir devons en cele desus dite cave'.[154] The castle is not said to be in the Schuf and by not including the Cave de Tyron amongst his possessions in the 'seignorie' of the Schuf (and in making this distinction clear by issuing a separate charter for the property) Julian clearly implies that the Cave de Tyron, while within the geographical boundaries of the Lordship of Schuf, was not part of the lordship itself.

The evidence of these charters indicates that there was a true Lordship of Schuf and that although the Lord of Sidon held the Schuf in the mid-thirteenth century, this was only in his capacity as Lord of Schuf, *not* as Lord of Sidon. It is also clear that the Cave de Tyron was within the geographical boundaries of the Schuf, but had never been part of the Lordship of the Schuf.

The history of the Lordship of the Schuf is almost entirely unknown prior to its sale, a fact which emphasizes the meagreness of surviving secular sources (if the fief had not been sold to a Military Order we would never have been aware of its existence, despite its large territorial extent). The area was dominated by the Cave de Tyron, however, and the history of this fortification, although it was not part of the lordship, provides some clues to its history.

In December 1133 the Muslims captured the Cave de Tyron.[155] The Franks must have captured the fortification

---

[152] *Reg. Hier.*, Nos. 1252–6, 1265–7, 1300, 1301. For recent work on the topography of the area, see Hilsch, 'Der Deutsche Ritterorden'.

[153] *Tab. ord. Theut.*, No. 108; *Reg. Hier.*, No. 1253.

[154] *Tab. ord. Theut.*, No. 110; *Reg. Hier.*, No. 1255.

[155] Qalanisi, ed. Gibb, p. 224; Ibn al-Athir, 'Kamil', i. 401; Abou'l Feda, p. 21.

sometime between 1133 and 1165, however, for in the latter year the Saracens took the fortress again.[156] The ownership of the castle at the time of its capture is not explicitly stated, but there are indications that it belonged to the Lord of Sidon. William of Tyre describes the Cave de Tyron at this time as being 'in territorio Sidoniensi situm', while it is significant that the garrison's commander (who was suspected of treason) was taken and hanged at Sidon, rather than at the royal court.

We also know that a rental agreement of 1158 which included casal Achi (later to be found in the fief of the Schuf) needed only the approval of the Lord of Sidon, and made no mention of either the Schuf or Gezin. It thus seems likely that until 1165 the eastern march of the Lordship of Sidon remained, when in Christian hands, in the possession of the Lords of Sidon.[157]

The Cave de Tyron was only recovered by the Franks in 1250 in a treaty concluded between St Louis and the sultan.[158] The Seigneury of the Schuf seems to have pre-dated the recapture of the Cave de Tyron, however; the fact that the seigneury existed at all implies that, although the Lord of the Schuf was also the Lord of Sidon in 1256, a previous owner of the lordship had been a person other than the Lord of Sidon, for if the possessor of the lordship had always been the Lord of Sidon there would have been no need to create the lordship. We also know that in 1256 John of Schuf held lands that were almost certainly held previously by his father, Andrew of Schuf.[159]

It is clear that the eastern march of the Lordship of Sidon was separated from the seigneury at some point after 1165, but before 1250. As the Lordship of the Schuf was constituted before the Cave de Tyron was regained, this would provide a likely explanation for the castle being in the possession of the Lord of Sidon, rather than in the Lordship of Schuf in 1256: the Cave de Tyron (not being in Christian hands) would not have been part of the original grant of land given to the Lord of the Schuf and thus, on its return to Frankish possession, would have reverted to the descendants of the last previous owner, the Lord of Sidon. The (unknown) family, the Lords of Schuf, seems to have died out

[156] William of Tyre, pp. 877–9.
[157] *ROL* 11 (1905–8), 181–3.
[158] Paris, *Chronica maiora*, vi. 196; *Reg. Hier.*, No. 1191.
[159] *Tab. ord. Theut.*, No. 115; *Reg. Hier.*, No. 1252.

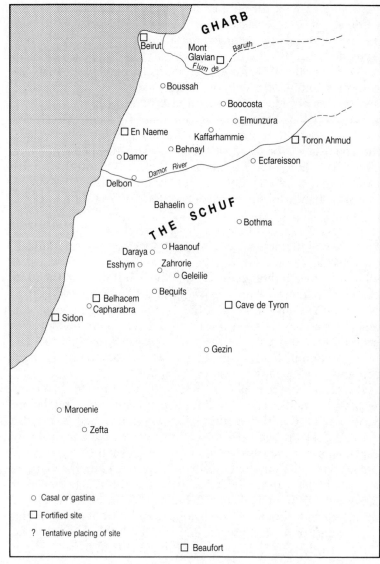

4. Beirut and the Toron Ahmud; Sidon and the Schuf

before 1256, at which time we find the seigneury in the hands of the Lord of Sidon.

We thus see that a hitherto unremarked lordship existed on the eastern borders of the kingdom by Sidon. The question remains as to why the Lordship of the Schuf was created, and by whom. Disputes between the Lord of Sidon and the king in the twelfth century may provide some answers. As we have seen, treason culminating in open rebellion could be followed by the dismemberment of the seigneury held by the traitor (e.g. the County of Jaffa). There is evidence of two very serious disputes between Gerard, Lord of Sidon, and the king, but historians have either dismissed the evidence as a fantasy, or overlooked its significance in this context.

It would appear that Gerard was driven out of the kingdom in 1161 for treason and piracy and was later executed by the king.[160] The dating of this incident causes great problems, however, for we know that Gerard was still alive and apparently enjoying royal favour in 1165. It is also the case that Gerard of Sidon must have been alive in 1169 in order to object to his son's marriage to Agnes of Courtenay, whose previous husband, Hugh of Ibelin, died only in that year.[161] Because of the problem of dating, the dispute between the king and Gerard has been dismissed as a fabrication.[162]

Another incident is recorded as having taken place between Gerard and King Amalric. Gerard disseised one of his vassals without consulting either his own vassals or the king. The wronged vassal appealed to King Amalric who supported him against Gerard. Gerard was eventually forced to return the fief to the vassal and the High Court placed on record, in the Assise sur la Ligece, the principle that a vassal could always have recourse to the royal court to appeal against any illegal action on the part of his lord.[163] Unlike Gerard's alleged piracy, the veracity of this incident has never been doubted, but its significance has only been commented on in relation to the Assise sur la Ligece, or as an example of lord–vassal relationships. It has also, of course, a

---

[160] See La Monte, 'The Lords of Sidon', pp. 192–3, for a discussion of the sources.
[161] For Gerard's presence after 1161, see *Reg. Hier. Add.*, No. 393c, and *Reg. Hier.*, Nos. 400, 412. See also William of Tyre, p. 870.
[162] La Monte, 'The Lords of Sidon', p. 192.
[163] John of Ibelin, pp. 214–15.

more specific significance for the relationship of the Lord of Sidon and the king, and proves that Gerard was on bad terms with Amalric. The other dispute between Gerard and the king is undoubtedly misdated (and possibly exaggerated) but, in view of Gerard's bad relations with the king, it is wrong to dismiss it entirely: if one merely supposes that the date of the alleged piracy was confused and that it should be placed, for instance, in *c*.1169–71 instead of 1161, the story gains credibility and, indeed, fits in with other evidence.

The succession to Gerard as Lord of Sidon is also doubtful though it failed to attract the attention of La Monte.[164] Eustace III, eldest son of Gerard, never inherited the Lordship of Sidon, though he is mentioned by William of Tyre and in the 'Lignages'.[165] Renaud, the younger son, became Lord of Sidon in his brother's stead and La Monte dates his lordship from 1171 to 1200. The passing over of Eustace III is extremely suspicious in the light of the evidence about their father's relationship with the king.

We know that the Lordship of the Schuf was created at some time between 1165 and 1250: during this period there is only one point when the succession to the Lordship of Sidon has come down to us in a confused form: the succession to Gerard. In view of Gerard's relationship with the crown and the unusual way in which the succession to Gerard was handled, it seems likely that the Lordship of the Schuf was created in the period *c*.1169–71. King Amalric had received direct benefits from the royal response to an earlier revolt: when the Count of Jaffa revolted King Fulk confiscated the fief and systematically dismembered it, ensuring that the military and political strength of the Counts of Jaffa was seriously diminished. I would suggest that Amalric temporarily confiscated the Lordship of Sidon and, while it was in the royal domain, carved out the Lordship of Schuf from the seigneury. Gerard's eldest son was passed over in the succession: his younger brother Renaud, who often appears in details of Amalric's entourage, probably proved more amenable to the royal will and was allowed to succeed to what remained of Sidon.

The resurgent military threat in the area may also provide us with a clue to the king's motivation in creating a new lordship.

[164] La Monte, 'The Lords of Sidon', p. 193.
[165] William of Tyre, p. 972; 'Les Lignages', pp. 455–6.

The Maronite historians Ibn Hajar and Salih ibn Yahya provide evidence that Muslim control of the area had grown to the extent where *iqta*s (fiefs) could be distributed from within the Schuf and military recruitment carried out.

Ibn Hajar, for instance, tells us that the emir Zahr ad-Dawla Shuja al-Mulk Jamal al-Umara Abu'l-Izz Karama ibn Buhtur at-Tanukhi had been engaged in warfare with the Franks on the coast and that he had been given the whole Gharb in *iqta* from Nur-ad-Din. Salih ibn Yahya gives more details and cites two documents issued by Nur-ad-Din to Karama. The first (dated 27 April 1157) is a decree, enjoining others to help Karama in his fight against the Franks: '. . . whoever assists him in fighting the infidels does so to our pleasure and receives our thanks, whoever disobeys him in this or rebels against him disobeys our orders . . .'.

The second document is a deed granting an *iqta* to Karama, dated 1 July 1161. The deed says he is assigned:

[for the upkeep of] forty horsemen and whatever he may be able [to levy] for campaigns. [His *iqta* shall include] most of the villages of the Gharb; and, from outside the Gharb: al-Qunaytra from the Biqa, Zahr Hmar from Wadi at-Taym, Tha'labaya, also from the Biqa, Barja from Sidon, B'asir; also al-Ma'asir al-Fawqa, ad-Damur, Sharun, Majda Ba'na, and Kafar'ammay.[166]

Faced with military activity emanating from within the Lordship of Sidon, Amalric may have felt that having an administrative unit dedicated to the defence of the eastern borders, and to the suppression of resistance within the kingdom, was an additional reason to detach the Schuf from the Lordship of Sidon.

Although this is a necessarily tentative reconstruction of events, the carving out of the Schuf fits all the known facts well and occurs at the one stage of the Lordship of Sidon's history when genealogical records are puzzling. The Lordship of the Schuf is indicative not only of the monarchy's capacity to take deliberate and considered action against its larger vassals, but also of historians' tendency to ignore those elements of the seigneurial

---

[166] Salibi, *Maronite Historians*, pp. 107–9; Barja is a village in the Karroub, north of Sidon; B'asir is a village in the Karroub, near Barja; Ma'asir al-Fawqa is a village in the Schuf.

framework that do not conform to the picture presented to us by John of Ibelin.

THE LORDSHIP OF TORON AHMUD

Another lordship that has never been recognized as such or commented upon by historians of the Latin East is that of Toron Ahmud. In 1261 John of Ibelin, Lord of Beirut, sold a large fief centred at the Toron Ahmud to the Teutonic Knights. The fief was described as:

un toron, qui est en la montaigne de Baruth, qui est nome Ahmud, et toz les casaus et toutes les gastines [deserted villages] et tote la terre et tot ce, qui est entre le flum del Damor et le ruisel ou flum, qui est devers la terre de Baruth, qui ist et sort des fontaines, qui sont en la devant dite montaigne de Baruth, et au chief de son cors vient et chiet ou flum del Damor meimes. Et outre celui ruisel devers l'autre terre de Baruth vos doins et otrei ausi en aumosne perpetuel franchemant et quitemant II charuees francoises de terre mesurees a la mesure selon l'usage dou reiaume de Jerusalem . . .

The Teutonic Knights were also told that their rights extended to:

totes les reisons et les dreitures, qui a ceaus casaus et gastines, qui sont entre le flum et le ruisel, apartienent, c'est a savoir dedenz le flum et le ruisel et de la ou le ruisel sor en amont vers orient, en homes, en fames, en enfanz, en terres laborees et non laborees, en plains, en montaignes, en montees, en valees, en bois, en riveres, en aigues, en pasturages, en arbres, en vignes, en cortilz, en jardins, en fors, en molins, en bainz, en fluns, en rinsiaus, en pescheries, en justises, en dreitures, en chemins et hors chemins, et en totes autres choses, qui ci sont moties et non moties, qui au devant dit toron et casaus et gastines apartienent or doivent apartenir dedans les devises desus moties; des quex devant diz toron et casaus et gastines o les apartenances desus moties et les II charuees francoises et le ruisel si come il sont desus devisez je, le devant dit J[ohan] d'Ybelin, seignor de Baruth, . . . dessessisant mei de totes reisons et dreitures et seignories, que je ou mes heirs y avons ou aveir porrions ou toron . . .[167]

This fascinating document provides evidence for the existence of a hitherto unknown, independent or semi-independent

[167] *Tab. ord. Theut.*, No. 120; *Reg. Hier.*, No. 1308.

lordship on the eastern borders of the Lordship of Beirut: the Seigneury of Ahmud. It is significant to note that Ahmud is said to be 'en la montaigne de Baruth' (a purely geographic description) but never 'in the territory of Beirut'. On the contrary, Ahmud's lands are twice described as being 'devers la terre de Baruth' (i.e. extending *towards* the Lordship of Beirut) clearly implying that the fief existed outside the lordship proper.

Other ambiguities in the document also tend to indicate independent status. On the one hand, John gave the Teutonic Knights all the lands pertaining to Ahmud, together with all its 'dreitures et seignories'. This seems an all-inclusive grant. On the other hand, however, he had to make specific mention, twice, that he was also giving the Brothers 'en aumosne perpetuel franchement et quitement II charuees francoises de terre'. It thus seems that these two carrucates were separate from Ahmud and, as they are being given by John, it seems likely that they remained in the hands of the Lords of Beirut even when Ahmud itself was independent. The Toron Ahmud would presumably have been in the hands of the 'Lord of Ahmud', who held, in addition, the 'dreitures et seignories' of the fief. It would appear that the Seigneury of Ahmud had come into the hands of the Lords of Beirut before 1261, but recognition of the original administrative boundaries had been maintained (hence the distinction made between the two carrucates and the fief proper, and the distinction between the 'terre de Baruth' and the fief of Ahmud).

The geographical location of Ahmud also makes independent status plausible. To the south the fief bordered on the independent Schuf–Gezin and, as we have seen, the eastern borders of the Latin Kingdom further to the south were also guarded by small independent seigneuries (e.g. Banias and Assebebe).

A further document of 1261 tells us the sale price of the transaction: '. . . Vm bezans sarracenas au pois d'Accre bien nombres et bien peses por lo toron, qui est nome Ahmit, qui est en la montaigne de Baruth, et por les casaus et les gastines et la terre et tot ce qui est entre le flum del Damor et le ruisel ou flum devers la terre de Baruth, qui sort des fontaines . . . et por les II charuees francoises de terre . . .'[168] Once again, the *toron* is said

---

[168] *Tab. ord. Theut.*, No. 122; *Reg. Hier.*, No. 1310.

to be 'en la montaigne de Baruth', but never in 'la terre de Baruth'. Geographical features in the document are again described as being towards the land of Beirut ('devers la terre de Baruth') but never in it.

It is interesting to note that by the acquisition of the seigneuries of the Schuf–Gezin and Toron Ahmud, the Teutonic Knights had acquired a substantial stretch of land covering much of the north-eastern borders of the kingdom that was effectively independent of any local secular authority: there is no record of any military service being owed to the Lords of Sidon or Beirut for the fiefs.

The motive of the Lord of Beirut in selling the fief, other than the obvious financial one, may be revealed when Lord John said that the Teutonic Knights were 'tenir et maintenir a toz jors mais ferm et estable' the *toron*.[169] It seems that the Lords of Sidon and Beirut could no longer afford to maintain an effective defence on their borders, and the Military Orders must have seemed an obvious successor to the independent, or semi-independent, lords of the march that had preceded them.

In the context of the Toron Ahmud it is interesting to recall that King Amalric had made a very deliberate attempt to acquire Beirut in the period 1165–74. The 'Lignages' tell us that Walter III, Lord of Beirut, and his two brothers were taken prisoner by the Saracens and only released because their mother was able to pay a large part of the ransom demanded.[170] Their mother replaced the brothers as hostage until the remainder of the money could be paid. They could not raise the additional funds, however (the 'Lignages' says because they were spend-thrifts: 'car it estoient grans despendeors'), and were unable to raise a loan, because the king had ordered everyone not to help them, presumably so as to recover the lordship and its prosperous port for the royal domain. Walter was thus forced to give up Beirut in return for Blanchegarde and a sum of money (some of which, in the form of revenues taken from the catena of Acre, he retained in 1174)[171]: '. . . et il li donerent la Blanche Garde en eschange et besanz aussi, de quei il paia sa dette et delivera sa mere'. Ironically, she only lived for one month after she was freed. In organizing this take-over the king was perhaps emulating his

---

[169] *Tab. ord. Theut.*, No. 120; *Reg. Hier.*, No. 1308.
[170] 'Les Lignages', p. 458.   [171] *Reg. Hier.*, No. 512.

brother's acquisition of Jaffa, by which the young Amalric had profited directly. Further, it is tempting to speculate that it was Amalric who created the independent Lordship of Ahmud: the similarity with Fulk's dismemberment of Jaffa is striking.

As in the case of the Seigneury of the Schuf, the Lordship of Toron Ahmud demonstrates the existence of a series of hitherto unrecognized border lordships created to decrease the power available to the larger tenants-in-chief.

THE SEIGNEURY OF JOSCELYN DE COURTENAY

The origins of the Seigneury of Joscelyn de Courtenay may be dated to *c.*1176, when Joscelyn married Agnes de Milly.[172] The Seigneury of Joscelyn de Courtenay as described by John of Ibelin consisted of: 'Le chastel dou Rei, IV. chevaliers. Saint Jorge, X. chevaliers. La terre sire Jofrei le Tor, VI. chevaliers. La terre sire Phelippe le Rous, II. chevaliers. La Chamberlaine, II. chevaliers'.[173]

It is also noteworthy that although the Seigneury of Joscelyn was formed mainly from the royal domain around Acre, these fiefs were only taken from direct royal control to be given to a close relative and loyal ally of the king. When Guy de Lusignan came to the throne, however, this familial relationship was weakened and the independent existence of the Seigneury of Joscelyn was no longer in the long-term interests of the monarchy.

It is significant that King Guy recognized this situation and took rapid (and successful) steps to ensure that familial links were strengthened and that the domain lands should eventually be controlled by the Lusignan family. An agreement was reached between Joscelyn and the king on 21 October 1186 concerning the marriage of Joscelyn's daughters. By the terms of this agreement Guy's younger brother, William of Valence, was to marry Joscelyn's elder daughter, who was to bring with her 'Torono et Castro Novo' (i.e. Chastel Neuf) and 'omni terra, quam a Iohanne camerario comparavit, et cum Cabor . . .'. The younger daughter was to marry one of Guy's nephews, bringing

---

[172] 'Les Lignages', p. 454, which is insistent that the lands Agnes brought with her were dowry rather than inheritance. For recent work on the Seigneury of Joscelyn de Courtenay see Mayer, 'Die Seigneurie de Joscelin'. [173] John of Ibelin, p. 422.

with her the rest of Joscelyn's lands ('reliqua terra sua et universa terra matris'). If the elder daughter should die before reaching marriageable age, it was agreed that William de Valence would be free to marry the other. If he chose to marry neither daughter, both would marry nephews of Guy.[174]

Thus, although the Seigneury of Joscelyn was carved out of royal domain, it was only released into the hands of a relative who was also a capable ally, and steps were soon taken to ensure that within a few years all its lands would once more be under the direct control of members of the royal family.

THE LORDSHIP OF CAYMONT

It is not known when the Lordship of Caymont was created. The first evidence for land ownership within the seigneury comes in 1182 when we find Baldwin IV including lands in Caymont in an exchange with Joscelyn de Courtenay.[175] As part of the agreement, the king gave Joscelyn the fief of John Banerius, consisting of 100 besants per annum from Acre and four carrucates of land in the territory of Caymont. In the absence of other information, the ability to give away a fief at Caymont may imply that the lordship was in the royal domain at this time.

CONCLUSIONS

It is clear that the monarchy could exercise extensive control over the feudal structure of the kingdom and chose to do so on numerous occasions. The reversion of a seigneury could be used to alter conditions to suit the crown: and almost all lordships reverted to the crown at one time or another. The County of Jaffa was effectively dismantled by using the opportunity provided by such a reversion, and much the same seems to have been true of the aftermath of Gerard of Sidon's dispute with the monarch. The separation of Toron and Nazareth from the Principality of Galilee is yet another example of this opportunity being exercised to the full.

The creation of smaller lordships, often at the expense of their more threatening neighbours, shows royal manipulation of the

[174] *Tab. ord. Theut.*, No. 23; *Reg. Hier.*, No. 655.
[175] *Tab. ord. Theut.*, No. 14; *Reg. Hier.*, No. 614.

feudal structure at its most effective. Fulk's response to the revolt of Hugh of Jaffa (the creation of a series of small lordships at the expense of the County which severely curtailed any future Count's potential for independent action) was a masterly stroke, but was by no means unique, as the proliferation of small lordships on the eastern borders of the Latin Kingdom testifies: Toron, Banias, Chastel Neuf, Toron Ahmud, Dera, Assebebe, and the Schuf. In so doing the monarchy simultaneously limited the scope for action available to the larger seigneuries and created a new layer of the nobility which was both directly beholden to the crown for its elevation to the baronage and, because of limited resources, more susceptible to royal pressure.

Partly as a result of an over-reliance on the lists of John of Ibelin, we have seen that there has been a tendency to put an earlier date on the creation of several lordships—Caesarea, Oultrejourdain, Bethsan, Ramla—than the evidence would allow. This has also been reflected in a tendency to ignore the fact that major lordships (such as the County of Jaffa and Ascalon, Toron, and Beirut) could spend substantial periods of time in the royal domain even after their creation. It is also the case that historians have sometimes been tempted to fill up the geographical gaps in John of Ibelin's feudal map of the kingdom by overestimating the physical extent of a given lordship as for instance, in the cases of Beirut, the Principality of Galilee, and Oultrejourdain.

The crown possessed, and showed no compunction in exercising, a series of very powerful political constraints over its nobility. In the twelfth century at least, any signs of baronial unrest were either crushed ruthlessly or, preferably, prevented from ever occurring.

3

Other Forms of Royal Control

THE crown could manipulate the nobility on the broadest political level through the creation of new seigneuries and the natural reversion of lordships to the king. These were not the only means of control, however; other methods, often more subtle, could also be employed, which would have had an important cumulative effect and would have impinged directly on the day-to-day running of every seigneury in the kingdom.

The geographical placement of fiefs was one way in which the king could maintain a greater degree of control over his potentially most troublesome vassals. Historians of the Latin East have overlooked the fact that the lordships could be formed of a dispersed collection of fiefs. This would ensure that the military and economic resources of any given seigneury were spread over a wide geographical area, thereby severely limiting the scope for independent political action. The corollary of this, of course, was that a lord planning independent action against the king's will would also find that at least part of his lands, and hence military potential, were outside his direct control. There is substantial evidence that this dispersal, and variations on the theme, was carried out extensively in the Latin Kingdom. Nor was this the only method of imposing constraints on the actions of the lords. Even when seigneuries left the direct control of the royal domain they often did so only to be given to a close relative of the king or to a trusted ally. Even further (though this was rare), the crown could attempt to take full control of a seigneury, whether or not (as we have already discussed with regard to Jaffa and Sidon) the tenant-in-chief had been in a state of rebellion. In short, in addition to the creation, reversion, and retention of seigneuries, the king had several other means of control at his disposal, each of which we now examine in detail.

1. THE DISPERSAL OF PROPERTIES WITHIN OTHER LORDSHIPS

The dispersal of properties held by the lord of one seigneury within the boundaries of other lordships was an effective way of diminishing the political and military independence of individuals. It could be argued that in a feudal society of this kind a scattering of properties would inevitably occur through the intermarriage of the great families, and that hence, far from being an act of royal policy of direct benefit to the king, this process was both natural and inevitable.

Against this, two points need to be made. Firstly, the consequences of this process were of value to the king, and it is thus, in a sense, irrelevant whether they were the product of a conscious act of will or not. Secondly, there is evidence that this process was, at least in part, a deliberate policy of the crown: a totally disproportionate level of such property dispersal is accounted for by the smaller lordships. It seems clear that in creating these lordships the kings of Jerusalem took pains to ensure that the properties belonging to these lords were spread throughout the kingdom.

The Lordship of Bethsan

The Seigneury of Bethsan, for instance, provides a striking example of the way in which a small lordship could be largely composed of fiefs scattered throughout other seigneuries. In 1128 Geoffrey de Flujeac gave the castle (described in rubric form as a 'castel') of Calansue to the Hospitallers, in the presence of King Baldwin II and his army. When Baldwin confirmed the gift of Calansue to the Hospitallers in 1129 he mentioned, interestingly, that the gift of 'Goffridus de Flaiaco' had been made together with 'Johannes de Bethsam' and his brother Hugh (with John of Bethsan presumably being Geoffrey's immediate overlord). As well as holding such a key fortified site the Lord of Bethsan's holdings in the Lordship of Caesarea alone may have been quite extensive, for we also see in a confirmation of 1154 that 'Johannes de Bethsan', with the consent of his brother Hugh, sold the Hospitallers casal Adeka, in the territory of Caesarea.[1]

---

[1] *Cart. gén. Hosp.*, No. 83; *Reg. Hier. Add.*, No. 121a; *Cart. gén. Hosp.*, No. 84; *Reg. Hier.*, No. 130; *Cart. gén. Hosp.*, No. 225; *Reg. Hier.*, No. 293.

The Lords of Bethsan also owned property in the neighbouring seigneury, the Principality of Galilee. In 1160 we find casal Bugaea, sited in Galilee, being given to the Hospitallers by 'Hugues de Besans' with the permission of Walter, Prince of Galilee (prince from March 1159–*c*.1170/4).[2]

The Lords of Bethsan seem to have been particularly reliant on fiefs held outside the boundaries of the lordship proper. We know of eight properties held by the Seigneurs of Bethsan: of the five properties which were within the territorial boundaries of the lordship proper, the Lords of Bethsan owned only one or two at any given time (Assera until 1149, Geluth and Tubania after 1152). Of properties outside the lordship, the Lords of Bethsan held Calansue until 1128, Adeka until 1154, and Bugaea until 1160. From 1171 the portion of the fief of Henry de Milly belonging to his daughter Helvis would have been in the hands of Lord Adam of Bethsan (approximately 21 casalia around St George de Lebeyne and a third of two other casalia), all of which were properties held outside the Lordship of Bethsan.[3] The known properties of the Lords of Bethsan (excluding the fief of Henry de Milly) are listed in Table 1.

The importance of external properties is perhaps not surprising given the limited size of the Lordship of Bethsan, and confirms the evidence available for other smaller lordships.

The Lordship of Haifa

The Lordship of Haifa was also heavily reliant on fiefs held in other seigneuries. Prior to 1168 we know that Pagan, Lord of Cayphas, held substantial estates in the Principality of Galilee. In April of that year Pagan agreed to give Fulk, Constable of Tiberias, 'Gybesovart et duas Gobias et Mogar et Gatregalee et Galafiee et Romane et Sellem et totam terram aliam, quam ipse tenebat a me' (i.e. which were held from Walter, Prince of

---

[2] *Cart. gén. Hosp.*, No. 288; *Reg. Hier. Add.*, No. 361*a*.

[3] St George de Lebeyne had been the portion of the fief of Henry de Milly left to his daughter Helvis (wife of Lord Adam of Bethsan). Helvis was also left a third of the casalia of Bouquiau and Saor (see Philip of Novara, 'Livre', pp. 542–3, and 'Les Lignages', p. 454). The fief of St George de Lebeyne was an extensive one: in 1220 a third of the fief was said to comprise seven casalia (see *Tab. ord. Theut.* No. 53; *Reg. Hier.*, No. 934). One can deduce that the entire fief consisted of approximately 21 casalia and their respective gastine. This would have been a major addition to the resources of the Lords of Bethsan.

TABLE 1. *Properties owned by the Lords of Bethsan*

Property	Location/ Lordship	Date	Owner
Calansue	Caesarea	pre 1128	Lord of Bethsan
		post 1128	Hospitallers
Assera	Bethsan	pre 1149	Lord of Bethsan
		pre 1149 onwards	Hospitallers
Tubania	Bethsan	pre 1152	Mount Thabor
		post 1152	Lord of Bethsan
Geluth	Bethsan	pre 1152	Mount Thabor
		post 1152	Lord of Bethsan
Adeka	Caesarea	pre 1154	Lord of Bethsan
		pre 1154 onwards	Hospitallers
Bugaea	Princ. Galilee	pre 1160	Lord of Bethsan
		post 1160	Hospitallers
Rehap	Bethsan	pre 1173	King
		post 1173	Teutonic Knights
Ardelle	Bethsan	pre 1173	King
		post 1173	Teutonic Knights

Galilee). In return, Pagan received a money fief of 850 besants per annum.[4] Interestingly, a later confirmation of the transaction refers to the entire estate which Pagan owned as that of 'Gibosevart' (or Gybesovart, which incidentally was listed first amongst the properties in the original transaction of 1168).[5] It would thus seem likely that Gybesovart acted as an administrative centre for the estate as a whole. Such a centre would certainly have been useful, given the distance between the estate and Haifa. Even in the latter half of the thirteenth century the Lords of Haifa retained fiefs in the Principality of Galilee. In 1259 the Brothers of Josaphat were in dispute with the Archbishop of Nazareth, the Lord of Haifa, and several others over the tithes of casal Anna. The location of this is unknown, but as the ecclesiastical protagonist of the monks was the Archbishop of Nazareth, it seems likely that the casal was in his diocese, i.e. in

[4] *Tab. ord. Theut.*, No. 4; *Reg. Hier.*, No. 447.
[5] *Tab. ord. Theut.*, No. 5; *Reg. Hier.*, No. 465.

the Seigneury of Nazareth or the Principality of Galilee.[6] The Lords of Haifa also seem to have held property in the Lordship of Toron. A document of 1236 survives in which 'Goffridus, dominus Cayphe' is listed amongst the 'hominum suorum' of Lady Alice of Toron. Presumably Geoffrey held a fief from Alice, as there is no record of any deeper link between the two lordships.[7] We also know that an earlier Lord of Haifa of the same name held possessions in Capharnaum, for in 1110 he gave the Hospitallers a villein with lands and houses at Haifa and Capharnaum.[8]

The Lordship of Mirabel

The already small Lordship of Mirabel was in the unhappy position of having much of its lands in the hands of other lords. In 1160 we find that Hugh of Ibelin, Lord of Ramla and, as such, overlord of Mirabel, retained lands in Mirabel: in that year he acquired some property which the monks of St Joseph and St Habukuk owned around Bethel in exchange for which he gave them lands in Mirabel.[9]

The Lordship of Ramla

Similarly, in 1181 Hugh of Flanders, Castellan of Ramla, sold his small castle of Chola, in the territory of Mirabel, to the Hospitallers for the sum of 3,000 besants.[10] An official of another seigneury was thus in possession of the only fortifications in the lordship, apart from Mirabel itself and its small outlying fort.

The Lordship of Scandaleon

There is some evidence that the Lord of Scandaleon may have held a fief in Hebron in the mid-twelfth century. In 1148 Patriarch Fulcher of Jerusalem confirmed that Humphrey, Lord of Toron, had given to the Brothers of St Lazarus a gift of 10 quintards of raisins and 10 besants, to be received annually

[6] *Chartes de Josaphat*, ed. Delaborde, No. 52; *Reg. Hier.*, No. 1271.

[7] *Tab. ord. Theut.*, No. 84; *Reg. Hier.*, No. 1073.

[8] *Cart. gén. Hosp.*, No. 20; *Reg. Hier.*, No. 57. See also *Cart. gén. Hosp.*, No. 225; *Reg. Hier.*, No. 293.

[9] *Cart. de St-Sépulcre.*, No. 64 (B.-B., No. 52); *Reg. Hier.*, No. 358; *Cart. de St-Sépulcre.*, No. 65 (B.-B., No 53); *Reg. Hier.*, No. 360.

[10] *Cart. gén. Hosp.*, Nos. 603, 606, 607; *Reg. Hier.*, Nos. 603, 604, 611.

from lands around Hebron.[11] Humphrey's wife and son confirmed the gift in the presence of Guy, Lord of Scandaleon. As Guy was related to Humphrey de Toron, and held fiefs in the Lordship of Toron, this may imply that the fief at Hebron was held by Guy from Humphrey, who in turn presumably held it from the Lord of Hebron (who, in 1148, would have been Hugh II). William of Tyre tells us that Guy de Scandaleon and Humphrey de Toron, the King's Constable, were related and that Humphrey entrusted the town of Banias into his care in 1157 (a difficult responsibility which he discharged admirably, successfully resisting a siege by Nur-ad-Din).[12] It is thus not surprising, in view of Guy's position, that he also held a fief in the Lordship of Toron. A document of October 1157 confirms that the Hospitallers owned 'duas vineas in territorio Toroni, quas Guido de Scandalione Hospitali tradidit'.[13] In 1180 there is evidence that Guy also held a fief in the County of Jaffa and Ascalon, for in that year a papal document confirmed that the Brothers of Mountjoy of Jerusalem owned 'palamarium cum terminis quos dedit vobis Guido d'Escadalione' in the territory of Ascalon.[14]

The Lordship of Arsur

A charter of 1176 gives us an insight into the landed holdings of the Lords of Arsur: in it King Baldwin IV confirmed that Casal Moyen, sited in the Lordship of Caesarea, was sold to the Hospitallers by Lord John of Arsur for the sum of 3,000 besants earlier in the same year.[15]

The Lordship of Beirut

It was not only the smaller lordships that were subject to such a dispersal of fiefs, however: the Lordships of Toron and Banias show that this process could have a major impact on the larger seigneuries as well. Banias was held from the Lord of Beirut, a major example of a dispersal of the influence of the secular seigneuries: the actions that precipitated the Saracen attack on Banias in 1132 were carried out solely by the Lord of Beirut, and

[11] *AOL* 2B, p. 127, No. 6; *Reg. Hier.*, No. 251.
[12] William of Tyre, pp. 832–3.
[13] *Cart. gén. Hosp.*, No. 258; *Reg. Hier.*, No. 325.
[14] *ROL* 1 (1893), 51–4, No. 1; *Reg. Hier. Add.*, No. 594a.
[15] *Cart. gén. Hosp.*, No. 497; *Reg. Hier. Add.*, No. 539b.

when Humphrey II attempted to give half of Banias to the Hospitallers it was specified that he held it from the Lord of Beirut.[16]

The Lordship of Sidon

For their part, the Lords of Sidon seem to have owned extensive lands in Tiberias: in August 1254 we find Lord Julian of Sidon's financial straits leading him to sell Casal Robert (in the Principality of Galilee) to the Hospitallers for 24,000 besants. Julian promised to defend the rights of the Order in any future dispute, and agreed that if the casal ever had to be returned to him he would repay to the Order the cost of any buildings it had erected, up to the sum of 6,000 besants.[17] The price charged, together with the building costs anticipated, seem to indicate that Casal Robert was a small town, possibly semi-fortified. The *Survey of Western Palestine* found traces of columns and medieval mouldings on the site, implying that the property was substantially more important than an ordinary casal.[18] It is interesting to note that the lord of one seigneury could own such significant properties in another lordship: this situation was perhaps not as unusual as one might expect, however, for, ironically, one finds that the senior vassal of Sidon witnessing the transaction is 'Pierre de Avalon, sire de Adelon', who was also Constable of Tiberias, and thus a senior vassal of the Principality of Galilee as well.

The Lordship of Caesarea

We know that the Seigneurs of Caesarea held extensive properties outside the boundaries of the Lordship of Caesarea and this seems to have been reflected in the duties of their administrative officials. In 1200–1 for instance, Soquerius, the scribanus of Caesarea, was specifically told that he would be provided with food by his lord while on his lord's duties whether inside or outside the lordship's boundaries.[19] Just as the Lords of Bethsan owned properties in the Lordship of Caesarea, so the Seigneurs of

---

[16] Qalanisi, ed. Gibb, p. 216; 'concessione Gualterii Berytensis, de cujus feodo movet . . .'; *Cart. gén. Hosp.*, No. 258; *Reg. Hier.*, No. 325.

[17] *Cart. gén. Hosp.*, No. 2688; *Reg. Hier.*, No. 1217.

[18] *Survey of Western Palestine*, i. 391–4.

[19] *Cod. dip. geros.*, i. 288–9; *Reg. Hier.*, No. 768.

Caesarea possessed a fief around Bethsan. In 1149 Queen Melisende confirmed that John, Lord of Bethsan, had previously sold casal Assera to the Hospitallers. Additional information about the feudal relationships governing the property (sited to the south of the town of Bethsan) is provided by the witness list to the confirmation for we are told that '. . . Thoma, et ejus uxor hoc voluerunt et concesserunt, quorum istud casale erat. Et Gualterius Cesarie, et filius ejus Eustachius, quorum istud feudum erat, hoc voluerunt et concesserunt . . .'.[20] It thus appears that Thomas held the property from the Lord of Caesarea (Walter 1 of Caesarea, 1123–c.1149) and therefore owed him feudal service for it (and that the Lord of Caesarea, in turn, owed service to the Lord of Bethsan for the fief).

The County of Jaffa and Ascalon

A charter of February 1182 provides evidence that the extensive fief of St George de Lebeyne (which had been part of the inheritance of Philip de Milly) belonged, at least in part, to the Counts of Jaffa and Ascalon, for in giving the property to Joscelyn de Courtenay King Baldwin IV specifically received the consent of Count Guy and Countess Sibylle.[21] The extent of the property is indicated by the large knights' service owed for it. John of Ibelin records the service as: 'Saint Jorge, X chevaliers'.[22]

The Lordship of Hebron

The Lords of Hebron owned several properties outside the boundaries of their lordship: in 1110, for instance, it was confirmed that 'Gauterius Baffumeth' had given casal Sussia (or Supheye, south of Montfort) to the Hospitallers.[23] Ownership of fiefs in other seigneuries was thus an important and very widespread constraint on the actions of the nobility.

2. FIEFS DEPENDENT ON THE ROYAL DOMAIN

Even more direct constraints on the ability of lords to take unilateral political action could be imposed by ensuring that a

---

[20] *Cart. gén. Hosp.*, No. 180; *Reg. Hier.*, No. 256.
[21] *Tab. ord. Theut.*, No. 14; *Reg. Hier.*, No. 614.
[22] John of Ibelin, p. 422.
[23] *Cart. gén. Hosp.*, No. 20; *Reg. Hier.*, No. 57. See also *Cart. gén. Hosp.*, No. 225; *Reg. Hier.*, No. 293.

substantial proportion of the fiefs held by the lords were dependent on the royal domain: at the first sign of trouble, they would thus lose a major part of their resources. As with the dispersal of properties in different lordships, the dispersal of properties within the royal domain lands was most prevalent amongst the smaller seigneuries: indeed, as we have discussed, the links between the smaller lordships and the crown were so close that some (Scandaleon, Haifa, and Blanchegarde) were made directly dependent on the royal domain at Acre.[24]

The Lordship of Scandaleon

Quite apart from owing service for the entire Lordship of Scandaleon to the royal domain at Acre[25] the Lords of Scandaleon were also dependent for their revenues on other parts of the royal domain. In 1179, for instance, King Baldwin IV confirmed that Lord Guy de Scandaleon had given the Hospitallers an annual rent of 40 besants which he received 'sur la loge' of the royal city of Tyre.[26] Similarly, in 1243, we know that Guy de Scandaleon's (unnamed) son owned property in the lands of the royal domain around Tyre.[27] Evidence survives of only one property owned by the Seigneur of Scandaleon within the Lordship of Scandaleon proper (casal Acref).[28] Like other small lordships, Scandaleon was clearly heavily dependent on resources derived from beyond its own boundaries, often within the royal domain.

Oultrejourdain and the Lordship of Hebron

In 1180 Reynald de Chatillon confirmed the previous donation of half of casal Bethomar (in the royal domain around Jerusalem) by Philip de Milly to the monastery of Josaphat. In the same document Reynald de Chatillon gave the other half of the casal to the Brothers.[29] As Philip and Reynald were lords both of Hebron and the Oultrejourdain it remains unclear which of these lordships Bethomar belonged to, however. The same is true of a house in Jerusalem (near the church of St Martin) which was said in c.1170 to belong to Philip de Milly.[30]

[24] John of Ibelin, p. 425.   [25] Ibid.
[26] *Cart. gén. Hosp.*, No. 555; *Reg. Hier. Add.*, No. 590a.
[27] Tafel–Thomas, ii. 374; *Reg. Hier.*, No. 1114.
[28] *Reg. Hier.*, Nos. 1399, 1435.
[29] *Chartes de Josaphat*, ed. Delaborde, No. 41; *Reg. Hier.*, No. 596.
[30] *Reg. Hier.*, No. 483.

The County of Jaffa and Ascalon

Even the Counts of Jaffa held fiefs in the royal domain. We know that in 1123 Count Hugh II of Jaffa owned a fief in the royal domain around Nablus, for in that year he gave a Samaritan casal there, called Saphe (or Saphet) to the monastery of Josaphat.[31]

The Lordship of Haifa

From 1168 onwards we find evidence that the Lord of Haifa held extensive money fiefs in the royal domain at Acre.[32] In April of that year Pagan, Lord of Haifa, agreed to give Fulk, Constable of Tiberias, a substantial estate in the Principality of Galilee. In return, Pagan received a money fief of 850 besants per annum, which Fulk had been accustomed to receive from the Templars and the king as recompense for the loss of his castle of Saphet. Pagan agreed to continue to render the service of one knight to Prince Walter of Galilee, which he had previously owed for the estate. The extensive fiefs belonging to Pagan outside the boundaries of the Lordship of Haifa are further demonstrated by a charter of 1169. In this document we find King Amalric confirming Pagan's possession of several money fiefs in Acre. We are told that Pagan had been given, by King Baldwin III, an annual revenue of 1,200 besants to be taken from the profits of the *Chaine* of Acre 'pro servitio duorum militum et primum feodum XX militum'. This had previously been held by his father-in-law, Joscelyn Pisellus. King Baldwin III had also given Joscelyn and his heirs (e.g. Pagan) a 'feodum C militum in Babilonia' if Egypt should ever be reconquered by Christians. In addition, Pagan received the sum of 600 besants a year from the profits of the *fonde* of Acre for the service of one knight, a grant which had also been made to Joscelyn by Baldwin III. With reference to the earlier exchange with Constable Fulk, King Amalric confirmed that he gave Pagan 500 besants per annum from the profits of the meat-market of Acre, a sum which he had previously given to Fulk of Tiberias in return for the castle of Saphet.[33] While apparently contradicting the charter of 1168, this probably means that the remainder of the 850 besants per annum given to Pagan in exchange for his estates in Galilee

---

[31] *Chartes de Josaphat*, ed. Kohler, No. 9; *Reg. Hier. Add.*, No. 102a.

[32] *Tab. ord. Theut.*, No. 4; *Reg. Hier.*, No. 447.

[33] *Tab. ord. Theut.*, No. 5; *Reg. Hier.*, No. 465.

(i.e. 350 besants a year) was paid to him directly by the Templars, rather than as a money fief in Acre. It is also interesting to note that a house owned by the Hospitallers in Acre in 1184 was described as being 'adjacet domus Marie de Caypha'.[34] Similarly, a charter of 1214 described a property in Acre as being 'a parte orientali domui que fuit Pagani de Cayphas . . .'.[35]

In 1229 the Emperor Frederick II ordered Balian of Sidon to dispossess a group of nobles including Rohard, Lord of Haifa, of their fiefs in Acre, without *esgart* or *conoissance* of court. After the dispossessed lords had appealed to the High Court their peers restored their fiefs to them by force.[36] It is interesting to note from this that Rohard was still in possession of substantial fiefs in Acre, probably the money fiefs discussed above.

It is apparent that fiefs held by the Lords of Haifa outside the territorial boundaries of the Seigneury of Haifa, whether in the royal domain or in other lordships, were, in economic terms at least, more important to the Lords of Haifa than those held within Haifa itself. Thus, if the Lord of Haifa attempted to take unilateral political action against the king he would immediately find that most of the revenues with which he enfeoffed his vassals were lost to him. In this context independent political action, for this lord at least, was impossible unless, as in 1229, he had the active support of his peers.

The Lordship of Blanchegarde

Blanchegarde was itself subordinated administratively to the royal domain at Acre, but its lords also held fiefs inside the royal domain. In 1174, for example, King Amalric conceded and confirmed to the Brothers of St Lazarus a grant of 40 besants to be collected annually from the revenues of the port of Acre. This was a payment which had previously been made to Walter of Beirut, now Lord of Blanchegarde, but which the latter now gave to the monks. It is not entirely clear in this instance whether this rent was part of the fief of Blanchegarde or held personally by Walter.[37] By the thirteenth century Blanchegarde and its surrounding lands had been captured by the Muslims, but the

---

[34] *Cart. gén. Hosp.*, No. 663; *Reg. Hier.*, No. 640.
[35] AOL 2B, p. 165, No. 1; *Reg. Hier.*, No. 871.
[36] Philip of Novara, 'Livre', pp. 517, 528; John of Ibelin, p. 325.
[37] AOL 2B, pp. 145–6, No. 28; *Reg. Hier.*, No. 512.

Lords of Blanchegarde continued to function, living on their fiefs in the royal domain. A Hospitaller document of March 1252–3 tells us of a 'donation de Raoul de Barut, seigneur de Blanche Garde, faite a l'ordre, de deux casaux apelles Capharbole et Labores, recevant par reconnaissance sept mille besans de l'ordre, ...'.[38] The high prices paid for the casalia indicate that they must have been in Christian hands in 1252–3. Capharbole may have been in the royal domain around Acre, as reference exists to 'un casal, qui estoit el terror d'Accre, que l'on nome Quafarbole', in which case, as the two casalia were sold for a joint sum, it is possible that Labores was situated nearby.[39]

The Lordship of Arsur

The Lords of Arsur also owned extensive fiefs around the royal domain at Acre. In 1255 John III of Arsur sold two pieces of land on the plain of Acre to the Hospitallers for the sum of 2,000 besants.[40] A document of the period 1266–9 survives which shows that the Hospitallers rented the town, castle, and Lordship of Arsur from Lord Balian I of Arsur for 4,000 saracen besants a year, with the exception of the properties which he held in Acre and the money revenues which he derived from the (lost) royal domain around Nablus.[41] We also know that a house in Acre was owned by an unnamed Lord of Arsur, presumably Lord John III.[42]

The Lordships of Ibelin and Ramla

The small Seigneury of Ramla was also dependent to a large extent on revenues derived from fiefs in the royal domain. We know that the patrimony of Baldwin II of Ramla, a vassal of the County of Jaffa, included extensive properties in the royal domain at Nablus, and this may have contributed to his decision to remain loyal to the king during the revolt of Count Hugh.[43] It is also the case that Hugh, Lord of Ibelin-Ramla, held extensive

[38] *Cart. gén. Hosp.*, No. 2593; *Reg. Hier. Add.*, No. 1198c.
[39] *Eracles*, p. 204.
[40] *Cart. gén. Hosp.*, No. 2753; *Reg. Hier.*, No. 1241.
[41] *Cart. gén. Hosp.*, No. 3047; *Reg. Hier.*, No. 1313.
[42] *Cart. gén. Hosp.*, No. 2662; *Reg. Hier.*, No. 1209.
[43] The properties we know of were Gemmail, Assir, and Beithbezim; *Chartes de Josaphat*, ed. Delaborde, No. 12; *Reg. Hier.*, No. 101; *Chartes de Josaphat*, ed. Kohler, No. 17; *Reg. Hier. Add.*, No. 129a.

fiefs in the royal domain. In 1155 he sold a series of properties to the Holy Sepulchre for the sum of 7,000 besants.[44] These properties included the casalia of Zibi[45] and Bethel,[46] both sited in the royal domain around Magna Mahomeria. In 1160 we see another example of the same lord's holdings in the royal domain, for in that year the Abbot of St Joseph and St Habukuk returned to Hugh the properties which Balian the Elder (Hugh's father) had previously given the Church near Bethel: namely, Bethel (presumably not Bethel itself, as this was already partly owned by the Holy Sepulchre)[47] and Beze (also known as Bazarim).[48]

The Lordship of Beirut

The Lordship of Beirut, territorially small but a substantial seigneury in terms of assets, held extensive properties in the royal domain, particularly around Acre. We know John of Ibelin, Lord of Beirut, to have held fiefs in Acre, for in 1206 he was forced to sell some of his urban property in the city for the sum of 2,700 besants in order to pay his debts to John le Tor.[49] This was indirectly confirmed in 1228 when Frederick II attempted to reclaim Beirut for the royal domain: while arguing his right to the fief, John said that, far from being an asset, he had had to expend the revenues of his other fiefs in Cyprus and elsewhere in the Kingdom of Jerusalem to defend the lordship.[50]

Just as the Lord of Beirut held fiefs in other parts of the kingdom, so did his vassals. Philip of Novara, himself a vassal of John, said that there were sometimes arguments between John and his rear-vassals on the matter.[51] It is also worth noting that the Mimars family were extremely prominent vassals of the Lordship of Beirut: Reynald de Mimars appears from witness lists to have been John of Ibelin's senior vassal.[52] Under the

[44] *Cart. du St-Sépulcre*, No. 56 (B.-B. No. 41); *Reg. Hier.*, No. 299.
[45] Prawer–Benvenisti Map, ref. 161/147.
[46] Prawer–Benvenisti Map, ref. 173/147.
[47] *Cart. du. St-Sépulcre*, No. 56 (B.-B., No. 41); *Reg. Hier.*, No. 299.
[48] *Cart. du St-Sépulcre*, No. 64 (B.-B., No. 52); *Reg. Hier.*, No. 358.
[49] *Tab. ord. Theut.*, No. 41, and see also chapter 4, section 5; *Reg. Hier.*, No. 812.
[50] 'Les Gestes des Chiprois', pp. 678–9.
[51] Philip of Novara, 'Livre', p. 538.
[52] See *Reg. Hier.*, Nos. 950, 951, 957, 963. The 'Renaldus de Murras' in *Reg. Hier.*, No. 965, is also almost certainly a copyist's error for Raynald de Mimars. The extent to which the family was trusted within the lordship is also indicated by the fact that 'Baylan de Mimars' was both first in precedence on witness lists of the seigneury, and also vassal-castellan of Beirut itself. See *Reg. Hier.*, Nos. 1250, 1307, 1308, 1310.

service owed for the royal domain at Nablus John of Ibelin tells us that the Mimars family were expected to meet a not insubstantial military commitment: 'La feme Hue de Mimars, IV. chevaliers'.[53]

Additions to fiefs held in the territory of the royal domain were made even in the thirteenth century. Henry of Cyprus gave Balian of Ibelin, Lord of Beirut (eldest son of John of Ibelin), a substantial fief in the royal domain at Acre, including the small castle of Casal Imbert:

je Henri . . . otrei et conferm en pardurable fie a tei Johan d'Ibelin, segnor de Baruth, et a tes heirs en creissement de ton fie de Baruth le don et le fie, que je donai a Balian d'Ybelin, ton pere, segnor de Baruth jadis, et a ses heirs en creissiment dou fie de Baruth, ce est assaveir: Casal Ymbert, le Fierge, le Quiebre, la Sebeque, Jasson, la Guille, Quafrenebit, la Meserefe, Douheyrap, Bene, Samah, la Gabasie . . .[54]

It has generally been supposed that seigneurial boundaries were rigidly fixed and that even when the same person was in possession of two seigneuries or large fiefs, the original administrative distinctions were always maintained. In most instances, of course, this was indeed the case. This fascinating document, however, shows that administrative boundaries could be changed and, in this case, extended. The phrase 'en creissiment dou fie de Baruth' clearly implies that the new territory was to be given as an actual increase in the size of the fief of Beirut, rather than as just another fief in the lord's lands. One thus has the circumstance whereby part of the Seigneury of Beirut would have been situated in the heart of the royal domain at Acre. Although there is no reason to suppose that Henry's motives in giving this fief to Balian were anything other than a desire to offer financial support to a hard-pressed vassal, the end result was that any future Lords of Beirut would find a substantial portion of their revenues being derived from an area dominated by direct royal vassals and royal influence.

By 1256 the Lord of Beirut, John, son of Balian and grandson of John 'the old Lord of Beirut', was so financially hard pressed that he was forced to lease most of the estate to the Teutonic

[53] John of Ibelin, p. 424.
[54] *Tab. ord. Theut.*, No. 105; *Reg. Hier.*, No. 1208.

Knights for the sum of 13,000 besants a year. The estate was said to comprise: Casal Imbert and everything pertaining to it, namely—le Fierge, le Quiebre, la Scebeique, Jashon, Kapharneby, Deuheireth, Benna, Samah, Laguille, Karcara, and four gastinae which were currently uninhabited: la Messerephe, la Ghabecie, la Quatranye, and la Tyre. It will be noticed that three properties additional to those mentioned in 1253 were leased to the Teutonic Knights in 1256: the casal or gastina Karcara, and the two uninhabited gastinae of Quatranye and la Tyre. These properties thus seem to have been in the possession of the Lords of Beirut before the original grant by King Henry.[55]

A later document sheds furthur light on the possessions of the Lords of Beirut in the royal domain around Acre. In 1261 the troubled times forced Lord John of Beirut to confirm the lease of the estate to the Teutonic Knights, but to add that in the event of the loss of Acre, the rent need not be paid. The rent was also to be reduced to 11,000 besants a year. The fief was said to comprise:

. . . tote ma terre, que je ai au terroer d'Acre, c'est a saver Casalimbert et le Fierge et le Quiebre o totes lor apartenances . . . sauves II charruees Francoises de terre, que je ai donees en aumosne perpetuel a la maison de l'ospital de saint Johan de Jerusalem . . . et bonees, des quels je les ai mis en saisine et en teneure, et sont jognant devers ponent a la terre de Manuet . . .

Clearly, in addition to the three properties we have already discussed, the Lords of Beirut had been in possession of other lands in Acre prior to the gift of King Henry (two carrucates which John had recently given to the Hospitallers, and possessions around Manueth).[56]

Most lords retained, at the very least, urban property in the royal domain. In 1262 we find evidence that Julian, Lord of Sidon, remained in possession of a house in Acre (a house is described as being 'a meridie domus domini Sydonensis') despite the fact that he had sold his lordship to the Templars and his

[55] 'Recherches', ed. Rey, pp. 38–40; *Reg. Hier.*, No. 1250.
[56] *Tab. ord. Theut.*, No. 119; *Reg. Hier.*, No. 1307. It is interesting to note that Casal Imbert, le Fierge, and le Quiebre were seen to be the main sites in the estate. Casal Imbert would have been the primary administrative centre, and it is possible that le Fierge and le Quiebre were minor, secondary administrative centres.

resources were almost exhausted.[57] Similarly, in 1153 William de Bures, Prince of Galilee, gave the Hospitallers a street in Jerusalem near the Hospital itself.[58]

The Lordship of Caesarea

The Lords of Caesarea owned several important properties in the royal domain, particularly around Acre. In February 1206 Lady Juliana of Caesarea gave the Teutonic Knights, amongst other gifts, the houses in Acre which had previously belonged to George Lormine.[59] In 1212 Lord Aymar and Lady Juliana used their houses in Acre and Tyre as partial security for a debt owed to the Hospitallers.[60] Evidence for the possession of lands in the lost royal domain around Nablus is also provided by John of Ibelin when he tells us that 'La dame de Cesaire' owed the service of two knights for lands held in that area.[61]

In December 1253 we find Lord John of Caesarea selling the Hospitallers the casal of Damor, in the territory of Acre, for 12,000 saracen besants of Acre weight.[62] If the Order could not get possession of the casal, John promised to give them an indemnity of 16,000 besants, to be taken from casal Cafresur. The latter part of the agreement sounds like a barely disguised loan arrangement, to go into effect if the original sale fell through: i.e. the Hospitallers would still give John the 12,000 besants, but in return he would give them 16,000 besants over a period of years, to be taken from the revenues of casal Cafresur.

Shortly afterwards (1 May 1255), John was forced to sell his remaining possessions in Acre to the Order.[63] These possessions were described as being a court, unspecified land, several houses (including the house of John himself), and an oven, mill, cellars, and a building 'in Accon in loco vocatum Rabattum'.

The fact that the seigneuries were dependent, to a greater or lesser extent, on revenues or lands in the royal domain must have provided a significantly inhibiting factor when contemplating independent political action, particularly for the smaller lordships:

[57] *Chartes de Josaphat*, ed. Delaborde, No. 54; *Reg. Hier.*, No. 1315.
[58] *Cart. gén. Hosp.*, No. 219; *Reg. Hier.*, No. 283.
[59] *Tab. ord. Theut.*, No. 40; *Reg. Hier.*, No. 810.
[60] *Cart. gén. Hosp.*, No. 1400; *Reg. Hier. Add.*, No. 859b.
[61] John of Ibelin, p. 424.
[62] *Cart. gén. Hosp.*, No. 2661; *Reg. Hier.*, No. 1210.
[63] *Cart. gén. Hosp.*, No. 2732; *Reg. Hier.*, No. 1234.

it must also have directly added to the force of royal influence in the internal affairs of the kingdom.

3. RETENTION OF ROYAL PROPERTY INSIDE THE LORDSHIPS

A logical extension of the dispersal of the lords' properties, and a process unremarked upon by historians of the Latin Kingdom, was the dispersal of royal lands. This distribution of property would allow royal influence to be carried directly into the lordships. Interestingly, the exact status of royal lands within a seigneury was never legally determined, although, as we shall see, these lands could sometimes be extensive.

Within the overall context of the king retaining lands outside what is generally thought to be the royal domain, I have distinguished two distinct policies, each of which would have had substantially different legal implications. First are lands held *within* a lordship's boundaries: often we can see the king making active efforts to obtain these lands, generally without reference to the lord of the seigneury. Second are lands which were effectively *withheld* by the king from a given lordship.

Historians of the feudal structure of the Latin Kingdom have often tended to make bold and inaccurate simplifications. Where lands, that were not defined by John of Ibelin as being in the royal domain, are close to a seigneurial centre, these lands have tended to be 'lumped in' with that seigneury. In many cases this is a rash assumption, however. As we shall see, there is extensive evidence that some of these lands were substantial pockets of royal domain that were neither part of the seigneuries nor a direct part of the larger administrative centres of the royal domain: Jerusalem, Acre, Tyre, and Nablus.

The Lordship of Oultrejourdain

Oultrejourdain provides a stricking example of the retention of royal domain both in a seigneury and in a territory assumed to have been in that seigneury. Arab chroniclers suggest that Baldwin II organized an expedition to the Wadi Mousa (Li Vaux Moys) in August–September 1127.[64] It was probably at this point (i.e. after the first Lord of Oultrejourdain had been appointed)

---

[64] Abou'l Modaffer, p. 566; Qalanisi, ed. Gibb, p. 182.

that Baldwin II built the castle of Li Vaux Moys. When this castle is first mentioned it is spoken of as if it is a royal castle.[65] The fortification had been lost to a joint Muslim expedition and peasant uprising in 1144, and Baldwin III led an expedition to retake it. When the castle was eventually captured it was Baldwin who appointed a garrison and reprovisioned it.

The theory that Li Vaux Moys was a royal castle is given further credence by two documents of the 1160s. In a charter of July 1161 Baldwin III gave Philip de Milly all the lands which Pagan the Butler had held, which he lists as being Montreal, Kerak, and Ahamant. The lands of Pagan are described as being 'a Zerca usque ad Mare Rubrum'. Baldwin then goes on to add to the lordship three other estates, which were obviously not part of the original lordship, namely the castle 'Vallis Moysis', the lands of Baldwin, son of Viscount Hulric of Nablus, and the lands of John Gothman. The sites of the estates of Baldwin, son of Hulric, and John Gothman cannot now be identified but, together with the castle of Li Vaux Moys, they demonstrate that major enclaves of royal domain were retained within what was to become the Lordship of Oultrejourdain at its fullest extent.[66] This view is supported by a charter of *c.*1160 in which two native Christian knights gave the Hospitallers casal Hara which, although its position cannot be identified exactly, seems to have been sited near the castle of Li Vaux Moys.[67] In this document the knights, two brothers called Joseph and John, confirmed that King Baldwin II had given the property to their father and that they in turn were giving it to the Hospitallers. There was no mention of a Lord of Oultrejourdain, either in confirming or conceding the original gift to their father, or the current gift to the Hospitallers. Their land would thus seem to have been in the royal domain around Li Vaux Moys.

A charter of November 1178 shows that it was Queen Melisende who had originally given the trans-Jordanian lands to Viscount Hulric, thus confirming that these were part of the royal domain.[68] Significantly, we also know that the fief of Viscount Hulric included possessions in the heart of what was the

[65] William of Tyre, pp. 721–2.
[66] *Tab. ord. Theut.*, No. 3; *Reg. Hier.*, No. 366.
[67] *Cart. gén. Hosp.*, No. 284; *Reg. Hier. Add.*, No. 365*b*.
[68] *Cart. gén. Hosp.*, No. 550; *Reg. Hier.*, No. 562.

Lordship of Oultrejourdain even from its inception: in 1152 Maurice, Lord of Oultrejourdain, described a possession of the Hospitallers as being next to the house of the Viscount of Nablus.[69] A later document confirms that the house was in Montreal itself.[70] There were two other Frankish castles sited close to Li Vaux Moys: Celle and Hormoz. In the absence of any direct evidence one can only speculate that, as they were both close to the royal castle of Li Vaux Moys, and as the area around Li Vaux Moys was in the royal domain, they too were under the control of the kings of Jerusalem until 1161.

Even the agreement of 1161 between Baldwin III and Philip de Milly did not mean that all royal rights in the area were relinquished, however, and it is tempting to hypothesize that the retention of castles on the caravan routes up to 1161 was at least partly due to a desire to administer royal economic rights in the region as fully as possible. The agreement of 1161 explicitly stated that two revenue-producing interests were *not* to be ceded to Philip, namely the right to levy tolls on caravans on their way between Egypt and Mesopotamia, and the taxes and other dues to be received from Bedouin not born in Oultrejourdain.[71] The agreement was made at a time when the monarchy was in a very strong bargaining position (the king appears effectively to have dictated the conditions to Philip de Milly) and the surrender of the last elements of royal domain in the lordship at such a time might seem to imply that the system of collecting royal taxes on merchants had become so regularized that the king could rely on collection, by whatever means, without having a major physical presence in the area.

Principality of Galilee

The Principality of Galilee provides another such example. It has always been assumed that the Terre de Sueth, as part of the trans-Jordanian territories by the Sea of Galilee, was controlled by the Princes of Galilee. Close examination of the sources throws doubt on this assumption, however, and indicates that at least part of this crucial area was alway retained under direct royal control.

[69] *Cart. gén. Hosp.*, No. 207; *Reg. Hier.*, No. 279.
[70] *Cart. gén. Hosp.*, No. 521; *Reg. Hier.*, No. 551.
[71] *Tab. ord. Theut.*, No. 3; *Reg. Hier.*, No. 366.

A royal presence in the area is apparent from the earliest days of the principality: royal aid had to be called in to subjugate the region.[72] In 1105 Frankish power in the Terre de Sueth was enforced by building a fortress on the strategic road running from Bethsan to Damascus. This fortress, known as Qasr Berdaouil, was named after King Baldwin I. It has been assumed that this venture was carried out by Hugh de St Omer, Prince of Galilee, but in view of the name of the castle it seems more likely that Baldwin built it.[73] Our only sources for its construction are Arab, and do not name the builder. Abou'l Modaffer writing of the year 499 (i.e. 13 September 1105 to 1 September 1106) says merely: 'Les Francs entrent dans la zone cultivee (saouad) de Tiberiade et se mettent a batir entre ces parages et la Batanee une forteresse nomme 'Aal, qu'ils rendent tres-redoutable . . .'[74] It was the king, rather than the Prince of Galilee, who settled the legal status of the Terre de Sueth and the Djebel Adjloun, concluding a treaty about the region with the Muslims in 1109.[75]

An exchange of properties in the area in 1147 also gives an indication of royal holdings in the Terre de Sueth. By this exchange the king gave the Hospitallers casal Altum (which appears to have been around Acre, near Coketum) and two nearby casalia. In return, the Order was to give the king the casalia which 'Gumfredus de Turre David' had previously given them in the Terre de Sueth. 'Gumfredus' was effective Castellan of Jerusalem and a senior member of the High Court. It is also the case that the exchange was made without reference to, or with the confirmation of, the Prince of Galilee (who was not even present as a witness to the charter).[76] It would thus appear that parts of the Terre de Sueth were retained directly in the hands of the king, or held as fiefs directly from him.

A siege of the Cave de Sueth in 1158 provides further evidence that the Kings of Jerusalem retained direct control of parts of the trans-Jordanian region. Nur-ad-Din had besieged the castle and it was Baldwin III who came to its aid. After relieving the siege,

---

[72] Albert of Aix, pp. 517–18; William of Tyre, pp. 448–9.
[73] Deschamps, *La Défense*, ii. 100–1, for instance, says Hugh de St Omer built the castle.
[74] Abou'l Modaffer, pp. 529–30; Qalanisi, ed. Gibb, pp. 71–2; Ibn al-Athir, 'Kamil', 1. 229–30.
[75] Qalanisi, ed. Gibb, p. 92; Abou'l-Mehacen, p. 491; Abou'l-Modaffer, p. 541.
[76] *Cart. gén. Hosp.*, No. 275; *Reg. Hier.*, No. 245.

we are told that it was Baldwin, rather than the Prince of Galilee, who placed men in the castle and reprovisioned it.[77] It thus seems likely that the Cave de Sueth was retained directly by the crown at this time.[78]

The County of Jaffa and Ascalon

Other cases of the retention or withholding of pockets of royal land abound. The Counts of Jaffa, for instance, had always had strong claims to the possession of Ascalon, and these claims had been recognized by the monarchy. The claims of Counts Hugh I (c.1110–c.1120), Hugh II (c.1120–34), and Amalric (1151–63) had all been recognized and confirmed by successive kings. In 1110, for instance, one finds that Hugh I had previously given the Hospitallers casal Melius, in the territory of Ascalon.[79] This gift was confirmed by King Baldwin III in 1154 and signed by the then Count of Jaffa and Ascalon, Amalric.[80] Thus, even at this early date (i.e. c.1110) one finds the Counts of Jaffa effectively laying claim to Ascalon. This must have met with royal approval as the charter of 1154 was a royal confirmation of gifts made.

Hugh II also seems to have been assured of his claims to Ascalon, as he gave the Hospitallers and the monastery of Josaphat properties that were described as being 'in the terrritory of Ascalon'.[81] Claims to Ascalon were so strong that its lands, even though they were in Egyptian hands, had already been subinfeudated. In January 1126 we find Count Hugh II confirming the gift to the Hospitallers, by his Constable, Balian the Elder, of casal Algie in the territory of Ascalon.[82] Clearly the Count's claims to Ascalon had been extended to his vassals, ensuring that they too had a stake in the capture of the city. The relationship was made explicit by King Baldwin III: a royal charter of 1152

---

[77] William of Tyre, pp. 841–2.

[78] William of Tyre says, in 1182, that it was held by Fulk of Tiberias, but speaks of Raymond of Tripoli, Prince of Galilee, 'ad cujus curam praedictum municipium respiciebat', pp. 1028–9. Nevertheless the king helped to recapture it when the Muslims seized it, pp. 1039–42.

[79] *Cart. gén. Hosp.*, No. 20; *Reg. Hier.*, No. 57. I find Rohricht's argument that 'Hugo de Puzath' is not the same person as Hugh I unconvincing, and instead follow J. La Monte, 'The Lords of Le Puiset on the Crusades', *Speculum* 17 (1942), pp. 100–18.

[80] *Cart. gén. Hosp.*, No. 225; *Reg. Hier.*, No. 293.

[81] *Chartes de Josaphat*, ed. Kohler, No. 9; *Reg. Hier. Add.*, No. 102a; *Cart. gén. Hosp.*, No. 77; *Reg. Hier.*, No. 113.

[82] *Cart. gén. Hosp.*, No. 74; *Reg. Hier.*, No. 112.   [83] *Reg. Hier.*, No. 276.

(*before* the capture of Ascalon) described Ramla as being 'in divisione Esqualon et Joppe', and was witnessed by Count Amalric.[83]

Despite recognition of the claims of the Counts of Jaffa, however, the king did not immediately relinquish all control of the recently captured city: on the contrary, there is evidence that the lands around Ascalon went largely to 'loyal supporters' of the king, or men who could make a contribution to the royal coffers. William of Tyre tells us that '. . . the king distributed possessions and the lands dependent on them both within and without the city to those who had well deserved them; to some, also for a price. The city of Ascalon he generously bestowed upon his younger brother Amalric, Count of Jaffa'.[84] It seems that there was an arrangement between the king and Amalric: the king would allow Amalric to own Ascalon (and take the long-term profits of ownership), as long as Baldwin could flood the area with his own appointees and make a substantial profit by 'one-off' payments from those willing to buy lands. The grant of fiefs to royal appointees indicates that substantial parts of the territory of Ascalon were carved out and made into royal domain land before handing the city over to Amalric.

The Lordship of Sidon

Beaufort, later to be an integral part of the Lordship of Sidon, and always assumed to have been part of the seigneury, was only added to the lordship after a period spent in the royal domain, and is a good example of a pocket of royal territory being withheld from a seigneury. The castle was abandoned to King Fulk in 1139 by the Muslims.[85] As we have seen, Fulk made an active policy of *not* handing 'windfalls' over to powerful barons, preferring to retain fortifications within the royal domain wherever possible. There is no evidence that Fulk gave the castle to the Lord of Sidon: it is only in witness lists of the Lordship of Sidon from 1158 onwards (i.e. long after Fulk's death) that we find the name 'de Belfort' appearing.[86] This would seem to indicate that the castle was in the hands of the Lords of Sidon by this date.

The castle of Beaufort was later to be an important and integral

---

[84] William of Tyre, p. 804.   [85] Deschamps, *La Défense*, ii. 178.
[86] ROL 11 (1905–8), 181–3.

part of the Lordship of Sidon. John refers to 'Le seignor de Seete et de Biaufor'[87] and 'La baronie de Seete, de qui Biaufort et Cesaire et Bessan sont . . .'.[88] Moreover, the knights' service owed by Sidon and Beaufort is given as a joint figure: 'De Seete et de Biaufort, XL. chevaliers'.[89] Beaufort was thus acquired by the Lord of Sidon at some point between 1139 and 1158, probably between 1143 and 1158, given Fulk's policy towards the higher nobility.

In 1158 we find an 'Aiguebertus de Belfort' as a senior vassal of the lordship witnessing a charter immediately after the Constable.[90] By 1253 the name 'de Beaufort' was in the possession of the family of the Lords of Sidon (in *Reg. Hier.*, Nos. 1253, 1256, 1257, 1265, 1300, and 1301 we find Philip, third son of Balian of Sidon and brother of the then Lord of Sidon, Julian, witnessing as 'Phelippe de Biaufort'). Prior to that date, however, there is no evidence that the castle was in the direct possession of the Lords of Sidon. Given that 'Aiguebertus de Belfort' was a senior vassal, it seems likely that he was enfeoffed with the castle, or was acting as its castellan. This view is reinforced by the presence as a senior vassal (third witness in an extensive list) of a certain 'Theodericus Bellifortis' in 1164.[91] If the latter was related to 'Aiguebertus', who was presumably dead by this time, this would argue for Beaufort being a hereditary sub-fief, rather than a castellany.

The king also held lands within the Lordship of Sidon itself. In 1174 King Amalric gave the Hospitallers an annual rent of 230 besants to be taken annually from a house which he had in Nablus, in return for the casal and the river of 'Amor' (or Damor), which was in the possession of the Order. This was an important property, sited within the Seigneury of Sidon.[92]

The Lordship of Hebron

We have seen that King Fulk was able to detach a new Lordship of Bethgibelin from the Seigneury of Hebron. Hugh II of St Abraham made the grant, but only at the request of the king. That Fulk was able to do so may suggest that substantial royal

---

[87] John of Ibelin, p. 420.   [88] Ibid. 422.   [89] Ibid. 422.
[90] ROL 11 (1905–8), 181–3.   [91] *Reg. Hier. Add.*, No. 393c.
[92] *Cart. gén. Hosp.*, No. 454; *Reg. Hier. Add.*, No. 517a.

possessions were retained in the lordship,[93] This is further suggested by the fact that, as well as 'requesting' Hugh to give the castle to the Hospitallers, Fulk himself added four nearby casalia to their possessions.

The Lordship of Toron

In 1161 there is also evidence of the king acquiring properties in the Lordship of Toron. As part of an extensive exchange of lands between Philip de Milly and Baldwin III in that year we find 'Dedit quoque et Maronem mihi et totum eciam illud, quod in montanis Tyri et Toroni in dominio habebat et quicquid alius ibidem ex ipso tenebat . . .'.[94] It is clear that Philip had been holding lands in Toron from Baldwin III and that these properties were now to be returned to the direct control of the king.

Smaller Lordships

It is significant to note that several smaller lordships seem in some way to have been given an intermediate administrative status between that of a tenant-in-chief and that of a fief-holder within the royal domain, allowing closer royal control. Thus, Haifa, Scandaleon, and Blanchegarde are all described by John of Ibelin as seigneuries with 'court et coins et justise', but their military service was owed to the royal domain at Acre, rather than directly to the crown as was the case with other lordships.[95] It appears that these lordships were all rear-fiefs of what John of Ibelin described as 'la seignorie d'Acre'.[96]

The retention of royal lands both within and just outside the seigneuries provided yet another check on the actions of the nobility: limiting the military and economic resources of the lords around their seigneurial centres, and providing islands of direct royal influence in contentious areas. In this context it is perhaps significant to note that a royal presence of this kind in and near the large border seigneuries of Oultrejourdain and the Principality of Galilee was so distinctive: royal control was retained longest where the potential for independent action by a seigneury was greatest.

---

[93] *Cart. gén. Hosp.*, No. 116; *Reg. Hier.*, No. 164.
[94] *Tab. ord. Theut.*, No. 3; *Reg. Hier.*, No. 366.
[95] John of Ibelin, pp. 420–1, 425.   [96] Ibid. 424.

4. INDIRECT CONTROL

There were several indirect ways in which the king could retain a high degree of influence in a lordship even when it had left his direct control. Foremost amongst these was the entrusting of seigneuries to close relatives or trusted allies of the crown.

The Lordship of Blanchegarde

Blanchegarde, for instance, carved out of the territory of Jaffa, was only allowed to leave direct royal control in 1151, when the king's brother, Amalric, became Count of Jaffa. In a charter of 1158 we find Amalric in control of Blanchegarde[97] and in 1165 (when Amalric was king) we find the castellan of Blanchegarde still concerned with the affairs of the County.[98] The territory of Blanchegarde was never returned to the County of Jaffa and Ascalon.

The Lordship of Beirut

Beirut had been acquired for the royal domain some time in the period 1165–74 but had been lost to the Muslims in 1187. When it was recovered in 1197 Queen Isabella gave it to her half-brother, John of Ibelin, who held it until his death in 1236.[99] As John also acquired the Lordship of Arsur in *c.*1207, through his marriage to Melisende, daughter of John I of Arsur, this placed two of the coastal seigneuries in the hands of a close relative of the crown.[100]

The Lordship of Toron

The Lordship of Toron had passed into the royal domain in 1180 through an agreement between the king and Humphrey IV, Lord of Toron.[101] By 1184 we know that some of the revenues of the lordship had been assigned to Agnes de Courtenay, the king's mother, though overall royal administration continued.[102]

In 1186 the Courtenays were given complete possession of the

---

[97] *Reg. Hier.*, No. 331; see also 'Papst-Kaiser', p. 46, no. 2.

[98] *Cart. gén. Hosp.*, No. 344; *Reg. Hier.*, No. 413. Semma was sited in the County of Jaffa and Ascalon.

[99] 'Les Gestes des Chiprois', pp. 678–9; 'Les Lignages', p. 458. Whether the whole lordship was immediately recovered is open to doubt, however: James of Vitry was only able to get there with an armed guard in the winter of 1216–17; James of Vitry, 'Lettres', p. 92.

[100] See La Monte, 'John d'Ibelin', pp. 419–20.

[101] William of Tyre, p. 1012; Ernoul, ed. Mas-Latrie, pp. 81–2.

[102] Ibn Jubair, p. 447.

fief, for in that year King Guy gave the lordship to Joscelyn de
Courtenay.[103] By this agreement Joscelyn was to be given
'Toronum et Castrum Novum' with everything pertaining to
them, and the rights to Banias, should it ever be recovered.
Joscelyn was also to receive the fief of Maron.[104]

Though Toron later left the hands of the royal relatives, the
Courtenays, this was only done at the express command of the
queen herself. Humphrey IV's wife, Isabelle, married Conrad of
Montferrat in 1190 and amongst her first acts as queen was the
restoration of her ex-husband's old fiefs: 'Je li renz toutes iceles
choses que il dona a mon frere, quant il me eposa; ce est assaver
le Toron et le Chastel Neuf, o toutes lor apartenances, et toutes
les teneures de son pere et de son ayol'.[105]

The thirteenth century provides us with another instance of
the king attempting (though this time unsuccessfully) to place the
Lordship of Toron in the hands of a relative or ally. By the treaty
of 1229 between Frederick II and the sultan, Toron was returned
to the Franks.[106] Perhaps inevitably, this led to disputes over the
ownership of the newly recovered fief. One claimant was Alice of
Armenia, daughter of Humphrey IV's sister, who had acquired
much of the Seigneury of Joscelyn de Courtenay. The other was
the Teutonic Knights. The Teutonic Knights undoubtedly had
the weaker case, though as supporters of the emperor they had his
backing. The only claim that the Brothers seem to have had
(based on surviving evidence) was the fact that they had
purchased many of the possessions and rights of Joscelyn de
Courtenay from his heirs. Joscelyn's lands were divided on his
death equally between his two daughters, Agnes and Beatrice. In

---

[103] *Tab. ord. Theut.*, No. 21; *Reg. Hier.*, No. 653.

[104] The military service of Maron presents certain problems. Riley-Smith has pointed
out that the military service of Maron seems to have increased (Riley-Smith, *Feudal
Nobility*, p. 9): in John of Ibelin's lists we find that a service of 3 knights is required, while
in this charter (i.e. *Reg. Hier.*, No. 653) a service of 'quatuor militum' is owed (John of
Ibelin, p. 423). This discrepancy is explicable. When referring in the same charter to the
service owed from Toron and Chastel Neuf, Guy is explicit in stating that the service
required will be the same as that owed by Humphrey II. In detailing the service he
required from Maron, however, Guy was careful to make no mention of the service which
had previously been owed for the fief: the implication must surely be that Guy had
decided to take advantage of the transfer of the fief to increase its military quota (i.e. 3–4
knights' service).

[105] *Eracles*, p. 154.

[106] *Hist. dipl. Fred. II*, iii. 86–7, 90–7, 102, 105; Ernoul, ed. Mas-Latrie, p. 465;
Eracles, p. 374; al-'Aini, pp. 188–90; al-Maqrizi, tr. Blochet, *ROL* 9 (1902), 525.

May 1220 Beatrice sold all her remaining possessions in the Latin Kingdom to the Teutonic Knights.[107] The confirmation of this agreement detailed just what these properties consisted of, namely the fief of Château du Roi, a third of the fief of St George, a third of Bokehel, and a third of a revenue of 800 besants at Acre.[108] What was clearly missing was a claim to any part of the Lordship of Toron. As we have seen, Queen Isabelle returned Toron to Humphrey IV in 1190 and the heirs of Joscelyn seem, by the evidence of these documents, to have recognized that they had lost the lordship.

The Teutonic Knights, however, were more territorially ambitious than Joscelyn's heirs; or it may simply be that by putting forward a claim to the lordship as a whole, they sought merely to invoke the compensatory clause in Guy's grant of Toron to Joscelyn in 1186.[109] In the event, they succeeded in achieving the latter. Frederick initially tried to give the entire lordship to them. A meeting of the High Court ruled for Alice, however, and when Balian of Sidon, the emperor's *bailli*, refused to put her into seisin, the vassals withdrew their service.[110] Frederick was forced to concede, and instead gave the Order the compensation due to the heirs of Joscelyn for the reversion of Toron to Humphrey IV or his heirs: namely, Maron and its casalia and the sum of 7,000 besants to be taken each year from the revenues of Acre.[111]

The case of the Seigneury of Joscelyn de Courtenay provides, as we have seen, a striking example of the way in which seigneuries might be given to trusted relatives. It is also interesting to note that the seigneury itself was created for Joscelyn by the king, his nephew. Active steps were taken to ensure that this close familial link would continue (i.e. the arrangements for Joscelyn's daughters to marry Guy de Lusignan's younger brother, William de Valence, and his nephews).[112]

The County of Jaffa and Ascalon

There were also instances when lordships were given to trusted

[107] *Tab. ord. Theut.*, No 52; *Reg. Hier.*, No. 933.
[108] *Tab. ord. Theut.*, No. 53; *Reg. Hier.*, No. 934.
[109] *Tab. ord. Theut.*, No. 21; *Reg. Hier.*, No. 653.
[110] John of Ibelin, pp. 112–13. 325–6.
[111] *Tab. ord. Theut.*, No. 66; *Reg. Hier.*, No. 1003.
[112] *Tab. ord. Theut.*, No. 23; *Reg. Hier.*, No. 655.

vassals who were not related to the monarchy. Mirabel, for instance, seems to have been given to Balian the Elder by King Fulk. As Balian was loyal to the king during his overlord's revolt in 1134, and as the creation of lordships at the expense of the County of Jaffa seems to have been undertaken as a matter of deliberate policy by Fulk it seems likely that the new lordship was given to him between 1135 and 1143.[113] The Lordship of Ramla, when it was set up in *c.*1134–6, seems also to have been given to a vassal of the County of Jaffa, Baldwin of Ramla, who had remained loyal to the crown during the revolt of 1134.[114]

The Lordship of Oultrejourdain

Such indirect methods of influence could also be exerted on a more limited level through purchase, or the exercise of royal rights *within* a given seigneury, for example through rights over the Bedouin population.

Royal links with the native population of Oultrejourdain seem to have been particularly strong. After the 1107 expedition to the area, Baldwin I returned with a number of native Christians to colonize parts of the Latin Kingdom: Oultrejourdain was not at that time under complete Frankish control.[115] Although it is not entirely clear whether this movement was voluntary, the previous record of co-operation between the native Christians and the Franks in this area would indicate that this was the case. Presumably these settlers would retain moral and possibly economic ties with the monarchy in their new homes.

Royal links with the native population of Oultrejourdain had pre-dated this colonization activity. During Baldwin I's expedition to the area, which left Jerusalem on 28 November 1100, native guides were used to help explore the region.[116] Similarly, the royal expedition to Oultrejourdain of February to April 1107 was guided by a native Christian, a certain Theodore.[117] Native help was forthcoming in later expeditions as well. In 1112–13 we find Bedouin helping the king to make a raid in Oultrejourdain which succeeded in capturing a Damascene caravan.[118] Royal rights

[113] See *Cart. gen. Hosp.*, No. 263; *Reg. Hier.*, No. 330 and *Cart. gén. Hosp.*, No. 327; *Reg. Hier. Add.*, No. 384a.
[114] See chapter 2, under The Lordship of Ramla.
[115] Albert of Aix, p. 644; Qalanisi, ed. Gibb, pp. 81–2.
[116] Fulcher of Chartres, pp. 376–84; Albert of Aix, pp. 535–6.
[117] Albert of Aix, p. 644; Qalanisi, ed. Gibb, pp. 81–2.
[118] Albert of Aix, p. 693; Qalanisi, ed. Gibb, pp. 130–1.

over some of the native population were maintained even after the establishment and expansion of the Lordship of Oultrejourdain: an agreement of 1161 between Baldwin III and Philip de Milly, the new lord, expressly reserved to the crown the rights over Bedouin not born in the lordship.[119]

The Principality of Galilee

In 1180 we find King Baldwin IV giving the Hospitallers a grant of 100 tents of Bedouin near Belvoir, i.e. within the Principality of Galilee.[120] The Bedouin were only given under the condition that they should come from outside the kingdom's borders and that they should never have been under the dominion of the king or any other lord: this migrant population was thus a source of profit to secular lords as well as the king and the Military Orders. It is striking to note that although a lord *could* have dominion over Bedouin, the king had retained this right in the heart of the single most powerful lordship in the kingdom.

5. DIRECT ACQUISITION

A far less subtle way of controlling a lordship was to engineer its direct acquisition by the crown. Because of the overt nature of the action, however, and the dubious legality that would generally accompany it, this was not a move that was often undertaken. If badly handled, this process, far from increasing royal control over the nobility, could inspire them to rebellion, as Frederick II discovered to his cost.

The Lordship of Beirut

Earlier Kings of Jerusalem had occasionally been able to engineer a direct acquisition, however, as the example of the Lordship of Beirut shows. Documentation exists from 1174 which tells us that Walter III of Beirut is no longer lord of that seigneury. King Amalric confirmed that Walter had given the Brothers of St Lazarus: 'XL bisancios apud Accon in redditu cathene, de ipsa assisia Galteri de Berito, Albe Custodie domino, quam ego ei pro Berito in cumcambio dedi . . . .'[121]

---

[119] *Tab. ord. Theut.*, No. 3; *Reg. Hier.*, No. 366; see Prawer, *Crusader Institutions*, p. 214, in which he argues that all Bedouin were directly subject to the king, unless specifically granted away.

[120] *Cart. gén. Hosp.*, No. 582; *Reg. Hier.*, No. 593.

[121] AOL 2B, pp. 145–6, No. 28; *Reg. Hier.*, No. 512.

The exact date at which Walter III sold Beirut to the king is not known. In April 1165 Blanchegarde was still in royal hands, for we find an 'Arnulfus, castellanus de Blancagarda' in that month: presumably the transfer took place sometime between April 1165 and February 1174.[122]

The reasons behind the collapse of such a prosperous lay lordship show just how fragile was the economic independence of the nobility: bad luck, or a single instance of mismanagement, could bring an entire seigneury to its knees, even in a time of peace and economic prosperity. As we have seen, when Walter III and his two brothers were captured by the Saracens, the ransom demanded forced him to give Beirut to the king in return for Blanchegarde and a sum of money.[123] He still retained some of this money, in the form of revenues drawn from the *catena* of Acre, in 1174.[124]

The desirability of Beirut is further made evident by the political conflicts of 1185–7 (no doubt also motivated by a wish to control the considerable port revenues of the lordship). In 1185 Raymond of Tripoli was given Beirut to defray the costs of the regency of the young heir to the throne, Baldwin V.[125] Immediately after the death of Baldwin V, however, Joscelyn de Courtenay seized Beirut and Tyre for Sibylla. At his first assembly of the baronage later in the same year, King Guy specifically announced that Beirut was to be taken from Raymond. When negotiations were started between Raymond and Guy early in 1187, Raymond demanded that Beirut be returned to him: Guy refused, thinking the price too high for a settlement.[126] Ownership of Beirut was soon to become academic, however, and in 1187 the lordship was swept away with most of the Latin Kingdom.

The Lordship of Toron

The direct take-over of a lordship by the king might be caused by higher motives than mere profit, however, as was probably the case with the acquisition of the Lordship of Toron. The Lordship was under major military pressure from the Muslims in the 1150s

---

[122] *Cart. gén. Hosp.*, No. 344; *Reg. Hier.*, No. 413.
[123] 'Les Lignages', p. 458.
[124] *AOL* 2B, pp. 145–6, No. 28; *Reg. Hier.*, No. 512.
[125] *Eracles*, p. 7; Ernoul, p. 21.
[126] Ernoul, pp. 34–5; *Eracles*, pp. 31–35.

and early 1160s and this situation rapidly got worse. In 1164 Banias itself fell, and this time was never to be recovered. A vassal of the lordship, Walter de Quesnoy, was left in charge of Banias, probably as castellan, and it was rumoured that he had betrayed the town: William of Tyre passed on the rumours, but expressed doubts about their veracity. [127]

A further blow came in 1167, when Chastel Neuf fell. The garrison retired from the castle, leaving Nur-ad-Din a free hand to destroy the fortifications. [128] The lack of resources available to Lord Humphrey II, and the increasingly untenable nature of border fortresses in the area is attested to both by the feeling amongst the garrison that resistance was futile and the fact that over ten years passed before Humphrey II felt able to rebuild the castle (in 1178). [129]

Humphrey II died in 1179 after being wounded near Banias. [130] Humphrey IV took over the lordship on the death of his grandfather. In 1180 King Baldwin IV stepped in and took over complete control of the Lordship of Toron. In that year the young Humphrey IV became betrothed to the king's sister Isabel. Following the betrothal, Humphrey IV exchanged the Lordship of Toron and his other fiefs with the king. As William of Tyre says:

Commutavit preterea patrimonium suum, quod in finibus Tyri per mortem avi paterni hereditario jure ad se fuerat devolutum, Toronum videlicet, et Castellum Novum et Paneadem cum pertinentiis suis, cum domino rege certis conditionibus, quarum tenor in archivis regiis, nobis dictantibus, per officium nostrum continetur introductus.

It is interesting to note that William, writing during the period in which the Lordship of Toron was a part of the royal domain, described Humphrey's possessions as being 'in finibus Tyri'. [131] It seems to have been this part of the administrative structure of

---

[127] William of Tyre, pp. 876–7; William of Newborough, p. 156. 'Annales de Terre Sainte', p. 432; Ibn al-Athir, 'Histoire des Atabecs', ii. 233–4; Abu-Shamah, iv. 126; Abou'l Feda, p. 35; Ibn al-Athir, 'Kamil', i. 540–1.

[128] Ibn al-Athir, 'Kamil', i. 551.

[129] For the rebuilding of Chastel Neuf see Deschamps, *La Défense*, ii. 130.

[130] William of Tyre, p. 999; Ibn al-Athir, 'Kamil', i. 635; see also al-Maqrizi, tr. Blochet, *ROL* 8 (1900–1), 530.

[131] William of Tyre, pp. 1012–13; Ernoul, ed. Mas-Latrie, pp. 81–2. I would not, however, place too much emphasis on the phrase 'in finibus Tyri' in isolation: William may have been referring to the ecclesiastical boundaries of his own province.

the royal domain that assumed responsibility for the new acquisitions.[132] Frustratingly, William knew the exact details of the exchange ('. . . certis conditionibus, quarum tenor in archivis regiis . . .'), but chose not to relate them. In the absence of such details this exchange has been interpreted as Humphrey IV being forced to concede to the wishes of a greedy king. Riley-Smith hypothesizes that Humphrey 'had been forced to surrender his fief of Toron and Chastel Neuf' because of Baldwin IV's suspicions of the allies of Raymond of Tripoli.[133]

There is, however, another way to interpret this transaction. We know from his later actions that Humphrey IV was a far less forceful leader of men than his grandfather. We have also seen that even under the extremely energetic and capable Constable Humphrey II the Lordship of Toron and the family's allied fiefs had suffered major losses. The king and the young Humphrey IV, who had only just come of age, may genuinely have reached a very just agreement whereby Humphrey could exchange turbulent properties on the border for money revenues and more stable properties elsewhere in the kingdom, while the king could ensure that the defence of this section of the border could be placed in more capable hands. Certainly, it is difficult to see the betrothal of the king's sister, Isabel, then aged only 8, as anything other than a mark of royal favour towards Humphrey. Moreover, although William of Tyre does not reveal details of what Humphrey received for the fiefs, later litigation sheds light on the earlier agreement: the details given in that litigation certainly do not seem punitive.

In an act of 1186 we find King Guy giving to Joscelyn de Courtenay Toron, Chastel Neuf, and, if it were ever recovered by Christians, Banias. The agreement then refers to 'Maronum cum omnibus pertinenciis suis prenominatis et illud concambium, quod dominus Henfredus iuvenis pro Torono et Castro Novo tenet et possidet'.[134] A later charter is even more explicit. In this document Frederick II gave the Teutonic Knights: '. . . Maronum, Quabrinquen, Belide, Cades, Lahare, Mees, duo Megeras, 7000

---

[132] It is also interesting to see that Toron, Banias, and Chastel Neuf, generally regarded by historians as a single entity, were merely described as 'patrimonium suum'. As I have argued in chapter 2, these were three separate lordships and were treated as such even when in the hands of the same lord (i.e. the de Toron family).

[133] Riley-Smith, *Feudal Nobility*, p. 105.

[134] *Tab. ord. Theut.*, No. 21; *Reg. Hier.*, No. 653.

bisantiorum sarracenatorum annuatim de reditibus catenae et fundae Acconensium percipiendos, quae omnia quondam Henfrido iuveni cambio pro Turone et Castro Novo'.[135]

The original agreement would thus seem to have been for an annual revenue of 7,000 besants and the substantial rear-fief of Maron. The king had exchanged stable revenues for a highly pressurized border fief: it seems more likely that he had little faith in Humphrey's abilities to defend the fief, and therefore felt obliged to take it over himself, than that he forced Humphrey to give up his patrimony for financial gain or internal political reasons.

6. CONCLUSIONS

In addition to the broad political controls provided by the creation and reversion of the lordships, the king possessed a wide range of controls of varying degrees of effectiveness and subtlety with which to influence the actions of the seigneuries on a more day-to-day basis. Lords could be severely constrained in their relationship with the monarchy and, when need arose, the king did not hesitate to use such constraints.

[135] *Tab. ord. Theut.*, No. 66; *Reg. Hier.*, No. 1003. It is also worth noting with regard to the Lordship of Toron that Baldwin IV may, in addition, have been concerned to prevent the possibility of Humphrey IV (as heir to the Oultrejourdain) possessing two great lordships at once.

4
Seigneurial Resources I:
The Example of Caesarea

THE Kings of Jerusalem exercised political control over the seigneuries both on a broad structural level and in more prosaic ways, such as through fief distribution. It might reasonably be argued, however, that the existence of such controls would not necessarily imply the impotence of the seigneuries: it could be said that given a certain level of resources, of whatever derivation, any of the more substantial lordships might still exert a major influence on the monarchy. At the very least, such a resource level would tend to bode well for the power and influence wielded by a lord *within* his own seigneury and it has been generally assumed that the lords of the Latin Kingdom were masters within their fiefs.

The Lordship of Caesarea has been singled out for particular comment in this respect. In contrast to the two 'weak' lordships which their lords were forced to sell to the Military Orders (Sidon and Arsur), Caesarea, and other lordships which remained in secular hands almost throughout the history of the kingdom, have been treated as examples of the way in which the power of the feudal nobility survived intact well into the thirteenth century.[1] A close examination of the land transactions carried out in the lordship, however, shows that this was far from being the case, and it is only because such an examination has not been done before that assumptions about the extent of secular resources, and hence power, have been able to persist.

1. METHODOLOGY AND SAMPLE

The Lordship of Caesarea provides a fascinating insight into the composition of a lay seigneury in the Latin Kingdom. A wealth of

---

[1] See e.g. Riley-Smith, *Feudal Nobility*, pp. 28, 30–1.

evidence exists for the lordship, but as it is so fragmentary and disparate it has never been analysed as a whole for this purpose.

Before undertaking any study of the composition of landed holdings in the lordship (and Caesarea is one of the few areas in the kingdom where statistically significant samples are available from which to draw conclusions as to composition) it is essential to make an accurate estimate of the total sample, of which surviving materials are merely representative. For the purposes of this study I shall use the casal as the basic unit of measurement for it is only when one estimates the number of casalia contained within the lordship that one can assess the significance of the results obtained by studying surviving charters and other evidence.

John La Monte, in his useful study 'The Lords of Caesarea in the Period of the Crusades', estimated that the whole lordship contained 45 casalia. He derived this figure by counting up the number of casalia listed by E. G. Rey as being in the lordship. This is obviously an unsatisfactory approach as it presupposes that Rey, writing in 1883, had access to all the materials now available (which was not the case); that references survived, and were available in 1883, for every casal in the lordship; and that Rey was scrupulously accurate.[2] None of these three preconditions was realistic and, I believe, led La Monte to underestimate substantially the number of casalia in the lordship. Rey himself never suggested that the casalia he listed were anything more than a survey of existing material. Benvenisti, in his work on population and settlement density, provides a more useful basis on which to work.[3] He estimated that the town of Caesarea, covering an area of approximately 120 dunaams, held a population of about 4,800 people, a density of 40 persons per dunaam. He also worked out the density of settlement in four other key areas: Tyre, Acre, Nablus, and Jerusalem. These calculations are summarized in Table 2.

Of these four areas, Acre seems to be the most closely comparable with Caesarea. Tyre was the subject of unusually high density, while Nablus and Jerusalem were inland sites. Benvenisti estimated the size of the Lordship of Caesarea to be 1,500 sq. km. On this basis, if we take Acre to be the closest parallel

---

[2] La Monte, 'The Lords of Caesarea', p. 145; Rey, *Les Colonies*, pp. 417–25.
[3] Benvenisti, *The Crusaders in the Holy Land*, pp. 15, 27, 137, 140.

TABLE 2. *Estimates of village density (Benvenisti)*

Area	No. of villages	Size of total area (sq. km.)
Tyre	65	340
Acre	83	970
Nablus	90	1 500
Jerusalem	104	2 000

to Caesarea, we arrive at a total figure of 163 casalia (using the same ratio of 11.69 sq. km. per casal).

A glance at the map of the Latin Kingdom, however (even as produced by Benvenisti), shows that the lordship was much smaller than the 1,500 sq. km. which Benvenisti asserted. The estimate of 1,200 sq. km. offered by G. Bayer and J. Prawer is the maximum that one can ascribe to the lordship and is the figure that I shall follow. On that basis the number of villages in Caesarea will have to be revised: if Acre is assumed to have been of similar density to Caesarea, then one can say that Caesarea would have had just over 100 casalia (i.e. 1,200 sq. km., divided by an average casal size of 11.69 sq. km. would give us a total of 102.65 casalia). I believe this to be the most reasonable estimate we can now make, and it is this which I shall assume to be the universe in future calculations: that the lordship had approximately 103 casalia, with an average size of 11.69 sq. km. each.[4]

The question of the *overall* composition of the lordship has always been the subject of confusion. John of Ibelin tells us that: 'La seignorie de Cesaire a court et coins et justise. Et a Cesaire a court de borgesie et justise.' The courts of Merle and Chateau Pelerin are both ascribed to the Lordship of Arsur in most variants, even though they were clearly within the territorial boundaries of the Lordship of Caesarea. The confusion over the status of these townships may in part reflect the semi-independent status of the Templars in those areas (Merle and Château Pélérin were both Templar properties): they were certainly never part of Arsur. La Monte adds to the confusion concerning the composition of the lordship with two extremely doubtful statements: 'The Lords of Caesarea may have been at one time the suzerains of the

[4] Prawer, *Crusader Institutions*, p. 180 n. 155.

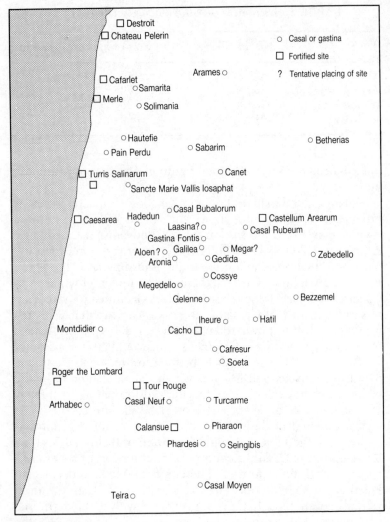

5. Caesarea

fief of Bethsan, which itself owed 15 knights' service, and was one of the more important arrière fiefs.' 'Not included in Sidon, but dependent thereon, were the important fiefs of Caesarea and Bethsan.' As far as I can see, there is no justification for either of these statements except in John of Ibelin's lists, which are extremely unreliable in matters of this kind. The Lords of Bethsan held property in the Lordship of Caesarea, and thus had to receive the Lord of Caesarea's confirmation for transactions carried out within his lordship, but this does not prove any deeper feudal relationship. The Lords of Caesarea were tenants-in-chief of the crown and thus unlikely to hold their fief from anyone else.[5]

2. LANDED TRANSACTIONS: 1101–1123

The town of Caesarea was captured on 1 May 1101 by Baldwin I, being one of the first major ports to be acquired after the first crusade. As we have seen, Caesarea was retained in the royal domain until it was given to Eustace Grenier, a Flemish knight who had arrived in the Near East some time between 1099 and August 1105. He acquired the office of Constable of the Latin Kingdom sometime between 1120 and 1123 and in the latter year was elected regent after the capture of Baldwin II. By September 1110 he had been given Caesarea as a lordship and later in the same year he was given the newly acquired Lordship of Sidon.[6] In September 1110 Baldwin I confirmed that Eustace had already given the Hospitallers a casal in the territory of Caesarea, as well as lands neighbouring Cacho. His 'milites' had already donated villeins (i.e. parts of casalia) to the Order, which was confirmed by Baldwin III in 1154. Baldwin also took the opportunity to confirm that Eustace had previously given the Hospitallers casal Bethtamis. Although the location of the casal cannot now be identified, it was sited somewhere in the Lordship of Caesarea.[7]

We find that, in 1112, the Archbishop of Caesarea exempted the Hospitallers from paying tithes in his archbishopric (following the example given by the Patriarch of Jerusalem earlier in the year) and in 1115 it was confirmed that Eustace had given the Hospitallers a house in Caesarea, together with more substantial properties in Sidon.[8]

[5] John of Ibelin, p. 420; La Monte, 'The Lords of Caesarea', p. 145; La Monte, 'The Lords of Sidon', p. 183; *Cart. gén. Hosp.*, No. 621; *Reg. Hier.*, No. 619.

[6] La Monte, 'The Lords of Sidon', pp. 185–90, and 'The Lords of Caesarea', pp. 145–6.

[7] *Cart. gén. Hosp.*, No. 20; *Reg. Hier.*, No. 57; *Cart. gén. Hosp.*, No. 225; *Reg. Hier.*, No. 293; *Cart. gén. Hosp.*, No. 20; *Reg. Hier.*, No. 57; *Cart. gén. Hosp.*, No. 225; *Reg. Hier.*, No. 293.

[8] For tithes see *Cart. gén. Hosp.*, No 29, and *Reg. Hier.*, No. 65. For the house in Caesarea see *Chartes de Josaphat*, ed. Delaborde, No. 6, and *Reg. Hier.*, No. 80.

In 1116 Eustace restored property to the monks of St Quarantene near Jericho, and let them use his water supplies twice a week, rather than once a fortnight as they had been accustomed to do; an interesting example of the value of water rights. It is impossible to say, however, whether these rights belonged to the Lordship of Caesarea or that of Sidon (or, indeed, whether they were just held as a personal fief by Eustace).[9]

Walter Grenier confirmed, in September 1131, that his father had given the Hospitallers, amongst other things: houses in Caesarea with two 'curtiles'; a casal in the lordship called Adelfie (Hautefie) with everything pertaining to it; in Cacho, houses and courtyards; 4 carrucates of land in Cacho; and 2 carrucates of land given by H. Lumbardus with Eustace's consent.[10]

In 1145 Walter also confirmed that his father had given the Holy Sepulchre half of casal Fiasse, and the lands adjacent to it. Interestingly, in the same document Walter mentioned that: '. . . sicuti idem pater meus divisit territorium a casale Sancte Marie Vallis Iosaphat et casale Sancti Petri Cesaree et casale de la Forest et casale Sabarini et casal Sancti Iohannis Sebaste et a meo casali, quod nuncupatur de Bufles . . .'.[11] As well as telling us something about the holdings of the Holy Sepulchre, this document also indicates several other elements of land ownership in the area: the monastery of Josaphat owned a casal in the lordship ('casale Sancte Marie Vallis Iosaphat'); the Archbishopric of Caesarea was the probable owner of casal 'Sancti Petri Cesaree'; the church of St John at Sebaste seems to have owned a casal in the lordship ('casal Sancti Iohannis Sebaste'); and the young Walter I of Caesarea owned casal Bufles (or Bubalorum) during his father's lifetime.[12]

In Table 3 (and those of similar type) we see the distribution of known lands within the lordship. This table is based only on data for casalia, and parts thereof. As many gifts are unspecific, I shall deem a 'part' of a casal (where otherwise undefined) to be 20 per cent of the whole. Those tables covering the early years of the

[9] *Cart. du St-Sépulcre*, No. 119 (B.-B., No. 94); *Reg. Hier.*, No. 82.
[10] *Cart. gén. Hosp.*, No. 94; *Reg. Hier.*, No. 139.
[11] *Cart. du St-Sépulcre*, No. 71 (B.-B., No. 59); *Reg. Hier.*, No. 237.
[12] It is interesting to note that Casal Bubalorum was still in the hands of the Lords of Caesarea in 1213, at which time it was used as security for a debt to the Hospitallers of 1,000 saracen *besants*; *Cart. gén. Hosp.*, No. 1414; *Reg. Hier.*, No. 866.

TABLE 3. *Land holdings:* c.1110–1123

	All casalia for which data exist		% all casalia for which data exist		% all casalia	
	c.1110	1123	c.1110	1123	c.1110	1123
Base:	8.6	8.6	8.6 100%	8.6 100%	103 100%	103 100%
Lay						
Lords of Caesarea	4.2	0.5	48.8	5.6	4.1	0.5
Relatives of Lords of Caesarea	1.0	1.0	11.6	11.6	1.0	1.0
Vassals	0.4	0.0	4.7	0.0	0.4	0.0
Military Orders						
Hospitallers	0.0	3.6	0.0	40.0	0.0	3.5
Other religious						
Josaphat	1.0	1.0	11.6	11.6	1.0	1.0
Holy Sepulchre	0.0	0.5	0.0	5.6	0.0	0.5
Archbishopric of Caesarea	1.0	1.0	11.6	11.6	1.0	1.0
Other religious	1.0	1.0	11.6	11.6	1.0	1.0

lordship cannot aspire to completeness or total accuracy, due to the limitations of the sources. They can, I believe, show general trends over time, however, and as we shall see, a very full picture can be built up by the thirteenth century.

It should be noted that although figures for the known possessions of the Lords of Caesarea and other lay individuals are included for the sake of completeness, they are in themselves almost meaningless for this period of the lordship's history. Rather it is the figures for the Hospitallers and other religious institutions that are important, for they tell us what the Lords of Caesarea and their vassals could not have owned.

The following points should be noted in each of the tables:

1. The base size at the top of the first four left-hand columns represents the number of casalia for which data exist at a certain time. Naturally, the further we go in examining the lordship, the greater the base size will become (i.e. as more data become

available). It follows from this that later tables will be statistically more reliable than early ones.

2. The first column represents the number of casalia at the beginning of a given period which we know to have been in the possession of certain groups.

3. The second column represents the same statistics as they pertain to the *end* of the period.

4. The third column represents the proportion of casalia at the beginning of a given period, which we know to have been in the possession of certain groups. Figures in this column are expressed in terms of a percentage of the total number of casalia whose ownership can be ascertained at that time.

5. The fourth column represents the same statistics as the third column, except that they pertain to the end of the period.

6. The fifth column expresses the number of casalia whose ownership can be ascertained at the beginning of the period, expressed as a proportion of the total number of casalia which I have calculated to be in the lordship (i.e. 103). The fifth and sixth columns of the table are of crucial importance, as they show the proportion of total lands out of lay hands at any given point.

7. The sixth column represents the same statistics as the fifth column except that they pertain to the end of the period.

8. The base size in the first two columns increases over time, but care has been taken to ensure that, wherever possible, double counting has not occurred e.g. if Cafarlet is mentioned in four periods of the lordship's history, it appears in the base size of the table pertaining to its first appearance (and increases the base size in the first four columns by 1) but does not increase the base size in succeeding tables (after its first inclusion any shifts in ownership are naturally represented by a change in the proportions *within* the columns).

3. LANDED TRANSACTIONS: 1123–c. 1149

It appears that Walter I of Caesarea (1123–c. 1149) took over the lordship on the death of his father in 1123, although we have no evidence that he used the title of Lord of Caesarea before March 1128. Prior to this, in April 1124, we find him with his mother and stepfather, Hugh of Jaffa, confirming gifts made by his father; appearing in three charters, with his mother and his brother

Eustace, in 1126; and in 1127 witnessing a charter of Constable Balian of Jaffa.[13]

For a short period in the 1130s it appears that Walter acted as regent of the Lordship of Sidon, as his brother Eustace seems to have died by September 1131, leaving his son Gerard in Walter's guardianship: in this year Walter referred to himself as 'G. cognomento Granerius, Cesareae et Sydonie Dei gratia dominus'. Gerard appears to have taken over the Lordship of Sidon by 1135, however, at which point we find Walter once again referring to himself merely as Lord of Caesarea.[14]

In 1128, as we have discussed above, Geoffrey de Flujeac gave the castle (described in rubric form as a 'castel') of Calansue to the Hospitallers, in the presence of King Baldwin II and his army, and in 1128 Pope Honorius II confirmed that the Brothers of the Holy Sepulchre owned, amongst other possessions, the 'castrum Feniculi', with its church and everything pertaining to it. Clearly, even at this early stage, minor fortifications within the lordship were leaving secular hands. One is tempted to ascribe this process to the financial problems that recurred throughout Walter's lordship (problems that became exacerbated under later lords).[15]

When Baldwin II confirmed the gift of Calansue to the Hospitallers in 1129, he mentioned, interestingly, that the gift of 'Goffridus de Flaiaco' had been made together with 'Johannes de Bethsam' and his brother Hugo (with John of Bethsan presumably being Godfrey's immediate overlord): as we have seen, the Lord of Bethsan's properties within the lordship may have been quite extensive. The extent of the Lordship of Bethsan's holdings in Caesarea may be judged by the confirmation in 1154 that 'Johannes de Bethsan', with the consent of his brother Hugo, also

---

[13] In March 1128 Walter witnessed a charter of King Baldwin II as 'Gualterius, Cesaree dominus', *Cart. du St-Sépulcre*, No. 44 (B.-B., No. 30); *Reg. Hier.*, No. 121. For April 1124 see *Cart. du St-Sépulcre*, No. 119 (B.-B., No. 94); *Reg. Hier.*, No. 104. For 1126 see *Cart. gén. Hosp.*, No. 74; *Reg. Hier.*, No. 112; *Cart. gén. Hosp.*, No. 77; *Reg. Hier.*, No. 113; *Chartes de Josaphat*, ed. Kohler, No. 12; *Reg. Hier. Add.*, No. 114b. For 1127 see *Chartes de Josaphat*, ed. Delaborde, No. 15; *Reg. Hier.*, No. 120.

[14] *Cart. gén. Hosp.*, No. 94; *Reg. Hier.*, No. 139; *Cart. gén. Hosp.*, No. 115; *Reg. Hier.*, No. 159.

[15] For Calansue see *Cart. gén. Hosp.*, No. 83, and *Reg. Hier. Add.*, No. 121a. For 'castrum Feniculi' see *Cart. du St-Sépulcre*, No. 16 (B.-B., No. 6), and *Reg. Hier.*, No. 124.

sold casal Adeka, in the territory of Caesarea, to the Hospitallers.[16]

In 1129 the Holy Sepulchre's possession of casal Fiasse was confirmed when Evremar, Archbishop of Caesarea, gave the Brothers the tithes of the casal, together with a tithe on its animals and other things which probably implies that all, rather than just half, of the casal now belonged to the Brothers.[17]

In 1131, while confirming the substantial gifts made by his father to the Hospitallers, Walter also conceded or gave the Order: a *curtile* (presumably in Cacho) which Walter, Viscount of Cacho, had given them, with his consent; the *curtile* which Alonis had exchanged with the Order; two carrucates of land in Cafarsalem, given to the Hospitallers by an unnamed vassal of Walter's; and two carrucates of land, given by Walter himself, in the marshes at Maresco. The latter lands were to come from the 'principio terre Rambaldi, que laboratur in Maresco . . .'. If this land failed, the Order was to receive better lands in Sabulone, where they would be given four carrucates; Calansue was also conceded by Walter.[18]

Walter's lordship appears to have been dogged by financial problems, though one can find no evidence of major building activities which might have caused such a situation: presumably he was just living beyond his means. In 1135 he had already consented to the sale of lands by a certain Isembard to the Hospitallers. Isembard sold to the Order casal Arthabec, in the territory of Caesarea, for 500 besants, together with all its trees, pasture, and water. The sale was authorized by Walter, described as 'Cesariensis dominus, in cujus territorio hoc casale est . . .', for which authorization he received 150 besants. In addition, a certain 'Arnulfus de Haynis, dominus Hysimbardi, similiter laudavit et auctorizavit . . .', for which he received 60 besants.[19] This transaction indicates the extended lines of dependence within the lordship and may also indicate the extent of Walter's financial problems, for an authorization fee of 30 per cent of the total sale price seems very high. Casal Arthabec itself is

[16] For the confirmation of 1129 see *Cart. gén. Hosp.*, No. 84, and *Reg. Hier.*, No. 130. For Casal Adeka see *Cart. gén. Hosp.*, No. 225, and *Reg. Hier.*, No. 293.

[17] *Cart. du St-Sépulcre*, No. 70 (B.-B., No. 58); *Reg. Hier.*, No. 126.

[18] *Cart. gén. Hosp.*, No. 94; *Reg. Hier.*, No. 139.

[19] *Cart. gén. Hosp.*, No. 115; *Reg. Hier.*, No. 159.

interestingly described as being 'ab oriente Kalensua, a meredie Calodia, ab occidente castellare [?] Rogerii Longobardi [probably Roger de Chatillon], ab aquilone casale Latinae' (i.e. probably belonging to Mary of the Latins).

In February 1136 Walter sold casal Betherias to the Hospitallers for the sum of 180 besants. Although one cannot be certain (sizes of casalia vary, for instance) this does look an extremely inexpensive price at which to sell an entire casal, and in view of his later financial record it is certainly possible that the sale was also in partial repayment of money borrowed from the Order.[20] In 1146 he sold lands in Cacho to the Hospitallers in order to pay off his debts and obtain the release from prison in Acre of his vassals who had been held captive as security for his debts: 'pro liberatione mea et hominum meorum qui pro debitis meis apud Acon sepissime tenebantur capti et semper fidei sue sponsione astricti, pro liberatione mea . . . .'. Part of the land which he sold to the Hospitallers had been previously bought by Walter from 'Petro, drugemanno de Caco', for 'ducentis bisantiis'. The final sale price to the Hospitallers, however, was 800 besants for properties including land, a house, and an 'area que sunt juxta cisternam communem'.[21] It therefore seems that the house and lands near Cacho were the property of Walter, while the outlying lands (comprising only a quarter of the total value of the package) had previously belonged to Dragoman Peter. Peter's landed involvement in the seigneurial subdivision of Cacho (which, as we shall discuss later, was a castle with a burgess court), together with his title as 'drugemanno de Caco', seems to imply that he had responsibilities over the whole subdivision.

In 1151/2 the Hospitallers bought the casal of Teira in the Lordship of Caesarea for the sum of 1,000 besants, and gave it to Robert of St Gilles. In exchange only 400 (rather than 500) besants were owed for Emmaus, which the Order had leased from Robert.[22] Walter died some time before 1154 (when we find his heir, Hugh, in possession of the lordship), and was buried beside his father in the church of Mary of the Latins.[23]

A number of witness lists survive from Walter's period as lord,

[20] *Cart. gén. Hosp.*, No. 118; *Reg. Hier. Add.*, No. 162b.
[21] *Cart. gén. Hosp.*, No. 168; *Reg. Hier.*, No. 243.
[22] *Cart. gén. Hosp.*, No. 202; *Reg. Hier.*, No. 274.
[23] *Cod. dip. geros.*, i. 205–6; *Reg. Hier.*, No. 342.

raising several points of interest concerning administration and land ownership in the seigneury. We find a Richard, *dapifer* of the lordship in 1129, and by 1131 it appears that he has been 'promoted' to Viscount of Caesarea (he signs as a witness before the new *dapifer*, Baldwin). There are records of a Walter, Viscount of Cacho in 1131 and 1135, and a Peter 'dragomannus de Chaco' in 1135, indicative of the subdivisional administration employed at that centre. We also find a 'Gualterius de Merula' appearing in 1131 before the Viscount of Cacho: it is probable that Walter had a fief at Merle.[24]

Table 4 shows the known proportions of landed holdings in the period 1123–c.1149. Once again, it is interesting to note the

TABLE 4. *Land holdings under Walter I: 1123–c.1149*

	All casalia for which data exist		% all casalia for which data exist		% all casalia	
	Early/ mid- period	End of period	Early/ mid- period	End of period	Early/ mid- period	End of period
Base:	17.6	18.6	17.6 100%	18.6 100%	103 100%	103 100%
Lay						
Lords of Caesarea	2.9	1.0	16.5	5.4	2.8	1.0
Relatives of Lords of Caesarea	0.8	0.8	4.5	4.3	0.8	0.8
Vassals	1.2	0.0	6.8	0.0	1.2	0.0
External lords	2.0	1.0	11.4	5.4	1.9	1.0
Military Orders						
Hospitallers	4.6	9.2	26.1	49.5	4.5	8.9
Other religious						
Josaphat	0.8	0.8	4.5	4.3	0.8	0.8
Holy Sepulchre	2.7	3.2	15.3	17.2	2.6	3.1
Archbishopric of Caesarea	0.8	0.8	4.5	4.3	0.8	0.8
Other religious	1.8	1.8	10.2	9.7	1.7	1.7

[24] For Richard and Baldwin, *dapifers* of Caesarea, see *Reg. Hier.*, Nos. 126, 139. For Walter, Viscount of Cacho, and Peter, Dragoman of Cacho, see *Reg. Hier.*, Nos. 139, 159. For Walter of 'Merula' see *Reg. Hier.*, No. 139.

seemingly inexorable rise in the proportion of the lordship held
by the Hospitallers: the proportion rose from 3.5 per cent in 1123
to 4.5 per cent in the early part of Walter's lordship, and ended at
8.9 per cent on his death.

In the context of Hospitaller land ownership there is every
reason to think, given the later history of the lordship, that the
Templars would have enjoyed as many possessions as the
Hospitallers in the lordship. In May 1262, for instance, the
Templars and Hospitallers came to an agreement over various
matters of dispute concerning properties in the Latin East, some
of which were in the Lordship of Caesarea. As part of this
agreement the Hospitallers gave up three carrucates of land at
Cafarlet (sited in the north of the Lordship of Caesarea), and all
they possessed in the Lordships of Sidon and Beaufort, to the
Temple, in exchange for all the Templar possessions in Valenia
and Margat, a manor at Sidon, and the casal of Cafarsset in the
Principality of Galilee.[25] The underlying principle behind this
agreement seems to have been the eminently sensible one that
each Order should concentrate properties in areas where it was
already very strong. The implication of this would seem to be that
the Hospitallers recognized Templar economic, if not political,
pre-eminence around Cafarlet (and Templar domination of the
area even closer to their centre at Château Pélérin must surely
have been unquestioned). We know (as we shall see) that the
Hospitallers had very substantial holdings in the lordship: for
Templar pre-eminence in the north of the lordship to be
recognized by the Hospitallers clearly implies that the Templars
had holdings on a similar scale to those of the Hospitallers, a
theme that we shall see developed more fully when discussing
fortifications. In the light of this it seems extremely likely that the
loss of the Templar records has left us with an unbalanced view of
land ownership in the lordship and that for every Hospitaller
casal one might reasonably expect there to have been one or
more Templar property.

It should, moreover, be noted that the Templars owned five
fortified places in the Lordship of Caesarea (including, after
1218, the strongest, Château Pélérin), while the Hospitallers
owned only three. The Templars would thus seem to have been

---

[25] *Cart. gén. Hosp.*, No. 3028; *Reg. Hier.*, No. 1318; *Cart. gén. Hosp.*, No. 3029;
Reg. Hier., No. 1319.

at least as prominent as the Hospitallers in the seigneury (and probably more so). It is also interesting to see that although there were shifts of property within the Lordship of Caesarea included in the agreement of 1262, neither the Templars nor the Hospitallers felt it necessary to seek the permission, or even mention, the Lord of Caesarea, perhaps indicative of the lord's increasing helplessness within his own fief. If one concedes that the Templars held at least as much property in the lordship as the Hospitallers, the two major Military Orders would, between them, have owned almost a fifth (17.8 per cent) of the lordship, even before the mid-twelfth century. Including other religious institutions, this would mean that almost a quarter of the lordship (24.2 per cent) was out of secular hands even when the lordship was at its strongest. This, in itself, may provide the reason for the increasing financial problems of the lordship: as time went on, the lords had ever fewer landed resources to call upon, and the only way to get themselves out of immediate financial problems was to sell lands to the Military Orders, thus exacerbating the problem for their successors.

4. LANDED TRANSACTIONS: c. 1154–1168

Hugh of Caesarea (c. 1154–68) was the younger son of Walter and Julianne (his elder brother, Eustace, had contracted leprosy); he first appears as Lord of Caesarea in a charter of 1154.[26] Unlike his father, who tended to keep away from the court, Hugh was a frequent witness to royal charters.[27] His last appearance was in an Act of 1168 in which he witnessed a charter of King Amalric at Acre.[28] On five charters he appears with his wife, Isabelle, the daughter of John Gothman, by whom he had Guy, Walter, and Julianne, all of whom succeeded to the fief.[29]

Several landed transactions survive from his period as Lord of Caesarea. In 1154 we find Pope Anastasius IV confirming that the monastery of Josaphat owned casal Betalla in the Lordship of

---

[26] *Cart. gén. Hosp.*, No. 225; *Reg. Hier.*, No. 293.

[27] 1154, *Reg. Hier.*, No. 293; 1155, *Reg. Hier.*, Nos. 299, 300, 307, 309; 1157, *Reg. Hier.*, No. 325; 1159, *Reg. Hier.*, No. 338; 1160, *Reg. Hier.*, Nos. 344, 354, 355; 1161, *Reg. Hier.*, No. 366; 1164, *Reg. Hier.*, Nos. 397, 400; 1165, *Reg. Hier.*, Nos. 412, 413, 416; 1166, *Reg. Hier. Add.*, No. 422a; *ROL* 11 (1905–8), 183–5; 1168, *Reg. Hier.*, No. 449. Hugh of Caesarea also witnessed charters for Hugh d'Ibelin in 1155 (*Reg. Hier.*, No. 301), and Walter of Tiberias in 1168 (*Reg. Hier.*, No. 448).

[28] *Reg. Hier.*, No. 449.   [29] *Reg. Hier.*, Nos. 361, 368, 373, 425, 426.

Caesarea and a house above the city itself. The Archbishop of Caesarea had given the monks the tithes of Betalla and the Brothers were confirmed as having a chapel in the village. In that same year, Lord Hugh gave the Hospitallers another tract of land at Cacho next to a garden which the Order already owned, where a corn press was sited, to add to their already extensive possessions in the area.[30]

In 1158 Pope Adrian IV confirmed that the Brothers of Mary of the Latins owned the 'turrem Latinam' in the territory of Caesarea, and a casal, which had previously belonged to 'Eustachii' (presumably Eustace Grenier or Hugh's brother Eustace) in the land of 'Cacto' (Cacho), together with other possessions which they had obtained by privileges from the Lords of Caesarea. The 'turrem Latinam' (Tour Rouge: see below) seems to be another example of minor fortifications held outside secular hands.[31]

In January 1160 Hugh gave to Mary of the Latins land and revenues for the salvation of the souls of his father and grandfather who were buried in that church. These lands used to belong to an otherwise unknown vassal, Stephen Barata. In the same year, Hugh also gave the Brothers of St Lazarus a 'viridarium' which had previously belonged to Stephen Loripes (otherwise unknown), a house which had belonged to his brother Eustace, and another house which had belonged to 'Arnaldi Gala'.[32]

To a certain Jacob, in 1161, he gave an annual *assise* of 25 besants and other goods, to be received at the cistern of Cacho, together with a house and gate that needed maintenance. This indicates that the administration of Cacho was still firmly in lay hands at this time, despite the accumulation of Hospitaller lands and properties around the settlement.[33]

In 1163 Hugh confirmed that a sale of lands to the Hospitallers had taken place outside the gate of St Stephen at Jerusalem, by

[30] For Betalla see *Chartes de Josaphat*, ed. Delaborde, No. 28, and *Reg. Hier.*, No. 290. For Cacho, see *Cart. gén. Hosp.*, No. 223 and *Reg. Hier. Add.*, No. 298a.

[31] *Reg. Hier.*, No. 331.

[32] For the gift to Mary of the Latins see *Cod. dip. geros.*, i. 205–6, and *Reg. Hier.*, No. 342. For the gift to the brothers of St Lazarus see *AOL* 2B, pp. 136–7, No. 18, and *Reg. Hier.*, No. 361.

[33] *Cod. dip. geros.*, i. 241; *Reg. Hier.*, No. 373. It seems likely that this James, who had some kind of administrative power in Cacho, is the James, Viscount of Cacho, that we find in 1175; *Cart. gén. Hosp.*, No. 470; *Reg. Hier.*, No. 533.

Agnes and Osmunde, daughters of Bertrand Pons, for 50 besants, and in that same year he also exchanged with the Order two casalia (Zafaira and Abeiria) for casal Adelfie, which had already been given to them by Eustace Grenier.[34]

King Amalric in 1166, confirmed the possessions of the canons of the Temple of the Lord, and amongst these were mentioned the casalia of Alemanni and Beledain in the territory of Caesarea, which had previously belonged to Arnoldus and Alexander, sons of Costa; the canons also owned a house in Caesarea which had formerly belonged to Theobald, canon of the church there, a shop which had also belonged to him, and another house next to the gate.[35]

In the same year Hugh sold to the Brothers of the Holy Sepulchre a valuable addition to their casal of Fiasse, namely, a mountain garden in which springs rose, which were channelled elsewhere by aqueduct. He also gave them an annual rent of sugar in compensation for the rights he retained to repair the aqueduct at any time, or build a new one, and to take water from the spring to use for sugar cane irrigation in one of his own nearby villages. The mountain garden was described as follows: 'incipit autem ex altera parte divisio terre huius a via, que venit de Braicaet versus casale Sancti Sepulcri et vadit versus orientem per caveam, que est inter duos montes . . . et sic per devexum montis recta linea versus spinam in planitie sitam, que terram casalis Dominici Sepulcri Faisse et Sabarim Hospitalis dividit, terminatur'.[36] It thus appears that casal 'Sabarim', mentioned in a charter of 1145, belonged to the Hospitallers.[37]

---

[34] For the lands at Jerusalem see *Cart. gén. Hosp.*, No. 312; *Reg. Hier.*, No. 391; *Cart. gén. Hosp.*, No. 314; *Reg. Hier. Add.*, No. 391a. For Adelfie see *Cart. gén. Hosp.*, No. 316; *Reg. Hier. Add.*, No. 391b. For the original grant of Adelfie (or Altafia) see *Cart. gén. Hosp.*, No. 94; *Reg. Hier.*, No. 139.

[35] *ROL* 8 (1900–1), 312–16; *Reg. Hier.*, No. 422a. These acquisitions confirm the high standing of the Costa family in the lordship: we find Arnald Costa featuring prominently on witness lists of the lordship in 1145 and 1146, and in 1160 and 1161 we find Peter Costa (his son?). In 1161 there is a Baldwin Costa, and in 1166 we find that Peter Costa has become Viscount of Caesarea and has been joined on witness lists by 'Johannes Costa'. In 1182 Peter and John Costa appear at the top of a list of witnesses, though by this time Peter was no longer Viscount of Caesarea (that position had been taken over by a certain 'Sibo'). We last hear of the Costa family in Caesarea in 1197. The casalia of Alemanni and Beledan are probably just an indication of the family's substantial landed holdings in the lordship.

[36] *Cart. du St-Sépulcre.*, No. 155 (B.-B., No. 139); *Reg. Hier.*, No. 425.

[37] *Cart. du St-Séplucre*, No. 71 (B.-B., No. 59); *Reg. Hier.*, No. 237.

Also in 1166 the Hospitallers bought casal Hadedun, together with two gastinae, the *curtile* of Urrici Tendille, the 'Salina terris Gervasii', and the houses which the natives had built on that land, from Lord Hugh for the sum of 2,000 besants. Casal Hadedun was described as follows:

vidilicet a regione occidentis habens dunas (. . . civitate vero casale) domini Hugonis Feustelli; a septentrione, sicut flumaria protenditur, per quoddam berchile vetus terminatur S. Michaelis (et alio) casali (domini) Engelberti ab oriente per quoddam bechile terminatur cum casali Templi Domini; a meredie per torone(m) Bufali terminatur (cum casali domini Amalrici et) cum Seraphie terra archiepiscopi usque ad magnum lacum.[38]

This description provides a wealth of land ownership detail: a certain 'Hugo Feustelli' owned a casal in the area;[39] as did a 'dominus Engelbertus';[40] the church of St Michael owned a nearby casal (the church of St Michael at Acre seems the most likely owner); the Temple of the Lord owned a nearby casal; a 'dominus Amalricus' owned a neighbouring casal;[41] and the Archbishop of Caesarea owned casal Seraphie and its surrounding lands.

A deed survives from 1167 recording the sale of a house in Caesarea for 30 besants and 12 nummi in full hereditary possession by one Isabella 'civitatis Cesaree Palestine Colona' (i.e. a burgess) to a certain Alberic. The terms of the sale stipulate complete freedom of alienation and state that the property is not burdened by any *cens*. The document also mentioned that the Hospitallers owned a house in the city.[42]

In 1182 Walter, then Lord of Caesarea, confirmed that Lord Hugh had previously (i.e. sometime between 1154 and 1168) given to the Hospitallers the Turris Salinarum, together with the hill on which it was built, to be held without any exactions: another example of fortifications leaving the direct ownership of the Lords of Caesarea.[43]

---

[38] *Cart. gén. Hosp.*, No. 350. *Reg. Hier.*, No. 426.

[39] Could this be the Seneschal Hugh that we find in *Reg. Hier.*, No. 432 of 1167?

[40] Possibly the senior vassal 'Engilbertus de Aria' that we find in 1166, *Reg. Hier.*, No. 425.

[41] We find him in the witness lists of the lordship in 1160 (*Reg. Hier.*, No. 361) and 1161 (*Reg. Hier.*, No. 373).

[42] *Reg. Hier.*, No. 432.   [43] *Cart. gén. Hosp.*, No. 621; *Reg. Hier.*, No. 619.

Witness lists also add to our knowledge of the administration and ownership of land in Caesarea in this period. The presence in such lists of a 'Petrus de Fossato, vicecomes de Calenzun' together with a 'Paganus de Calenzun' in 1166 indicates that at least part of the settlement of Calansue was still operating as a subdivision of the secular lordship nearly forty years after it had been given to the Hospitallers.[44]

Table 5 shows the distribution of known landed holdings within the seigneury for the period c.1154–68. Once again, the proportion of lands held in non-lay hands has risen. The Hospitallers alone were in possession of 12.8 per cent of the lands by 1168. If one adds in other religious institutions one finds the total rises to 30 per cent. If one assumes the Templar possessions to be roughly comparable to those of the Hospitallers, it seems

TABLE 5. *Land holdings under Hugh of Caesarea:*
c.1154–1168

	All casalia for which data exist		% all casalia for which data exist		% all casalia	
	Early/ mid- period	End of period	Early/ mid- period	End of period	Early/ mid- period	End of period
Base:	35.4	37.8	35.4 100%	37.8 100%	103 100%	103 100%
Lay						
Lords of Caesarea	5.6	2.0	15.8	5.3	5.4	1.9
Relatives of Lords of Caesarea	0.8	0.8	2.3	2.1	0.8	0.8
Vassals	5.0	3.0	14.1	7.9	4.9	2.9
External lords	1.0	1.0	2.8	2.6	1.0	1.0
Military Orders						
Hospitallers	9.2	13.2	26.0	34.9	8.9	12.8
Other Religious						
Josaphat	1.8	1.8	5.1	4.8	1.7	1.7
Holy Sepulchre	4.4	4.4	12.4	11.6	4.3	4.3
Archbishopric of Caesarea	1.8	1.8	5.1	4.8	1.7	1.7
Other religious	5.8	9.8	16.4	25.9	5.6	9.5

[44] *Reg. Hier.*, No. 426.

likely that almost half (42.8 per cent) of the lordship's lands were in religious hands.

5. LANDED TRANSACTIONS: 1174–1189/91

The existence of Guy, eldest son of Hugh and Isabelle, is known only through his presence in two charters. The first of these was a charter of King Amalric (of July 1174) which was witnessed by Guy, as Lord of Caesarea, and his brother Walter. The other was a charter of Baldwin d'Ibelin of Ramla, Guy's stepfather, in 1176, to which Guy of Caesarea appears as a witness amongst other barons of the kingdom.[45]

Property evidence for the lordship in this period comes from a charter of 8 March 1173 in which Pope Alexander III confirmed that Mary of the Latins owned 'turrem Latine in territorio Cesaree cum pertinentiis suis, in eodem territorio casale, quod fuit Eustachii, cum pertinentiis suis, terram in Cacho, terras quoque et possessiones, quas privilegiis dominorum Cesaree confirmatas legitime possidetis . . . .'.[46]

In 1176 King Baldwin IV confirmed that casal Medium (also known as Madianum) sited near Calansue, had been sold to the Hospitallers by John of Arsur for 3,000 besants. In the following year the Master of the Hospitallers confirmed that the inhabitants of Calansue had been granted the right to water their animals at the Order's cistern by Raymond du Puy.[47]

In 1179 we find amongst the possessions of the Church of Mount Sion of Jerusalem, confirmed by the Pope, the casalia of Sidia, Caforana, and Canet in the territory of Caesarea, together with half of the tithes from the casalia and a house in Caesarea itself.[48] Walter II of Caesarea (c.1182–1189/91) first appeared with the title of Lord of Caesarea in 1182. Walter aligned himself with the baronial party which supported the cause of Raymond of Tripoli against that of Guy de Lusignan: he is mentioned by William of Tyre as one of the barons who participated in the 1183 campaign against Saladin, but refused to fight under the command of Guy who had been newly appointed *bailli* of the

[45] *Tab. ord. Theut.*, No. 7; *Reg. Hier.*, No. 517; *Cart. gén. Hosp.*, No. 495; *Reg. Hier.*, No. 539.   [46] 'Papst-Kaiser', p. 57.
[47] For Casal Medium see *Cart. gén. Hosp.*, No. 497; *Reg. Hier. Add.*, No. 539b. For Calansue, see *Cart. gén. Hosp.*, No. 510; *Reg. Hier.*, No. 554b.
[48] Rey, *Les Colonies*, pp. 281–4; *Reg. Hier.*, No. 576.

realm.[49] Walter survived the disastrous engagement at Hattin (if, indeed, he was present) as we find him with Raymond of Tripoli and Joscelyn de Courtenay in July 1187, drawing up a treaty with the Genoese to help defend Tyre. He became a supporter of Conrad de Montferrat on the latter's arrival in Tyre, and witnessed five of his acts and treaties between October 1187 and May 1188. He died at some point during the siege of Acre (i.e. between July 1189 and 12 July 1191).[50]

During this period the town of Caesarea suffered greatly at the hands of the Saracens. In mid-July 1187 the Muslims took Caesarea without effort. The town was looted, the cathedral ruined, and the remaining Frankish inhabitants killed or taken into slavery. The fall of Acre led Saladin to review his position in Caesarea, and he decided to abandon it, together with other towns which he felt unable to garrison effectively.[51]

Of the landed transactions during Walter's period as Lord of Caesarea, we know that he made a substantial sale of land to the Hospitallers in 1182. This sale consisted of a casal called Galilea, in the territory of Caesarea, for the sum of 5,000 besants. He also confirmed that the Order was in possession of the 'Turris Salinarum', described as being sited next to the sea. The positioning of casal Galilea gives an indication of the surrounding land ownership. It was described as follows: 'ab oriente pertinenciis castelli Arearum, ab occidente terre Daidonis, a meridie casali domini Amalrici cum Aronia et pertinentiis Cossye, a septentrione casali Templi Domini et casali S. Anne'.

That Galilea comprised a substantial tract of land is indicated both by the price paid and by the fact that the land contained no less than five gastinae which had previously been casalia in their own right ('infra vero hos terminos continentur gastine, que olim fuerunt casalia, quarum capud est Galilea prememoratum'): namely Gedida, Megar, casal Rubeum, gastina Fontis, and Laasina. This was confirmed by the king in 1182, at which time all service to the crown for the property was remitted.[52]

---

[49] William of Tyre, p. 1054.

[50] *Reg. Hier.*, Nos. 659, 665–8, 675; 'Les Lignages', p. 456.

[51] Abu Shamah, iv. 301; Baha'-ad-Din, tr. Wilson, p. 116; Ibn al-Athir, 'Kamil', i. 690; Abou'l Feda, p. 56; 'De Expugnatione Terrae Sanctae', p. 229; Roger of Howden, ii. 341.

[52] *Cart. gén. Hosp.*, No. 621; *Reg. Hier.*, No. 619; *Cart. gén. Hosp.*, No. 645; *Reg. Hier.*, No. 618.

Casal Montdidier was leased to the Hospitallers, together with Tour Rouge (Turriclee) by the Brothers of Mary of the Latins at some point before 1189, for in that year we find the Bishop of Valenia being ordered to solve a dispute over the rents payable. We also know that Walter made gifts to the Hospitallers on his deathbed, for in October 1197 his sister Julianne confirmed that he had given the Order casal Adelfie (Hautefie) as an eleemosynary gift.[53]

Table 6 shows the distribution of land ownership within the seigneury in the period 1174–1189/91. It is interesting to note that even before the disaster of Hattin the Hospitallers owned 17.7 per cent of the lordship. With the other religious institutions

TABLE 6. *Land holdings under Guy of Caesarea and Walter II: 1174–1189/91*

	All casalia for which data exist		% all casalia for which data exist		% all casalia	
	Early/ mid- period	End of period	Early/ mid- period	End of period	Early/ mid- period	End of period
Base:	44.8	44.8	44.8 100%	44.8 100%	103 100%	103 100%
Lay						
Lords of Caesarea	3.0	1.0	6.7	2.2	2.9	1.0
Relatives of Lords of Caesarea	0.8	0.8	1.8	1.8	0.8	0.8
Vassals	3.0	3.0	6.7	6.7	2.9	2.9
External lords	2.0	1.0	4.5	2.2	1.9	1.0
Military Orders						
Hospitallers	13.2	18.2	29.5	40.6	12.8	17.7
Other Religious						
Josaphat	1.8	1.8	4.0	4.0	1.7	1.7
Holy Sepulchre	4.4	4.4	9.8	9.8	4.3	4.3
Archbishopric of Caesarea	1.8	1.8	4.0	4.0	1.7	1.7
Other religious	14.8	12.8	33.0	28.6	14.4	12.2

[53] For Tour Rouge see *Cart. gén. Hosp.*, No. 879; *Reg. Hier. Add.*, No. 682a. For Adelfie see *Cart. gén. Hosp.*, No. 1002; *Reg. Hier.*, No. 736.

this figure rises to 37.6 per cent. If one deems the number of properties of the Templars to be approximately the same as the Hospitallers one finds that 55.3 per cent of the lordship was in religious hands before the battle of Hattin: the Lordship of Caesarea was thus largely out of the lords' hands even before the Muslim inroads of 1187.

After 1187 it is also noteworthy that the proportion of lands held by non-military religious institutions falls for the first time, with the properties concerned being absorbed by the Hospitallers. One would assume that this process was also repeated in the north of the lordship, with the Templars taking on properties that non-military religious institutions were beginning to find untenable.

6. LANDED TRANSACTIONS: 1193–1213

Walter's sister, Julianne, married twice: firstly Guy of Beirut and secondly Aymar de Lairon. Guy appears in only two charters, both dated before Walter's death, and there is nothing to indicate that he ever held the title of Lord of Caesarea, though he may have done so. Julianne had four children by Guy: Walter III, Bernard, Isabelle, and Berte.[54]

Aymar de Lairon, Julianne's second husband, appears as Lord of Caesarea for the first time in 1193, when he witnessed a charter of Henry of Champagne as 'Azemarus, Cesariensis dominus'. In 1194 he appears again (as 'Azmarus Cesariensis'), and in 1197 confirmed the deathbed grants made to the Hospitallers by Walter II.[55] It seems that Julianne died sometime between 1213 and 1216 and that Aymar lost the title he had held through his wife, as we find him in 1216 as Marshal of the Hospital.[56] Caesarea itself had been returned by treaty to the Franks in 1192.[57]

Several landed transactions survive from this troubled period. A pancart of the Teutonic Knights, dated by Rohricht as *c*.1173– *c*.1243, says that a 'domina Iuliana' gave the Order two houses

---

[54] See La Monte, 'The Lords of Caesarea', pp. 152–3.

[55] *Cart. gén. Hosp.*, No. 954; *Reg. Hier.*, No. 709; *Tab. ord. Theut.*, No. 30; *Reg. Hier.*, No. 720; *Cart. gén. Hosp.*, No. 1002; *Reg. Hier.*, No. 736.

[56] *Cart. gén. Hosp.*, No. 1462; *Reg. Hier. Add.*, No. 885a.

[57] *Eracles*, pp. 198–200; Ernoul, p. 153; Baha'-ad-Din, tr. Wilson, p. 381; Abu-Shamah, v. 77.

which had belonged to George Lorrinnive (also known as Lormine) and the 'woltam Bernardi Falcille' with everything pertaining to it, together with an urban gastina which lay between the same houses and the tower of Mallart. She also gave the Brothers another smaller tower, 'que est opposita in cantone civitatis a porte orientali', and a *platea*.[58]

In 1199 the Archbishop of Caesarea conceded to the monks of Josaphat all the tithes of casal Taranta, which lay within the Lordship of Caesarea. From this it seems extremely likely that the casal itself already belonged to the Brothers. This grant is indicative of the relatively healthy finances of the archbishopric, the only Latin see not to encounter serious financial problems after 1187.[59]

A fascinating document survives from the period 1200–1 by which Aymar ceded to a certain Soquerius Scribanus, and to such descendants as he would have by his wife, the feudal grant which had belonged to his uncle, Johannes Scribanus. This grant consisted of a divided carrucate of land ('carrucatam terre divisam') in Cafarlet, together with a threshing floor and a house, and various grants at other casalia belonging to the Lord of Caesarea. These were:

Samaritano	Zebedello	Hatil
Solimania	Trassim	Bezzemel
Bufalis	Allar	Gelenne
Megedello	Aloen	

He also received grants at four other casalia in the lordship, namely Soeta, Pharaon, Mezgebino (or Seingibis), and Cafeto. These casalia (where sites are still known) were spread throughout the lordship.[60]

In February 1206 Julianne made a series of 'gifts' to the Teutonic Knights which provide an insight into the ownership of landed property in and around the city of Caesarea itself. In view of the financial problems facing the Lords of Caesarea at this time

---

[58] *Tab. ord. Theut.*, No. 128; *Reg. Hier.*, No. 510; Rohricht's dating of this charter can be made more accurate: Julianne would almost certainly not have been in a position to make such a grant before the death of her brother in c.1189–91 and it also seems that the actual gift of these properties to the Teutonic Knights took place in 1206; *Reg. Hier.*, No. 810. The charter may thus be dated c.1189–c.1243 or, even more likely, 1206–c.1243.

[59] *Chartes de Josaphat*, ed. Kohler, No. 58; *Reg. Hier. Add.*, No. 765a.

[60] *Cod. dip. geros.*, i. 288–9; *Reg. Hier.*, No. 768.

one may reasonably wonder whether this was not in fact a disguised sale.[61] These gifts and confirmations consisted of the houses in Acre which belonged to George Lorrinnive; the *woltam* of Bernard Falcille; the gastina between the above houses and that of Peter de Beugrant, sited between a public road and a road running down to the sea;[62] the tower of Mallart, with an adjacent street, which extended up to the gastina of the Temple of the Lord; and another small tower opposite the tower of Mallart, sited on the eastern part of the city walls. It was specially stated that these defensive works were to be returned into the hands of the Lady of Caesarea in time of war. This would indicate that the defence of the city of Caesarea, if not the lordship, was still in the hands of the lay lords. The Teutonic Knights also owned a field which had belonged to the Lady Brime. This field was bordered on the west by a garden belonging to the Hospitallers, and on the south by the field of 'Lord Amalric'. On the east it was bounded by the road which divided the field from that of Lord Simon (a senior vassal whom we find as a witness in 1197 (*Reg. Hier.*, No. 736), 1200–1 (*Reg. Hier.*, No. 768), 1206 (*Reg. Hier.*, No. 810), and 1207 (*Reg. Hier.*, Nos. 818 and 819). On the north the field was bounded by the road dividing the field from that of the Lady Grosse.

It was also confirmed that John Charle gave the Teutonic Knights two fields and a garden.[63] One of the fields was said to be bordered by the 'agullia' of St Peter, and on the east by the field which belonged to Raynald de Gibeleth (a vassal of Caesarea in the 1160s: *Reg. Hier.*, Nos. 361 and 373), where there had also been a vineyard. On the south the field was separated from the garden of the Archbishop of Caesarea by a road. The other field was sited on the east of the first, touching on the south the same field of Raynald de Gibeleth. To the north it adjoined another field belonging to John Charle (i.e. a field which he had not given to the Teutonic Knights). It was also said to be next to the

---

[61] *Tab. ord. Theut.*, No. 40; *Reg. Hier.*, No. 810.

[62] Peter de Beugrant seems to have been a senior vassal of the lordship; presumably he was a descendant of the 'Rainaldus Belgrant' we find as a vassal of the lordship in 1160 (*Reg. Hier.*, No. 361), 1162 (*Reg. Hier.*, No. 375), and possibly 1200–1 (*Reg. Hier.*, No. 768).

[63] We find John Charle in witness lists of 1206 (*Reg. Hier.*, No. 810) and 1213 (*Reg. Hier.*, No. 866). His descendants, such as Elyas Charle, were also leading vassals of the lordship in the mid-thirteenth century: *Reg. Hier.*, Nos. 1210, 1233, 1238.

field of Lord Walter of Caesarea (presumably Julianne's son), in which there was a vineyard. The garden which John Charle gave was said to be bounded to the west by the city walls; to the east by a road which divided it from the garden of P. Gasta; to the south by the field which was the garden of John Lermine, a vassal who appears in 1206 (*Reg. Hier.*, No. 810), and to the north by the archbishop's garden.

By this grant we are told the ownership of a relatively large number of vineyards, gardens, and fields around the city of Caesarea. It is interesting to note the composition of ownership, as shown in Table 7.

TABLE 7. *Some small-scale property ownership around the city of Caesarea: 1206*

	Total properties	Fields	Gardens
	15	10	5
Teutonic Knights	4	3	1
Hospitallers	1	0	1
Church of St Peter	1	1	0
Archbishopric of Caesarea	2*	0	2*
Lord Amalric (unknown)	1	1	0
Lord Simon (vassal)	1	1	0
Lady Grosse (unknown)	1	1	0
John Charle	1	1	0
Lord Walter (son of Julianne)	1	1	0
P. Gasta (unknown)	1	0	1
John Lermine (vassal)	1	1	0

* or possibly 1.

The proportion of properties in the sample owned by the Teutonic Knights is, of course, upweighted dramatically because of the nature of the evidence (the charter describes the area where Teutonic properties are sited, after all). The data do allow the information in Table 8 to be derived, however.

Even given the inaccuracies inherent in drawing conclusions from such a relatively small sample, it is apparent from the Table

TABLE 8. *Sample of land holdings around Caesarea by social grouping: 1206*

	Properties	
	No.	%
Total	15	100
Military orders	5	33
Other religious bodies	3	20
Vassals	3	20
Other individuals (probably vassals)	3	20
Lords of Caesarea (and relatives)	1	7

that the proportion of property around the town of Caesarea still held in the hands of the Lords of Caesarea was slight. Moreover, all the grants of non-urban land made to the Teutonic Knights had come from vassals rather than lords, so the previous distribution would not have been any more favourable to the lords. This small element of landed holdings is probably a result of divestments forced on the lords by financial problems.

One should not underestimate the importance of the land in the immediate environs of Caesarea. It was extremely fertile and, in all probability, in one of the relatively few secure areas of the lordship at the turn of the twelfth and thirteenth centuries. According to the document *Reg. Hier.*, No. 768, the Lords of Caesarea owned at least eleven casalia, but there is nothing to indicate which, if any, of these properties were economically viable or even in Christian hands. The uncertainty of the political situation may well account for the fact that although we know the Lords of Caesarea to have been in financial straits, and to have borrowed money from at least one of the Military Orders, there is no record of their having sold any casalia in this period. While this may be due to an understandable desire to retain real property wherever possible, it is also possible that outright sales were not undertaken because of the depressed market for land since, if properties were in disputed territory or in the hands of the Muslims, potential purchasers would have been buying only the *possibility* of collecting future revenues, rather than present exploitation rights. In these circumstances it would be wiser to use the (potential) property rights as security for loans, rather than sell them outright, and it was this course which the Lords of Caesarea took. In this context, properties in the fertile and secure area around Caesarea would have been extremely desirable and hence have retained a high saleable value: the Lords of Caesarea may have divested themselves of their properties around Caesarea to meet their immediate financial needs, while using the vulnerable casalia as collateral to finance short- to medium-term loans, needed to bridge unexpected financial difficulties. Cafarlet, for instance, was used as security for a debt and was later recovered.[64]

In February 1207 we find Lady Julianne giving the Hospitallers the house (which had once belonged to George the Knight) of Robert Hohais, which was sited between Cafarlet and the casal of Roger de Chastellion, together with three carrucates of land in Cafarlet. George the Knight appears in the witness lists of the 1160s as 'Georgius Herminius' and 'Georgius'.[65]

In the same month Julianne also gave the Hospitallers the two casalia of Pharaon and Seingibis. Also mentioned as being in the vicinity of these casalia was Phardesi, a casal belonging to 'domini Gormundi' (unknown), and Calansue, which was said already to belong to the Hospitallers. By this grant Julianne became a *consoror* of the Order and asked to be buried in their cemetery.[66]

The indebtedness of the Lords of Caesarea was demonstrated in two documents of 1212 and 1213. In the first of these Aymar and Julianne borrowed 2,000 besants and a quantity of corn from the Hospitallers, using casal Turcarme and their houses in Acre and Tyre as surety for the debt. In 1213 the casalia of Cafarlet, Samarita, and Bubalorum were given to the Order as surety for a debt of 1,000 saracen besants by Aymar, until the debt could be repaid from the revenues of these casalia. This latter document is also interesting because it provides rare evidence of the existence of demesne land in the Latin Kingdom. The casalia are to be

---

[64] See this chapter, section 9, under Cafarlet and Arames.
[65] For the gift to the Hospitallers see *Cart. gén. Hosp.*, No. 1250; *Reg. Hier.*, No. 818. For George the Knight see *Reg. Hier.*, Nos. 375, 425.
[66] *Cart. gén. Hosp.*, No. 1251; *Reg. Hier.*, No. 819.

given as surety 'cum rusticis et omnibus eorum pertinentiis, exceptis tantum carrucis propriis et corveis . . . '.[67]

Possession of lands by Julianne, or an earlier Lady of Caesarea, in the lost royal domain around Nablus is also evidenced by John of Ibelin recording that 'la dame de Cesaire' owed the service of two knights for lands held in that area.[68]

TABLE 9. *Land holdings under Julianne of Caesarea and Aymar de Lairon: 1193–1213*

	All casalia for which data exist		% all casalia for which data exist		% all casalia	
	Early/ mid- period	End of period	Early/ mid- period	End of period	Early/ mid- period	End of period
Base:	64.0	65.0	64.0 100%	65.0 100%	103 100%	103 100%
Lay						
Lords of Caesarea	19.0	13.6	29.7	20.9	18.4	13.2
Vassals	4.0	4.0	6.3	6.2	3.9	3.9
External lords	1.0	1.0	1.6	1.5	1.0	1.0
Military Orders						
Hospitallers	18.2	24.2	28.4	37.2	17.7	23.5
Teutonic Knights	0.0	0.4	0.0	0.6	0.0	0.4
Other Religious						
Josaphat	2.8	2.8	4.4	4.3	2.7	2.7
Holy Sepulchre	4.4	4.4	6.9	6.8	4.3	4.3
Archbishopric of Caesarea	1.8	1.8	2.8	2.8	1.7	1.7
Other religious	12.0	12.8	20.0	19.7	12.4	12.4

Table 9 shows the ownership distribution of properties, where known, throughout the lordship in the period 1193–1213. The apparent rise in the holdings of the Lords of Caesarea at the beginning of the period is a reflection of our increased knowledge (due almost entirely to *Reg. Hier.*, No. 768 of 1200/1), rather

[67] *Cart. gén. Hosp.*, No. 1400; *Reg. Hier. Add.*, No. 859b; *Cart. gén. Hosp.*, No. 1414; *Reg. Hier.*, No. 866. [68] John of Ibelin, p. 424.

than to any real increase in land ownership. It is noteworthy that the seemingly inexorable rise of Hospitaller possessions continued apace, reaching 23.5 per cent of total holdings by 1213. If one assumes that the Templars owned a similar number of casalia as the Hospitallers, it may be that over two-thirds of the lordship (68.5 per cent) was in religious hands by 1213.

7. LANDED TRANSACTIONS 1216-1239/41

Walter III was, by the standards of his time, of advancing years when he entered into possession of the Lordship of Caesarea: he was aged at least 40. As a result of this he was invariably referred to as the 'old Lord of Caesarea'. From 1206 he used the title 'Constable of Cyprus', a title which he held for the rest of his life.[69] Walter accompanied John de Brienne on the Fifth Crusade, against Damietta, and in his role as Constable of Cyprus commanded a company of 100 knights.[70]

In December 1217, at the same time as the Templars and Teutonic Knights were building Château Pélerin, Duke Leopold and John de Brienne began to improve the fortifications of Caesarea. By February 1218 the rebuilding was complete, despite Muslim harassment. In November 1219, however, the Muslims launched a surprise attack on the town, while the Crusaders, Walter III included, had their attention on the attack on Damietta.[71] There appears to have been some friction between John de Brienne and Walter about this, indicative of the serious financial problems besetting the seigneury. The town seems to have been retained in the hands of the king after rebuilding, as Walter had not reimbursed John for the work: presumably Walter had broken an agreement with the king to pay for at least part of the building work. When the town was attacked in 1219, however, the garrison held out for only four days before evacuating the town by sea, and escaping to Acre. The

---

[69] As Constable of Cyprus Walter would undoubtedly have held fiefs in the Kingdom of Cyprus. He appears as a witness on many of the charters of the period: *Reg. Hier.*, Nos. 721, 722*a*., 740*b*, 746–8, 810, 812, 844, 846, 892, 896, 900, 901, 903, 912, 938.

[70] *Eracles*, pp. 322, 339–340.

[71] For the rebuilding of 1217–18 see *Eracles*, pp. 325, 332; Ernoul, ed. Mas-Latrie, p. 421; James of Vitry, ed. Bongars, pp. 1130–1, and id., 'Lettres', pp. 99–102. For the attack of 1219 see *Eracles*, p. 334; James of Vitry, ed. Bongars, p. 1144; Abu-Shamah, v. 178; *Roger de Wendover*, ii. 261.

Muslims moved into Caesarea unopposed and demolished its fortifications.[72]

In 1227 the refortification of Caesarea was begun once again, this time by German Crusaders awaiting the arrival of Frederick II. Work began in May 1228 and was still in progress when Frederick arrived in Acre in September. By the Treaty of Jaffa, ratified on 18 February 1229, the Muslims recognized Crusader possession of Caesarea.[73] Walter now had free possession of the fief that others had devoted so much energy to restoring to him, but did not live long to enjoy it: he died at the battle of Nicosia on 24 June 1229.[74]

Given the degree of military instability, it is perhaps not surprising to find that we have only one reference to any landed holdings in the lordship during this period, and that even this is only a confirmation. In 1227 the Pope, in confirming the properties of the Church of Bethlehem, noted that they owned 'in the archbishopric of Caesarea, Belveir . . .' and later in the same document that they owned 'in the city of Caesarea a house and in the same territory, the casal Belveir . . .'. The repetition of casal Belveir seems to indicate that Bethlehem had been in possession of the village for some time: the papal scribe seems to have been copying two previous confirmations of ownership.[75]

After the death of his father at the battle of Nicosia, John, 'the young Lord of Caesarea', became one of the most prominent Ibelin supporters. In 1231 he was dispossessed of his fiefs around Acre by Balian of Sidon, who seems to have been *bailli*. This dispossession was ineffective, however, as John remained in control of his lands and was able to sell some of them to raise money for the baronial cause.[76] In 1232 the Ibelins were able to raise money for their cause by selling Arames and Cafarlet. The *Eracles* tells us that John sold Cafarlet to the Hospitallers for the sum of 16,000 besants, while Arames was sold by John of Ibelin to the Templars for 15,000 besants. Philip of Novara tells us that 'the young Lord of Caesarea sold part of his land of Caesarea, and my lord John d'Ibelin, who was later Count of Jaffa, sold a great

[72] *Eracles*, p. 334; Ernoul, ed. Mas-Latrie, p. 423; James of Vitry, ed. Bongars, p. 1144.

[73] For the work of 1227–8, see *Eracles*, p. 365; Ernoul, ed. Mas-Latrie, pp. 459, 461, and *Roger de Wendover*, ii. 326. For the treaty of 1229 see *Roger de Wendover*, ii. 367.

[74] See La Monte, 'Lords of Caesarea', p. 156.   [75] *Reg. Hier.*, No. 983.

[76] Philip of Novara, 'Livre', pp. 517, 528; John of Ibelin, p. 325.

manor of his which was at Acre and they loaned the money to the king' (c. April 1232).[77] This sale is more complicated than it appears at first sight, but we shall at the moment take it at face value and discuss it in more detail later, when looking at the fortifications of the lordship. Suffice it to say at the moment that the sale shows once again the lack of readily available money for the Lords of Caesarea and represents, whoever the real recipient was, an important diminution in the power of the lords and the extent of their lordship.

In 1234 Peter, the Archbishop of Caesarea, conceded and confirmed to the Brothers of St Lazarus the house and church of Painperdu (sited between Chateau Pelerin and Caesarea) with everything pertaining to it, in return for 'octo cereos et iiii rotularum' to be received each year in the Cathedral of St Peter of Caesarea. This grant of alms at a time when the other dioceses of the Latin Kingdom were in dire financial straits indicates that the Archbishopric of Caesarea remained in a reasonable financial condition, while the finances of the lordship deteriorated. One must assume that a higher proportion of the archbishopric's revenues were derived from sources outside the lordship proper, such as Acre, and even further afield.[78]

The casalia of Montdidier and Turriclee had been rented to the Hospitallers before 1189 by the church of St Mary of the Latins. By 1236 the Hospitallers had lost possession of the properties, however, as a surviving rent renewal of that year stipulated that the Templars, who had been holding them from the monks, should be moved.[79]

Table 10 shows the distribution of property in the lordship during the period 1229–1239/41.

8. LANDED TRANSACTIONS: 1249–1264

Marguerite, eldest daughter of the young Lord of Caesarea, succeeded to the lordship at some point before 1249, when she appears with her husband John L'Aleman in a charter selling six

---

[77] *Eracles*, p. 398; 'Les Gestes des Chiprois', pp. 711–12.

[78] For the grant of alms see *AOL* 2B, p. 154, No. 37; *Reg. Hier.*, No. 1051; *AOL* 2B, p. 155, No. 38; *Reg. Hier.*, No. 1066. For the finances of the Latin Church at this time see Hamilton, *The Latin Church in the Crusader States*, pp. 292–3.

[79] *Cart. gén. Hosp.*, No. 879; *Reg. Hier. Add.*, No. 682a; *Cart. gén. Hosp.*, No. 2141; *Reg. Hier. Add.*, No. 1072a; *Cart. gén. Hosp.*, No. 2142; *Reg. Hier.*, No. 1072.

TABLE 10. *Land holdings under Walter III and John of Caesarea: 1229–1241*

	All casalia for which data exist		% all casalia for which data exist		% all casalia	
	Early/ mid- period	End of period	Early/ mid- period	End of period	Early/ mid- period	End of period
Base:	67.0	67.0	67.0	67.0	103	103
			100%	100%	100%	100%
Lay						
Lords of Caesarea	14.6	13.6	21.8	20.3	14.2	13.2
Vassals	4.0	4.0	6.0	6.0	3.9	3.9
External lords	1.0	1.0	1.5	1.5	1.0	1.0
Military Orders						
Hospitallers	24.2	23.2	36.1	36.1	23.5	23.5
Templars	0.0	1.0	0.0	1.5	0.0	1.0
Teutonic Knights	0.4	0.4	0.6	0.6	0.4	0.4
Other Religious						
Josaphat	2.8	2.8	4.2	4.2	2.7	2.7
Holy Sepulchre	4.4	4.4	6.6	6.6	4.3	4.3
Archbishopric of Caesarea	1.8	1.8	2.7	2.7	1.7	1.7
Other religious	13.8	13.8	20.6	20.6	13.4	13.4

casalia around Acre to the Teutonic Knights.[80] John was still alive in 1264 (at his son's death in that year, Hugh was described as 'heir' of Caesarea), but it is never explicitly stated in the sources that he was still Lord of Caesarea when it finally left Christian hands in 1265.[81]

The ineffectiveness of the Lords of Caesarea was indicated still further in this period; lands had to be sold to maintain John and Marguerite, and the refortification of Caesarea itself was left to St Louis. In 1250 Louis arrived in the East and, after repairing Acre, spent a full year strengthening Caesarea, only moving on to

[80] *Tab. ord. Theut.*, No. 100; *Reg. Hier.*, No. 1175. These casalia had never been part of the Lordship of Caesarea, having been fiefs belonging to John L'Aleman before his marriage.

[81] 'Les Gestes des Chiprois', p. 758; *Eracles*, p. 448; 'Les Lignages', p. 457.

Jaffa in the spring of 1252. All those who worked on the walls in person, including Louis, received a papal indulgence.[82]

On 27 February 1265 Baybars appeared outside Caesarea with siege equipment secretly prepared as he affected to hunt around Arsur. The assault was successful, and the defenders were forced to retreat to the citadel. On 5 March 1265 the survivors agreed to surrender in return for their lives. Unusually for Baybars, these terms were adhered to (possibly because he had no way to prevent a seaborne exit) and the Franks sailed for Acre. The Muslim army then spent two weeks demolishing the walls of Caesarea while a detachment captured and destroyed Haifa.[83]

Several landed transactions survive from this period as the last effective Lord of Caesarea struggled to keep his administration in order and maintain his social and military commitments. In 1248 the Hospitallers leased the rights (lands?) of St Mary of the Latins at Cacho, together with the casalia of Montdidier and Tour Rouge, for a rent of 800 gold saracen besants of Acre weight. There was a penalty clause, whereby 50 besants would become payable if the rent was late and it was stated that the agreement should be renewed every 25 years: clearly, both parties were anticipating that the Hospitallers would take over the long-term administration of the properties.[84]

In December 1253 John sold the Hospitallers the casal of Damor, in the territory of Acre, for 12,000 saracen besants of Acre weight. If the Order could not get possession of the casal, John promised to give them an indemnity of 16,000 besants, to be taken from his casal Cafresur. The latter part of the agreement sounds like a barely disguised loan arrangement, to go into effect if the original sale fell through: the Hospitallers would still give John the 12,000 besants, but in return he would give them 16,000 besants over a period of years. Cafresur was described as extending to the east as far as casal Socque, which also belonged to Lord John; to the west as far as Cacho; to the south as far as 'Turrarme' and 'Casal Neuf', which belonged to the Archbishop

[82] St Louis's fortifications are those impressive monuments which still remain on the site; Paris, *Chronica Maiora*, v. 257, vi. 205; 'Rothelin', p. 628; John of Joinville, pp. 257–8, 283.
[83] al-Maqrizi, tr. Quatremere, i: 2, 7–8; al-'Aini, p. 219; 'Annales de Terre Sainte', pp. 451–2; *Cart. gén. Hosp.*, pp. 291–3, No. 3308 *bis*; *Reg. Hier. Add.*, No. 1358a; *Cart. gén. Hosp.*, No. 3173.
[84] *Cart. gén. Hosp.*, Nos. 2482, 2491; *Reg. Hier.*, No. 1164.

of Caesarea; and to the north to casal 'Theure', which belonged to Lord 'Isambert'.[85] The Lords of Caesarea continued to maintain some landed holdings, therefore (in this case Cafresur and Socque). The identity of Lord Isambert is unknown, though he was probably a vassal of the lordship. It is also worth noting the relatively substantial holdings of the archbishop, a partial explanation for his lack of financial problems.[86]

In April 1255 John sold casal Roger de Chatillon to the Hospitallers for the suspiciously low sum of 50 besants (particularly so in view of its position on the fertile coastal plan). As we shall discuss later, casal Roger de Chatillon (or Roger the Lombard) was a fortified site and it is certainly possible that John felt financially unable to garrison or provision the site any longer. The Hospitallers, in return for a nominal purchase price, may have agreed to discharge John's responsibilities for him and so doubtless they enjoyed the revenues of the surrounding lands.[87]

It is interesting to see that casal Roger de Chatillon is described as extending to the east to the Hospitaller casal of Hautefie and extending to the north to the Templar casal of Cafarlet. The property was thus in the heart of an area already dominated by the Military Orders.[88]

Within weeks of the sale of casal Roger de Chatillon, John sold all his remaining possessions in Acre to the Hospitallers (1 May 1255). These possessions were listed as being: a court, land, and several houses (including the house of John himself), together with an oven, mill, cellars, and buildings, all 'in Accon in loco vocatum Rabattum'.[89] In return for these properties, the Order was to take over several of John's responsibilities and obligations which implies that he could no longer discharge them himself. These obligations were: to pay Isabelle d'Adelon (wife of his brother Hugh) the sum of 600 saracen besants each year; to pay a priest in the church of St Nicholas, in the cemetery of Acre, 40 saracen besants per annum; to pay a priest in the chapel of St Mary in the Cathedral of Acre 40 saracen besants each year; to pay a priest in the Holy Sepulchre (celebrating at the altar of St

---

[85] *Cart. gén. Hosp.*, No. 2661; *Reg. Hier.*, No. 1210.

[86] See Hamilton, *The Latin Church in the Crusader States*, pp. 292–3.

[87] *Cart. gén. Hosp.*, No. 2725; *Reg. Hier.*, No. 1233.

[88] Casal Hautefie (or Adelfie) had already been confirmed as being the property of the Hospital by Lady Julianne of Caesarea in 1197, *Cart. gén. Hosp.*, No. 1002; *Reg. Hier.*, No. 736.   [89] *Cart. gén. Hosp.*, No. 2732; *Reg. Hier.*, No. 1234.

Peter) 40 saracen besants per annum if Jerusalem should ever be recaptured; to pay 10 saracen besants to the clergy of the Cathedral of Acre; to pay 5 saracen besants to the clergy of the Holy Sepulchre; and to pay 5 saracen besants to the church of St Nicholas. This shows that John had been committed to the payment of 100 saracen besants per annum to various religious institutions in Acre (including those in exile from Jerusalem), in addition to the 600 saracen besants to be paid to his sister-in-law. The loss of his own house, in addition to the admission of failure to maintain his family's benefactions to their favourite churches, must have been a humiliating step for him to take. No greater indication of his financial ruin could be given. Even after the Hospitallers had agreed to pay her 600 saracen besants a year, Isabelle d'Adelon seems, like other members of her family, to have been in financial straits. Within four years of the agreement (6 March 1259/60) Isabelle remitted the rent in exchange for a one-off payment of 1,500 gold saracen besants, an arrangement that seems to have been very much to the advantage of the Hospitallers: for the cost of only 2½ years' rent the Order had discharged its duties to Isabelle in perpetuity.[90]

In May 1255 John gave the Hospitallers the rights of pre-emption on a property called 'le moulin Rout', which was sited in Caesarea. There are two likely possibilities about the background to this action: either the document was drawn up as part of a formal offer to the Order to purchase the property, or the Hospital was already leasing the property from John. In such cases it was common for the lessor to be offered rights to pre-emption.[91] In either case, this indicates a desire on the part of John to raise ready cash by the alienation of his property in the lordship; yet more evidence of the inability of the lay authorities to maintain the solvency of the fief under sustained Muslim pressure.

In August 1256 we find that the Hospitallers and the Convent of St Anne were disputing the borders of casal Galilea (belonging

---

[90] *Cart. gén. Hosp.*, No. 2914; *Reg. Hier. Add.*, No. 1271a.

[91] *Cart. gén. Hosp.*, No. 2731; *Reg. Hier. Add.*, No. 1235a; La Monte, 'The Lords of Caesarea', p. 159, describes 'Rout' as a casal. There is no documentary evidence to support this assertion, however, and it seems more likely that 'moulin Rout' was a rural mill in the possession of the Lords of Caesarea, unattached to any particular casal (if it had been a casal, or even part of one, it is highly unlikely that such a fact would have been omitted). The exact location of the property is now unknown.

TABLE 11. *Land holdings under Marguerite of Caesarea and John L'Aleman: 1249–1264*

	All casalia for which data exist		% all casalia for which data exist		% all casalia	
	Early/ mid-period	End of period	Early/ mid-period	End of period	Early/ mid-period	End of period
Base:	72	72	72 100%	72 100%	103 100%	103 100%
Lay						
Lords of Caesarea	16.6	14.6	23.1	20.3	16.1	14.2
Vassals	5.0	5.0	6.9	6.9	4.9	4.9
External lords	1.0	1.0	1.4	1.4	1.0	1.0
Military Orders						
Hospitallers	24.2	26.2	33.6	36.4	23.5	25.4
Templars	1.0	1.0	1.4	1.0	1.0	1.0
Teutonic Knights	0.4	0.4	0.6	0.6	0.4	0.4
Other Religious						
Josaphat	2.8	2.8	3.9	3.9	2.7	2.7
Holy Sepulchre	4.4	4.4	6.1	6.1	4.3	4.3
Archbishopric of Caesarea	1.8	1.8	2.5	2.5	1.7	1.7
Other religious	14.8	14.8	20.6	20.6	14.4	14.4

to the Hospitallers) and the casal of Davie (belonging to the Convent), both in the Lordship of Caesarea, and had gone to arbitration to settle the matter.[92] The matter was soon made academic, however, for in 1265 the Lordship of Caesarea was divided into iqtas by Baybars and distributed to his emirs.[93] From that point on the Lords of Caesarea lived in Cyprus. Table 11 shows the distribution of land ownership in the last years of the lordship's history as a Frankish possession.

[92] *Cart. gén. Hosp.*, No. 2826; *Reg. Hier. Add.*, No. 1249d.

[93] Riley-Smith in Lyons and Riley-Smith, *Ayyubids, Mamlukes and Crusaders*, pp. 80–2, 208–10, has undertaken the valuable task of enumerating the fiefs distributed by Baybars, correlating them, where possible, with the Frankish name for the fief, and mapping those fiefs whose location is known. Almost all the fiefs were in the Lordship of Caesarea, though some of the most southerly ones were in the Lordship of Arsur.

TABLE 12. *Percentage of lordship held by Military Orders and other religious bodies*

	Lordship in religious hands (%)	Lordship in religious hands, assuming equal presence of Templars and Hospitallers (%)
c.1110–1123	7.0	10.5
1123–c.1149	15.3	24.2
c.1154–1168	30.0	42.8
1174–1189/91	37.6	55.3
1193–1213	45.0	68.5
1229–1241	47.0	69.5
1249–1264	49.9	74.3

Far from being the powerful political force that it has hitherto been assumed to be, the Seigneury of Caesarea was largely out of the direct control of its lords long before the battle of Hattin. This can be clearly seen when tracking the percentage of the lordship held in the hands of the Military Orders and other religious bodies (see Table 12). These findings are, as we shall see, reinforced by an examination of the fortifications in the lordship.

9. THE FORTIFICATIONS OF THE LORDSHIP

In view of the unbalanced nature of extant materials (in particular, the loss of the Templar documents and the survival of those of the Hospitallers), it is worthwhile looking in detail at the fortifications of the Lordship of Caesarea, of which there were many. We have seen that the Hospitallers had substantial properties in the lordship: by correlating the number of casalia owned with the number of fortifications possessed by them one will be able to arrive at a better understanding of their strength in the lordship. More importantly, by examining the number and size of Templar fortifications one can make an estimate, even if inaccurate, of their influence in the seigneury given that fortifications tended to be administrative centres as well as military strongholds. An assessment of the ownership of the fortifications of the lordship also gives another means of tracking the military and economic independence of the Lords of Caesarea: as their resources diminished one would naturally expect them to be forced to relinquish more of their responsibilities for the lordship's defence.

Caesarea

Caesarea itself remained in lay hands until it was captured by Baybars in 1265, and this fact, above all others, has encouraged the misleading view that the Lordship of Caesarea remained relatively independent while others were being surrendered to the Military Orders. It is worth noting, however, that after 1186 the Lords of Caesarea were totally unable to defend even the town of Caesarea without extensive external assistance. In 1217 it was Duke Leopold and John de Brienne who repaired the town's defences, and in 1227 the rebuilding work was carried out by German crusaders awaiting the arrival of Frederick II. The only other major strengthening of the town's defences was carried out by St Louis in 1250–2. The Lords of Caesarea must have been in almost continual financial straits, even without having the expense of paying for their own defensive works. Moreover, even though Caesarea received extensive aid from external sources, its defences were never very effective, despite the impressive remains that still exist today: whenever a Muslim attack was made in earnest (as in 1187, 1219, and 1265) Frankish resistance crumbled in days rather than weeks. It seems that the Lords of Caesarea could no more afford to garrison the town adequately than they could spare the expense of rebuilding and repairing it. At best, the Lordship of Caesarea was, after 1187, a hollow shell: the Military Orders moved in to occupy the economic and military vacuum that its decline created.

Calansue

The remains of Calansue (as they existed in the nineteenth century) consisted of a crusader tower and a crusader building sited to the east of the tower, with walls 6 metres high and vaults below the main floor. The building had an upper storey and a loophole in the southwest corner.[94]

The property, described in rubric form as a 'castel', was given

---

[94] *Survey of Western Palestine*, ii. 199.

to the Hospitallers by a certain Geoffrey de Flujeac in 1128, in the presence of King Baldwin II and his army. For a property to be described as a castel and to have its ownership transferred in the presence of the king and barons would certainly seem to imply that certain fortifications existed on the site before that date. If so, this would be the earliest recorded instance of the Hospitallers taking over such a site. That is not to say that Calansue was a major military position, however, as the ambiguity with which it was described by contemporaries demonstrates.[95]

In 1129 King Baldwin II confirmed that Calansue had been given to the Order, referring to it as a 'casal called Calansue'. He also noted that Geoffrey de Flujeac had only been able to make the gift with the consent of John of Bethsan and his brother, Hugo. The property would thus appear to have belonged to the Lord of Bethsan before 1128, despite the fact that it was in the Lordship of Caesarea.[96]

Walter Grenier, Lord of Caesarea, conceded the gift in September 1131, referring to the property merely as 'Calumzum'. It is interesting to note that properties in this charter are described in two different ways: Adelfie, with no fortifications, was described as a casal, while Chaco and Cafarsalem, both fortified sites, were merely referred to by name (as was Calansue). This may be another indication that the site was fortified at the time of its transfer to the Hospitallers.[97]

In 1176 it was once again implied that the status of Calansue was something more than just a casal: the rubric of a confirmation by King Baldwin IV in that year described a property as being 'Casal Moyen pres de Kalenson'.[98] In the period 1177–87 the Master of the Hospitallers confirmed the facility, given to the inhabitants of Calansue by Master Raymond, of watering their beasts at the Order's cistern.[99] In 1207 a charter referred to various places in the Lordship of Caesarea as 'casalia' (Pharaon, Seingibis, and Phardesi) while Calansue was referred to merely as 'Calanchun'.[100]

[95] *Cart. gén. Hosp.*, No. 83; *Reg. Hier. Add.*, No. 121a; an eighteenth-century rubric.
[96] *Cart. gén. Hosp.*, No. 84; *Reg. Hier.*, No. 130.
[97] *Cart. gén. Hosp.*, No. 94; *Reg. Hier.*, No. 139.
[98] *Cart. gén. Hosp.*, No. 497; *Reg. Hier. Add.*, No. 539b.
[99] *Cart. gén. Hosp.*, No. 510; *Reg. Hier. Add.*, No. 554b.
[100] *Cart. gén. Hosp.*, No. 1251; *Reg. Hier.*, No. 819.

The accumulation of evidence would seem to indicate that Calansue was more than a village, but less militarily significant than a castle (perhaps merely consisting of a tower and some outworks), and had been such prior to its possession by the Hospitallers in 1128. Hospitaller ownership of the town does not seem to have been complete, however, and this incompleteness may in itself explain some of the ambiguities in the nomenclature used by contemporaries. In 1166 we find a 'Petrus de Fossato, vicecomes de Calenzun' and a 'dominus Paganus de Calenzun' witnessing a charter for Lord Hugh of Caesarea.[101]

It will be remembered that the original grant of 1128 was for *castel* Calansue, and it may well be that the *casal* of Calansue, the unfortified village or small town, remained in the hands of the Lords of Caesarea, while the fortifications belonged to the Hospitallers. The *Survey of Western Palestine* thought that the substantial building to the east of the tower at Calansue was a hall. The vaulted cellars and the loophole would argue against the building being a church, while a dichotomy of power in the town in the twelfth century would make the existence of a hall as a base for the Lord of Caesarea's viscount an extremely strong possibility. The viscount may have administered the town from the hall, while the Hospitallers were in possession of the tower.[102] This dichotomy would also explain the rather formalized way in which the water privileges of the inhabitants of Calansue were confirmed in 1177–87: the Hospitallers may just have been allowing watering rights to be extended to the beasts of the inhabitants of *casal* Calansue.[103]

The split responsibility for Calansue did not survive the upheavals of the turn of the century, however. In 1207, when Calansue was back in Christian hands, the property seems to have been under the control of an Hospitaller called 'Symon de Calenchum' and it is possible that Calansue was an administrative centre for Hospitaller possessions in the south of the Lordship of Caesarea at this time (perhaps under the control of Caesarea, where we know there to have been an Hospitaller *auberge* in the

---

[101] *Cart. gén. Hosp.*, No. 350; *Reg. Hier.*, No. 426.

[102] Survey of Western Palestine, ii. 199; Benvenisti, *The Crusaders in the Holy Land*, p. 198.

[103] *Cart. gén. Hosp.*, No. 510; *Reg. Hier. Add.*, No. 554b.

middle of the thirteenth century). Calansue was captured by Baybars and given as a fief to an emir in 1265.[104]

The history of Calansue seems to have been the usual one of declining lay power in the lordship. Before 1128 the property was owned by a vassal of the Lord of Bethsan, who presumably owed service for it (the Lord of Caesarea was called upon to confirm the gift). From 1128 to 1187 the small unfortified town of Calansue remained in secular hands, under the immediate control of a viscount of the Lord of Caesarea, while the Hospitallers were in possession of fortifications (perhaps a tower) and possibly had colonists of their own on the site. From *c.*1207 to 1265 the Hospitallers owned the whole of Calansue.

Roger the Lombard

This was described by the *Survey of Western Palestine* as consisting of the remains of a vaulted building. There was a small tower 6.3 metres square on one side of the building and it was thought that the building formed one side of a small fortress. There was a well and a trough below the building, together with six circular rock-cut granaries.[105]

The remains give the impression of a minor administrative centre, presumably the centre of the fief of the otherwise unknown Roger the Lombard. The only surviving reference to the site is dated 1135, when casal Arthabec was described as being 'castellaris Rogerii Longobardi ad occidentem'. The wording in this charter may imply that Roger was still in possession of the site in 1135. Its later history is entirely unknown.[106]

Tour Rouge

Tour Rouge has been the subject of a recent historical and archaeological study. The crusader structure consisted of a rectangular tower, measuring 20 metres by 16 metres, with walls over 2 metres thick. There appears to have been a walled

---

[104] *Cart. gén. Hosp.*, No. 1250; *Reg. Hier.*, No. 818; *Cart. gén. Hosp.*, No. 1251; *Reg. Hier.*, No. 819; Lyons and Riley-Smith, *Ayyubids, Mamlukes and Crusaders*, pp. 80–82, 208–210.

[105] *Survey of Western Palestine*, ii. 142.

[106] *Cart. gén. Hosp.*, No. 115; *Reg. Hier.*, No. 159.

enclosure (about 60 metres by 60 metres) in which were sited other buildings.[107]

The tower may be traced back to the Turris Latinae, confirmed by the Pope in 1158 as belonging to the abbey of Mary of the Latins, in the Lordship of Caesarea.[108] The tower, by now called 'Tour Rouge' or 'Turriclee', was leased to the Hospitallers, together with casal Montdidier and lands in Cacho, some time before 1189, at which time the Bishop of Valenia was called in to solve a rent dispute.[109] By 1236 the Hospitallers seem to have lost possession of the tower for a condition of the lease renewal of that year was that the Templars should vacate the property.[110] The lease was renewed in 1248, when the tower and the other properties were rented to the Hospitallers, for 800 gold saracen besants per annum, for as long as the cities of Tyre and Acre were held in Christian hands. This agreement was renewed in 1267.[111] The tower and the other possessions had been in Muslim hands for two years, but as Tyre and Acre were still under Christian rule, the Order would have been obliged to continue to pay rent for the properties: the Order may have recouped some of its losses from 1283 onwards, however, when it was agreed with the Muslims that the Order's farms in the Lordship of Caesarea should remain in their hands.[112] Tour Rouge had been given as an *iqta* to an emir in 1265.[113]

There is no firm archaeological or historical evidence as to the date of the building of Tour Rouge, but it does seem more likely that the original structure was built by a Lord of Caesarea or one of his vassals than by Mary of the Latins. Once again, the history of the tower shows the gradual shift of power out of secular hands: although possibly built and owned by a Lord of Caesarea, from before 1158 to before 1189 the tower belonged to the abbey of Mary of the Latins. From before 1189 to before 1236 the Hospitallers leased the tower from the Brothers of Mary of the

---

[107] Pringle, 'Excavations at Al-Burj Al-Ahmar', pp. 16–19, and *The Red Tower (Al-Burj al-Ahmar)*.   [108] *Reg. Hier.*, No. 331.

[109] *Cart. gén. Hosp.*, No. 879; *Reg. Hier. Add.*, No. 682a.

[110] *Cart. gén. Hosp.*, No. 2141; *Reg. Hier, Add.*, No. 1072a; *Cart. gén. Hosp.*, No. 2142; *Reg. Hier.*, No. 1072.

[111] *Cart. gén. Hosp.*, Nos. 2482, 2491, for the agreement of 1248; *Reg. Hier.*, No. 1164; *Cart. gén. Hosp.*, No. 3283, for the agreement of 1267; *Reg. Hier.*, No. 1356.

[112] *Cart. gén. Hosp.*, No. 3832; *Reg. Hier.*, No. 1450.

[113] Lyons and Riley-Smith, *Ayyubids, Mamlukes and Crusaders*, pp. 80–2, 208–10.

Latins who were unable to maintain it. From before 1236 to 1236 the Templars took possession of the tower, and from 1236–65 the Hospitallers regained the property.[114]

Cacho

A crusader castle was built at Cacho in the early years of the kingdom's history. We first hear of Cacho in 1110, when King Baldwin I confirmed that the Hospitallers had been given lands next to Cacho by Eustace Grenier.[115] In 1131 the Lord of Caesarea confirmed the gift of four carrucates of land and houses with courtyards to the Hospitallers by Eustace Grenier, the gift of a *curtile* to the Order by Walter, Viscount of Cacho, and two carrucates of land which had been given to the Order by a certain 'H. Lumbardus', with the consent of Eustace.[116] The appearance of a Viscount of Cacho in this charter shows that the town was a secondary centre of lay administration in the lordship. This is confirmed by the presence on a witness list of 1135 of a certain 'Petri, drogomanni de Chaquo' and 'Gualterii, vicecomitis de Chaquo'.[117]

In 1146 the Hospitallers expanded their already substantial holdings in Cacho with the purchase of lands, a house, and open space by the communal cistern, for 800 saracen besants from the Lord of Caesarea, who was, not unusually, in debt. The land which the Hospitallers bought had previously belonged to Peter, the Dragoman of Cacho.[118] In 1153 Pope Eugene III confirmed the gifts to the Order in Cacho, and in 1154 a piece of land, adjoining an existing garden of the Order at Cacho, was given to the Order by Lord Hugh of Caesarea.[119]

In 1161 we find Lord Hugh taking a direct interest in the administrative affairs of Cacho, giving a certain James 'de Chaquo' (who was later probably also the Viscount of Cacho) a

---

[114] Benvenisti, *The Crusaders in the Holy Land*, p. 338, claims that Tour Rouge was in the possession of the Templars until 1189, at which point it is supposed to have passed to the monastery of Mary of the Latins until 1248. These assertions directly contradict all the surviving evidence.

[115] *Cart. gén. Hosp.*, No. 20; *Reg. Hier.*, No. 57. This gift was also confirmed by Baldwin III in 1154; *Cart. gén. Hosp.*, No. 225; *Reg. Hier.*, No. 293.

[116] *Cart. gén. Hosp.*, No. 94; *Reg. Hier.*, No. 139.

[117] *Cart. gén. Hosp.*, No. 115; *Reg. Hier.*, No. 159.

[118] *Cart. gén. Hosp.*, No. 168; *Reg. Hier.*, No. 243.

[119] For the confirmation of 1153 see *Cart. gén. Hosp.*, No. 217; *Reg. Hier. Add.*, No. 280*b*. For the gift of 1154 see *Cart. gén. Hosp.*, No. 223; *Reg. Hier. Add.*, No. 298*a*.

fief and extra money to supervise the rebuilding of the town gates.[120] Despite the extensive possessions of the Hospitallers in and around the town, Cacho, or at least its Cour des Bourgeois, was clearly still under the direct supervision of the Lord of Caesarea and his officials, and in 1175 we find James, 'Caco viscecomitis', as a witness to a charter of the Lord of Ramla.[121]

All this had changed by 1187. The extensive sales of land made to the Hospitallers by Lord Walter II of Caesarea (who was Lord of Caesarea for most of the period 1175–87) show the financial straits that the lordship was in at this time and it seems almost certain that Cacho was sold to the Templars in this period (though the documentary evidence, as one might expect with the Templars, has not survived). The Templars seem to have garrisoned the town by 1187, however, and the seigneurial administration of Cacho, which had been so prominent until 1175, is seen no more. The detachment which was destroyed by the Muslims at the battle of Cresson on 1 May 1187, for instance, was partly composed of the Templar garrisons of Cacho and La Feve.[122]

The fate of Cacho in the turmoil of the late twelfth and early thirteenth centuries is not known, but in 1248 the Hospitallers leased the rights of the Abbey of St Mary of the Latins at Cacho, together with Montdidier and Tour Rouge, for an annual rent of 800 gold saracen besants.[123] The lease was renewed in 1267, though by this time Cacho had been overrun by Baybars.[124] In 1253 we know the Lord of Caesarea to have still been in possession of rights in Cacho, but there is no mention of the castle.[125] There is no evidence that the Templars lost their possessions in Cacho (including the fortifications) until 1265, however.

The history of Cacho seems to bear remarkable similarities to that of Calansue. In both cases the Lord of Caesarea seems to have originally been in possession of a Frankish settlement and fortifications (a tower and perhaps outbuildings in the case of Calansue, and a small castle at Cacho). In both towns the Lords of

[120] *Cod. dip. geros.*, i. 241; *Reg. Hier.*, No. 373.
[121] *Cart. gén. Hosp.*, No. 470; *Reg. Hier.*, No. 533.
[122] Ernoul, p. 38; *Eracles*, p. 39.
[123] *Cart. gén. Hosp.*, Nos. 2482, 2491; *Reg. Hier.*, No. 1164.
[124] *Cart. gén. Hosp.*, No. 3283; *Reg. Hier.*, No. 1356.
[125] *Cart. gén. Hosp.*, No. 2661; *Reg. Hier.*, No. 1210.

Caesarea gave up more and more of the lands surrounding the settlements to the Military Orders and other religious institutions. They were probably forced to do so by the financial problems that we know they were experiencing, even in the twelfth century. Eventually, even the fortifications (with all the power they represented) were surrendered. Although we know a Viscount of Cacho to have existed in 1175, the Templars may have taken possession of the castle long before this: the presence of the viscount at the most proves that the Lord of Caesarea retained rights over all (or some) of the Frankish settlers of the town of Cacho, and that he held a *Cour des Bourgeois* there. The history of Cacho, like that of Calansue, is one of a gradual decline of seigneurial authority.

Castellum Arearum

We first hear of Castellum Arearum in 1182, but no clue is given as to its ownership.[126] It is possible that the castle was the centre of the fief of the Area family, vassals of the Lordship of Caesarea.[127] The castle was overrun in 1265 by Baybars and given to one of his emirs.[128]

Merle

Merle in the nineteenth century was in much better condition than today. The *Survey of Western Palestine* found the ruins of a mound, with towers going towards the south, and the remains of a harbour and a colonnaded building near it, together with a large cistern. The tower was separated from the town by a deep moat. The tower's base was approximately 6 metres by 12 metres. It formed the corner of a fortress, and the foundations of another tower were visible. It was thought that most of the buildings, and certainly the tower, were crusader work.[129]

[126] *Cart. gén. Hosp.*, No. 645; *Reg. Hier.*, No. 618; *Cart. gén. Hosp.*, No. 621; *Reg. Hier.*, No. 619.

[127] We find an 'Engelbertus de Aria' in 1146 (*Reg. Hier.*, No. 243), 'Aeris de Area' in 1160 (*Reg. Hier.*, No. 342) and 1162 (*Reg. Hier.*, No. 375), and 'Engilbertus de Aria' in 1166 (*Reg. Hier.*, No. 425).

[128] Lyons and Riley-Smith, *Ayyubids, Mamlukes and Crusaders*, pp. 80–2, 208–10; Deschamps, *La défense*, ii. 23, believed Castellum Arearum to have been a Templar stronghold, but the references he gives hold no clue to the castle's owners. I can find no evidence to support this contention. Was he thinking of Arames, perhaps (i.e. 'Castellum Harames' in *Reg. Hier.*, No. 1450)?

[129] *Survey of Western Palestine*, ii. 7–8.

Merle was a secondary seigneurial centre with a 'court de borgesie et justise'. Unfortunately, the text of John of Ibelin is mistaken in describing Merle and Chateau Pelerin as being possessions of the Lordship of Arsur: they were both within the Lordship of Caesarea.[130] The family of de Merle was presumably the first owner of the fief and we find a 'Gualterius de Merula' amongst the vassals of the Lords of Caesarea in 1131.[131] That the family were substantial landholders is also indicated by John of Ibelin when he tells us that from 'Eude dou Marle, IIII chevaliers'' service was due for lands held around Nablus.[132] A 'Widone de Merlon' was listed as amongst 'de baronibus' in royal charters of 1133 and 1135.[133]

Merle was captured by Saladin in 1187, at which time the chroniclers referred to it as 'Merla Templi', which is evidence that the fief already belonged to the Templars. It was finally abandoned by the Franks shortly before the fall of Chateau Pelerin in 1291. Once again we have an important site being taken over by the Military Orders even before the catastrophe of 1187.[134]

Cafarlet and Arames

Cafarlet was a small castle built on a sandstone hill. It was of the 'castrum' type, 58 metres long by 50 metres wide. There were round towers at the corners of the square, walled enclosure.[135]

In 1131 Walter Grenier, Lord of Caesarea, gave the Hospitallers two carrucates of land 'in Cafarsalem'.[136] In 1200/1 we know that the *scribanus* of the Lord of Caesarea had, amongst his possessions, a house, a threshing floor, and a carrucate of land 'in Kafarleto'. At this point Cafarlet was clearly still in the possession of the Lords of Caesarea.[137] In 1207 the Hospitallers were given a house, three carrucates of land, and two other pieces of land between Cafarlet and casal Roger de Chatillon. In this document,

---

[130] John of Ibelin, p. 420.
[131] *Reg. Hier.*, No. 139.   [132] John of Ibelin, p. 424.
[133] *Cart. du St-Sépulcre*, No. 85 (B.-B., No. 73); *Reg. Hier.*, No. 149; *Cart. du St-Sépulcre*, No. 86 (B.-B., No. 74); *Reg. Hier.*, No. 157.
[134] See Benvenisti, *The Crusaders in the Holy Land*, p. 189.
[135] *Survey of Western Palestine*, ii. 29; Benvenisti, *The Crusaders in the Holy Land*, pp. 282, 329–31.   [136] *Cart. gén. Hosp.*, No. 94; *Reg. Hier.*, No. 139.
[137] *Reg. Hier.*, No. 768.

composed by the scribes of Cafarlet's owner, Julianne, Lady of Caesarea, the property is explicitly referred to as 'casale Capharleth', implying that the site was still not fortified at this stage.[138] In 1213 Cafarlet was given to the Hospitallers by the Lord of Caesarea as partial security for a debt of 1,000 saracen besants.[139]

When we next hear of Cafarlet, it was back in the hands of the Lords of Caesarea and its value had increased enormously: in 1213 Cafarlet and two other casalia were needed as security for a debt of 1,000 saracen besants. In 1232, however, *Eracles* tells us that Cafarlet on its own was sold to the Hospitallers for 16,000 besants.[140]

One possible explanation for the extremely high price paid for the property in 1232 is that the fortification of the property had taken place in the mean time. This would have been a logical time for the construction to have taken place: in 1217 John de Brienne and Duke Leopold were rebuilding Caesarea, and in 1227 a German crusader army was working on Caesarea. It is certainly possible that one or both of these two major building expeditions would have seen the need to improve the defences of the lordship as a whole, rather than just the town of Caesarea.

Much the same is true of Arames. Before 1232 there is nothing to indicate that the property had any defences at all, but in 1232 it was able to command a price of 15,000 besants when it was sold to the Templars.[141] When we next hear of Arames (in 1283) it is referred to as a canton of Château Pélérin. It was agreed at that time that Arames should be apportioned to the sultan.[142]

It is surely no coincidence that the two properties which were sold, and which raised large sums of money for the Ibelin cause, were both fortifications as well as agricultural properties and that the fortification of two previously (as far as we know) unfortified positions should have taken place in a period when two major secular building enterprises were undertaken in the lordship.

The Hospitallers seem to have exchanged or sold Cafarlet to the Templars, as it was certainly in the hands of the Templars by 1255; the Hospitallers seem to have retained some of the

---

[138] *Cart. gén. Hosp.*, No. 1250; *Reg. Hier.*, No. 818.
[139] *Cart. gén. Hosp.*, No. 1414; *Reg. Hier.*, No. 866.
[140] *Eracles*, p. 398 (May 1232).   [141] *Eracles*, p. 398.
[142] al-Maqrizi, tr. Quatremere, ii:3. 227; *Reg. Hier.*, No. 1450.

acquisitions they had made around Cafarlet in the twelfth century, however, as they only agreed to renounce these in 1262.[143]

The history of Cafarlet and Arames, both relatively minor forts, indicates yet again the weakness of the resources available to the Lords of Caesarea. Before 1232 the two sites were agricultural properties: Cafarlet belonged to the Lords of Caesarea, while Arames belonged to the lord of another seigneury. At some time before 1232 the two properties were fortified, probably by Crusaders helping the Lords of Caesarea. In 1232 castle Arames was sold to the Templars and entered into their possession until 1283. Castle Cafarlet was sold to the Hospitallers in 1232 and remained in their possession until 1255 (when they sold or exchanged it with the Templars). Thus, two more defensive positions, even with their building costs presumably defrayed by external bodies, proved too costly for secular lords to maintain, and were acquired by the Military Orders.

Destroit

In the nineteenth century the ruins of Destroit consisted of a small tower (15 metres square with 2.4 metre thick walls) surrounded by a fortified courtyard. There was a fosse to the east of the tower and stables to the north. There was also a rock-cut cistern at the base of the tower. Along the middle of the east wall was a row of 13 mangers. The remains indicated that the position could hold 15–20 men with their horses at any given time.[144]

The tower of Destroit was built on the defile where King Baldwin I was wounded in 1103 and which was a notorious refuge for bandits in the early days of the kingdom.[145] In October 1220 the tower was dismantled by the Templars on the approach of the Muslims: the latter then went on to complete the task with greater thoroughness and to destroy the surrounding

---

[143] *Cart. gén. Hosp.*, No. 2725; *Reg. Hier.*, No. 1233; *Cart. gén. Hosp.*, No. 3029; *Reg. Hier.*, No. 1319; Benvenisti, *The Crusaders in the Holy Land*, pp. 329–31, thinks that Cafarlet had been sold to the Templars in 1232. However, *Eracles*, the only evidence for the sale, explicitly says that the property was sold to the Hospitallers. Templar strength in the north of the lordship, and Hospitaller strength in the south, makes the exchange or sale of most of Cafarlet an understandable move (a precursor of the agreements of 1262) and one which does not contradict the only available evidence.

[144] *Survey of Western Palestine*, i. 309–10.

[145] William of Tyre, pp. 484–5.

woods.[146] The tower is proof of the Templar presence in the north of the lordship from the earliest days of the kingdom.

Château Pélérin

The castle of Château Pélérin was protected by two exterior and three interior lines of defence. The outer line of fortifications of the castle itself was the town wall. This wall included a square tower whose plan resembles that of Destroit. This tower is older than the rest of the wall and seems to have been used in the twelfth century as an independent fort, which was incorporated into the wall when Château Pélérin was built in the thirteenth century. It has been estimated that Château Pélérin and its town covered an area of 90 dunaams and had a total population of about 3,600 inhabitants. This would undoubtedly have increased in time of war, however, as we know the population to have been much greater than this during the siege of 1220.[147]

The fact that Château Pélérin was built largely by the Templars and came into their possession as soon as it was completed would seem to indicate that the Order had substantial possessions in the north of the lordship. This is backed up by the existence of Destroit as a Templar fort in the twelfth century, and by the existence of a very similar fort on the site of Château Pélérin. A glance at the map of the lordship would also seem to indicate a strong Templar presence in the north. In the south, where the Hospitallers were strongest, one finds a mass of crusader place-names. In the north, however, particularly around Château Pélérin, one finds almost none. As the Templars' records have been lost, while those of the Hospitallers have survived, it seems almost certain that the Templars owned substantial tracts of land in the north of the lordship.

This is also indicated by the evidence of the peace treaty of 1283. In this agreement the remnants of the Latin kingdom are referred to in terms of 'cantons'. The Templar castle of Château Pélérin is defined as having 16 cantons attached to it, while Sidon has 15, Carmel 13, and Haifa 7. Only Acre is said to have more cantons than Château Pélérin: clearly, the Templars owned extensive tracts of land there, and it is also very likely that these possessions, as with those of the Hospitallers, were built up

[146] James of Vitry, 'Lettres', pp. 138–41; Abou'l Feda, p. 94.
[147] Benvenisti, *The Crusaders in the Holy Land*, pp. 26–7.

piecemeal over the twelfth and thirteenth centuries.[148] The history of Château Pélérin is relatively well documented. In February 1218, while John de Brienne and Duke Leopold were refortifying Caesarea, the Templars, Teutonic Knights, and Walter d'Avesnes were building the castle. The preliminary building work continued until 15 April 1218.[149] At the end of a naval combat in 1258 between the Muslims and the Genoese, two Muslim ships took refuge there, only to be captured by Venetian ships.[150]

In 1220, after the capture of Caesarea, the Muslims approached Château Pélérin and, as we have seen, precipitated the destruction of Destroit. In stark contrast to the weakness of Caesarea, however, the siege of Château Pélérin lasted for a month and was then abandoned, as success was not in sight.[151] The defensibility of the Château is also emphasized by the behaviour of Frederick II in 1229: he went to the castle and was so impressed by its strength that he told the Templars he wanted to take it over. The Order responded by telling him to leave before he was made their prisoner.[152]

In 1250 Château Pélérin was mentioned in the peace treaty concluded after the disaster at Mansourah and was referred to as a separate entity from Caesarea: 'Jopen, Azothum, Caesaream, Castrum Peregrinum, . . .'.[153] The peace treaty of 1283 confirmed that the Franks should retain the castle of Château Pélérin and its town, but also stated that half of its surrounding territory (a substantial proportion of the surviving Latin lands) should be given to the Muslims. It is interesting to note that although Caesarea was also mentioned in the treaty (the Hospitallers were to retain their farms in the lordship) there was no question of Caesarea and Château Pélérin being linked in any way. Arames, formerly in the Lordship of Caesarea, was described as being in the territory of Château Pélérin, rather than that of Caesarea.[154] The castle survived until the end of the Latin

[148] *Reg. Hier.*, No. 1450.

[149] Ernoul, ed. Mas-Latrie, p. 422; James of Vitry, 'Lettres', p. 108; *Eracles*, pp. 325, 331–2; 'Table chronologique de Hethoum', p. 484; 'Les Gestes des Chiprois', p. 665.

[150] 'Les Gestes des Chiprois', p. 746.

[151] James of Vitry, 'Lettres', pp. 138–41; Abou'l Feda, p. 94.

[152] *Eracles*, pp. 373–4; Ernoul, ed. Mas-Latrie, p. 462.

[153] Paris, *Chronica maiora*, vi. 191–7; *Reg. Hier.*, No. 1191.

[154] al-Maqrizi, tr. Quatemere, ii:3. 224–30; *Reg. Hier.*, No. 1450; *Cart. gén. Hosp.*, No. 3832.

Kingdom: Acre fell on 28 May 1291 and on 14 August the knights of Château Pélérin, devoid of hope, evacuated the castle and sailed for Cyprus.[155]

The relationship of Château Pélérin to the Lordship of Caesarea is an enigmatic one. It has generally been assumed that it was an integral part of the seigneury but the surviving texts of John of Ibelin are confused about the relationship. The standard text says 'Le seignor d'Arsur a court et coins et justise . . . Et a Chastiau Pelerin a cour de borgesie et justise.' This is obviously untrue. It is only the variant readings D, E, and T which say that 'le seignorie de Cesaire au Chasteau Peloin a court et coins et justise'. If anything, this confusion may indicate that the status of Château Pélérin was ambiguous, even for contemporaries.[156]

There are, however, firm indications that Château Pélérin enjoyed at least semi-independent status in the thirteenth century. Firstly, the only surviving documentary link between the Château and Caesarea is in the confused lists of John of Ibelin. Secondly, the castle of Château Pélérin was built by the Templars. The possibility of the castle being given to the Lords of Caesarea, who could not even afford to renew the relatively weak defences of Caesarea itself, does not seem to have been considered. Thirdly, in the peace treaties of 1250 and 1283 Caesarea and Château Pélérin are treated as separate entities. In the latter case, as we have seen, a possession in the Lordship of Caesarea (Arames) is specifically described as being in the territory of Château Pélérin, while the Hospitaller possessions are still described as being in the territory of Caesarea.

There is a strong case for arguing that the power of the Lords of Caesarea in the thirteenth century was so weak that the north of the lordship was effectively detached from the lordship proper from 1217 onwards, and that the Templars enjoyed at least semi-independence. As we have seen in dealings between the Military Orders, the Hospitallers recognized Templar preponderance in the north of the seigneury, and it would be surprising if the much weaker Lords of Caesarea were not forced to do likewise.

One is left with the apparently insoluble problem of the extent of Templar possessions in the north. The north of the lordship, where there are few surviving place-names, occupies approxim-

---

[155] 'Les Gestes des Chiprois', p. 818; al-Maqrizi, tr. Quatemere, ii:3. 126; Abou'l Feda, p. 164.   [156] John of Ibelin, p. 420.

ately 25 per cent of the total lordship (about 300 square kilometres): using the same model developed earlier in this chapter, one would expect this area to contain approximately 26 casalia. Given the Templar preponderance in this region in the thirteenth century, one would assume that the vast majority of these properties would be in Templar hands from 1217 onwards and a substantial proportion of them to have been owned by the Templars in the twelfth century. It is also likely that the Templars, like the Hospitallers, possessed some other, more scattered, possessions in the lordship, of which we now have no record.

Turris Salinarum

This was a small fortification on the coastal road from Caesarea to Haifa, standing near to the mouth of 'li flum as cocatrix'. The tower was in the possession of the Lords of Caesarea before the period *c.*1154–68, when it was given, together with the surrounding hill, by Lord Hugh to the Hospitallers. This grant was confirmed by Lord Walter in 1182.[157]

Castrum Feniculi

This was a small fortification close to the Turris Salinarum. In 1128 Pope Honorius II confirmed that the Holy Sepulchre owned 'in episcopatu Cesaree Palestine castrum Feniculi cum ecclesia et omnibus pertinentiis suis . . .'. The 'castrum' was still in the possession of the Holy Sepulchre in 1162, for in that year a dispute between them and Josaphat was described as being 'de querela terrarum, sue videlicet et nostre, apud castrum, quod dicitur Feniculi . . .'. The later history of the fortification is unknown.[158]

Overview of Fortification Ownership

Table 13 summarizes fortification ownership in the seigneury; several points emerge from it. Of the ten fortifications known to have existed in 1186, only one, Caesarea itself, can be proved to have been in the hands of the Lord of Caesarea or his vassals.

---

[157] *Cart. gén. Hosp.*, No. 621; *Reg. Hier.*, No. 619.
[158] *Cart. du St-Sépulcre*, No. 16 (B.-B., No. 6); *Reg. Hier.*, No. 124; *Cart. du St-Sépulcre*, No. 69 (B.-B., No. 57); *Reg. Hier.*, No. 375; Rohricht (*Reg. Hier.*, No. 375) is mistaken in describing Feniculi as a casal.

The ownership of a further two fortifications remains unknown. Five of the remaining positions were owned by the Military Orders, and two owned by other religious institutions. The majority of the lordship's fortifications were thus out of secular hands even before the collapse of 1187.

By 1264 the preponderance of the Military Orders had become overwhelming. Of the twelve fortifications that probably existed in that year, only one, Caesarea again, was in the hands of the lord, and even that was due only to huge amounts of external aid. The strongest fortification in the lordship (Château Pélérin), together with all other fortifications of which we know the ownership, were in the hands of the Military Orders.

The Templars appear to have been the dominant Military Order in the lordship. Despite the disappearance of their records, we know that they owned Château Pélérin and four other fortifications. The Hospitallers, on the other hand, held only three fortified sites. This, together with the other evidence we have already reviewed, would indicate that one should assume that the Templars possessed at least as many properties in the lordship as the Hospitallers.

TABLE 13. *Summary of Fortification Ownership*

	Ownership 1186	1264
Calansue	Hospitallers	Hospitallers
Roger the Lombard	?	?
Tour Rouge	St Mary of the Latins	Hospitallers
Cacho	Templars	Templars
Castellum Arearum	?	?
Merle	Templars	Templars
Cafarlet	n.a.	Templars
Château Pélérin	n.a.	Templars
Destroit	Templars	n.a.
Turris Salinarum	Hospitallers	Hospitallers
Castrum Feniculi	Holy Sepulchre	?
Caesarea	Lord of Caesarea	Lord of Caesarea
Arames	n.a.	Templars

Note: n.a. = not applicable.

10. CONCLUSIONS

The view of the Lordship of Caesarea as an independent lay lordship, successfully maintaining its independence until the final collapse of 1265, clearly needs revision. Almost from the beginning the Lords of Caesarea were in financial difficulties. Even *before* 1187 over half the lordship's lands and most of its outlying fortifications were in the hands of religious institutions, primarily the Military Orders.

By the mid-thirteenth century the secular element of the lordship had disintegrated so far that the lord's influence in many parts of his own lordship must have been minimal. A very plausible reason for the fact that the Lordship of Caesarea remained in lay hands, while those of Arsur and Sidon were sold to the Military Orders, is that there was not enough left to make a sale worthwhile for the lord or attractive to a potential buyer: the seigneury was just a shadow of its former self.

5

Seigneurial Resources II: The Example of Galilee

THERE is clear evidence that almost all the lordships of the Latin Kingdom were in financial straits even in the twelfth century, and that after the collapse of the first kingdom those that survived were greatly reduced: Caesarea is merely the seigneury for which most documentation still exists.

The Principality of Galilee, superficially the most powerful of the lordships, provides a striking example of the gradual loss of seigneurial strength. Tancred started this process through his generosity to the Church: William of Tyre was fulsome in his praise of Tancred's actions, saying that he established churches at Nazareth, Tiberias, and on Mount Thabor, and endowed them with ample patrimonies.[1] At a time when Frankish power was still expanding eastwards, such generosity, which was at least in part a confirmation of properties thought to have been owned by the Church in earlier days, must have seemed to pose no threat to the future stability of the principality.

MOUNT THABOR

The monastery of Mount Thabor was the largest single religious landowner in the principality. In March–August 1100 Tancred conferred on the monks extensive estates, which were said to have belonged to the monastery in the previous Muslim or Byzantine periods. These estates consisted of about twenty-six named properties, though at least two of these (Panya Naame and Alma de Suchem or Defurchaim) do not appear to have been in the Principality of Galilee.[2] From this impressive beginning, religious landholdings in the principality mushroomed.

[1] William of Tyre, p. 437–8.
[2] *Cart. gén. Hosp.*, ii. 897–8, No. 1; Alma de Suchem was sited near Tyre (still a Muslim possession in 1100) while Panya Naame was sited to the east, again in Muslim hands.

In July 1103 Pope Pascal II gave Mount Thabor a confirmation of their possessions. These were now said to consist of approximately forty-seven properties, so about twenty properties in the principality appear in the confirmation of 1103 which had not been included in the confirmation by Tancred.[3] These sites were presumably acquired by Mount Thabor in the intervening period, a combination of the pious zeal of the new settlers and the possible reallocation of properties which had belonged to the Greek dioceses, given that the Abbot of Mount Thabor had now assumed archiepiscopal powers.[4]

The sites enumerated by papal scribes are by no means relayed at random. It seems that they were working from documents now lost, for although the charter of 1103 has its own internal geographical logic, it owes nothing to the grant of 1100, which one might have expected to have been copied. Rather, sites in the later document are grouped in broad geographic areas, and, one suspects, grouped by individual donation. Thus one sees that the first part of the confirmation (from 'Baria' to 'Erbeth') deals exclusively with twenty-two casalia on the western side of the Jordan/Sea of Galilee, all in the Principality of Galilee. The second part of the document (from 'Caimun' and 'Desurchain') deals exclusively with three casalia in other lordships in the Latin Kingdom, Caymont, and Tyre. The third part deals with two casalia called 'Alme', one near Saphet and the other near Banias. The fourth part deals with the Brothers' possessions to the east of the Jordan/Sea of Galilee ('Neeme' to 'Ayu', comprising a total of fifteen casalia), while the fifth part deals with five casalia, at least four of which comprised a compact block of land on the western shore of the Sea of Galilee. Because of this internal logic (particularly striking in view of the normally poor knowledge of middle-eastern geography in papal documents), and other reasons which we shall examine below, it seems clear that a series of now lost donation/confirmation documents was used to produce this list. With this in mind, several features of the papal confirmation are of interest.

Towards the end of the first group, for instance (i.e. from 'Baria' to 'Erbeth'), comes a set of three casalia: Cara, Nurith, and Sulem. These properties comprise a relatively compact estate to

---

[3] *Cart. gén. Hosp.*, ii. 892, No. 2; *Cart. gén,. Hosp.*, No. 2832; *Reg. Hier.*, No. 39.
[4] i.e. acquired between the issuing of *Reg. Hier.*, Nos. 36 and 39.

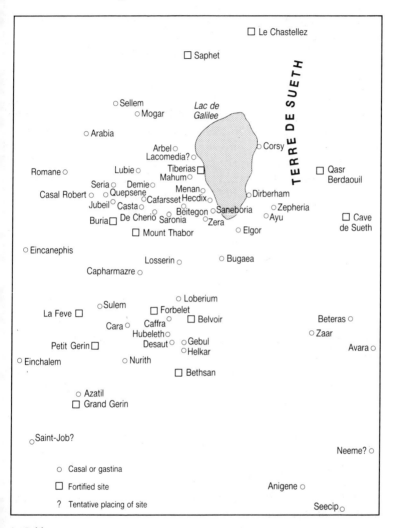

6. Galilee

the south-south-west of Mount Thabor, and as they were not mentioned in the confirmation of 1100, were presumably acquired in the period 1100–3 (or, more likely, 1100–2 given the time taken for documentation to reach Rome). Their geographical proximity, consecutive placement in the charter, and absence from the confirmation of 1100 lead one to hypothesize that the three were given *en bloc* to Mount Thabor by the Prince of Galilee or one of his vassals in this period.

The fourth group of properties (i.e. 'Neeme' to 'Ayu') contains four casalia, again in consecutive order, which were not mentioned in 1100: Avara, Zaar, Elleeram, and Beteras. These properties were all sited to the east of the Jordan and were all close to each other. It thus seems that these casalia comprised another donation made to the Brothers after 1100. Appropriately enough, as Frankish expansion eastwards continued, success was reflected in donations made to the Church.

Further down the group we see Anigene and Seecip, once again listed consecutively, geographically close together, and both acquired since 1100. The same is true of Elgor, Zepheria ('in terra Auram'), and Ayu: all are listed consecutively, close together geographically (all near the eastern shores of the Sea of Galilee), and all acquired since 1100. Once more it looks as though a block donation had been made to Mount Thabor since 1100, as the Frankish presence in the Terre de Sueth became more significant.

The fifth group of sites comprises five casalia (Zera, Alcotain, Menan, Hecdix, and Saneboria), four of which constitute a very compact block on the south-western shores of the Sea of Galilee. The location of the fifth, Alcotain, is unknown, but it is not unreasonable to assume that it was nearby. All had been acquired since 1100 and probably constituted a single grant by the Prince of Galilee or one of his vassals.

It thus seems that Mount Thabor, and no doubt others as well, profited directly from the expansion into the Terre de Sueth, receiving several extensive grants of land there and elsewhere in the Principality of Galilee, in the period 1100–3. One sees that by 1103, in a period of Frankish confidence and when secular control of the principality must have seemed complete and assured, the Church had already acquired huge tracts of land: and this was a process which, as we shall see, had only just begun.

OUR LADY OF THE VALLEY OF JOSAPHAT

The monastery of Josaphat also acquired several properties in Galilee over the years. In 1115 Baldwin I confirmed that the

Brothers had been given possessions by William de Bures, at that time only a vassal of the principality, though he was later to become prince (1120–42). Josaphat was now said to own casal Jerraz ('in territorio Gordi situm') and houses in Jerusalem which had previously belonged to William.[5]

Another confirmation given to Josaphat in 1115 shows that the monastery owned even more property in Galilee. A certain Lambert, a vassal of William de Bures, had given the Brothers casal Soesme on the River 'Diaboli', Prince Joscelyn had given casal Casrielme, and two villeins in Tiberias and Theobald de Nigella donated casal Zebezeb.[6] A confirmatory document of 1130 tells us that the grant of Zebezeb was only made through the concession of William de Bures, and that casal Soesme was sited beyond the Jordan.[7] It is clear that the vassals of Galilee were, like the princes, generous in their early dealings with the Church.

In 1121 William de Bures gave Josaphat 'in territorio Tyberiadis, prope civitatem, quandam currucatam terre et unum Sirium cum sua sequentia ad eamdem terram operandam libere'.[8] On the same day, 1 February 1121, William also gave Josaphat the hospital of St Julian of Tiberias which he had built in his own domain.[9]

More gifts to the monastery were to follow. In 1126 we find William giving Josaphat casal Saint-George, sited next to Medan.[10] It is interesting to note that Josaphat had previously been given the Frankish church at Saint-George, which implies the presence of a Frankish population: it seems that the Brothers were probably being given a Frankish settlement.[11] In 1129 William also gave the monastery casal Saint-Job.[12]

[5] *Chartes de Josaphat*, ed. Delaborde, No. 5; *Reg. Hier.*, No. 79.
[6] *Chartes de Josaphat*, ed. Delaborde, No. 6; *Reg. Hier.*, No. 80.
[7] *Chartes de Josaphat*, ed. Delaborde, No. 18; *Reg. Hier.*, No. 134.
[8] *Chartes de Josaphat*, ed. Delaborde, No. 10; *Reg. Hier.*, No. 92.
[9] *Chartes de Josaphat*, ed. Delaborde, No. 11; *Reg. Hier.*, No. 93.
[10] *Chartes de Josaphat*, ed. Delaborde, No. 14; *Reg. Hier.*, No. 115.
[11] *Chartes de Josaphat*, ed. Kohler, Nos. 2, 3; *Reg. Hier, Add.*, No. 56a.
[12] *Chartes de Josaphat*, ed. Delaborde, No. 16; *Reg. Hier.*, No. 131. In a confirmatory charter to Josaphat in 1130 King Baldwin III makes the geographical position of the casalia of Saint-Job and Saint-George a little clearer. They are described as being 'ultra mare Tyberiadis', making the possibility that one of them contained Frankish settlers all the more interesting; *Chartes de Josaphat*, ed. Delaborde, No. 18; *Reg. Hier.*, No. 134. See also the concordat reached by Josaphat with the bishop, *Chartes de Josaphat*, ed. Delaborde, No. 40.

HOLY SEPULCHRE

Other religious bodies also benefited from secular gifts. In 1132 William de Bures continued to show his generosity to the Church by giving to the Holy Sepulchre the casalia of Gebul and Helkar, together with the rights from fisheries on the Sea of Galilee for eight days during Lent, and boon work from four fishermen for one day in the year.[13] Similarly, in a document dated c.1148 the Prince of Galilee gave casal Caffra to the Church of the Ascension.[14]

BETHLEHEM

In a pancart of 1227 we are told that the Bishopric of Bethlehem owned a property known as Haim, sited in the Bishopric of Tiberias; a casal in Galilee, called Bedar; a house in the town of Tiberias and a casal in its territory called Aim (presumably the same as Haim), with everything pertaining to it on this side (i.e. the west) and beyond the river which flows to the Sea of 'Cedeleae' (presumably the Sea of Galilee).[15] As these lands were in Muslim hands when the pancart was issued (and had been since 1187) these properties had been in the possession of the bishopric since the twelfth century, a point confirmed by the repetition of casal Haim, implying that at least two confirmations of ownership had been issued before 1227. Bedar was located west of Nazareth and although the exact site of Haim is unknown, it was probably close to the Jordan.[16]

THE MILITARY ORDERS

In 1110 King Baldwin I confirmed that Duke Godfrey had given the Hospitallers casal Hessilia. This property, though it cannot be exactly located, seems to have been in Galilee.[17] We also know the Hospitallers owned several properties in the principality by 1110: a casal in the Terre de Sueth called Dirberham which had

---

[13] *Cart. du St-Sépulcre*, No. 74 (B.-B., No. 62); *Reg. Hier.*, No. 142.
[14] Caffra is sited west of Belvoir; *ROL* 3 (1895), 53, No. 58; *Reg. Hier. Add.*, No. 252a; *Cart. gén. Hosp.*, No. 422; *Reg. Hier.*, No. 492.
[15] *Reg. Hier.*, No. 983.　　　　[16] Prawer–Benvenisti Map, ref. 165/235.
[17] *Cart. gén. Hosp.*, No. 20; *Reg. Hier.*, No. 57; *Cart. gén. Hosp.*, No. 225; *Reg. Hier.*, No. 293.

been given to them by Peter de Lens; casal Capharmazre, donated by Arnulf Loferencus; and villeins and lands which were given to the Order by Hugh and Gervaise in 'Thabaria' (presumably Hugh de St Omer and Gervaise de Bazoches, Princes of Galilee from March 1101 to August 1106, and September 1106 to 1108, respectively).[18]

Prince William, in 1131, confirmed to the Hospitallers all the goods that they possessed in the territory of Tiberias, but unfortunately only the rubric of this document has survived.[19] In 1147 we know the Hospitallers to have been in possession of unspecified casalia in the Terre de Sueth, which had previously been given to them by 'Gumfredus de Turre David'.[20] In 1150 the Archbishop of Nazareth exempted them from the payment of tithes on corn, wine, vegetables, and beasts throughout his province, with the exception of the diocese of Tiberias. Presumably, therefore, the Hospitallers owned extensive properties around Tiberias.[21]

In 1154 Ermengarde, Viscountess of Tiberias, gave St Lazarus of Tiberias 'duas carruatas terre in terra que dicitur Mahum, et quamdam villam nomine Caliphum, cum omnibus heredibus suis'.[22] In 1160 Hugh de Bethsan gave the Hospitallers casal Bugaea, sited just west of the Jordan, south of the Sea of Galilee,[23] and in 1165 Prince Walter gave the Order the casalia of Delehaoa and Desaut, both sited close to Belvoir.[24]

In April 1168 Prince Walter confirmed the possessions of the Hospital in Galilee. These were said to be the castle of Belvoir and the casalia of Loberium, Losserin, de Cherio, and Hubeleth, all of which had been recently bought by the Order to build up their estates around Belvoir, together with Delehaoa and Desaut.[25]

In a charter dated *c*.1171 the Hospitallers gave a number of houses and shops in Jerusalem, with 16 tenants and producing an annual rent of 130 besants, to the Monastery of the Mount of

---

[18] Dirberham is sited just east of the Sea of Galilee. Capharmazre is sited just south of Mount Thabor.　　　[19] *Cart. gén. Hosp.*, No. 93; *Reg. Hier. Add.*, No. 137c.

[20] It is likely, though not certain, that the Hospital had been given three casalia there by 'Gumfredus', for they exchanged them with the king for three villages; *Cart. gén. Hosp.*, No. 275; *Reg. Hier. Add.*, No. 245.

[21] *Cart. gén. Hosp.*, No. 196; *Reg. Hier. Add.*, No. 259a.

[22] *AOL* 2B, pp. 132–3, No. 13; *Reg. Hier.*, No. 297.

[23] *Cart. gén. Hosp.*, No. 288; *Reg. Hier. Add.*, No. 361a.

[24] *Cart. gén. Hosp.*, No. 345; *Reg. Hier.*, No. 414.

[25] *Cart. gén. Hosp.*, No. 398; *Reg. Hier.*, No. 448.

Olives. In return, the Order received casal Caffra, sited just to the
north-west of Belvoir. Once again, the Hospitallers seem to have
been taking active steps to build up their estates around their new
fortifications.[26]

In 1174 Princess Eschiva of Galilee gave the Hospitallers a hill
called Lacomedia, sited just to the north of Tiberias itself. In
addition, the Order was given all the land which ran from the hill
to the shore of the Sea of Galilee, together with the lake itself for
a distance out as far as a man could throw a stone weighing
20 besants. They were given fishery rights over this area and the
right to build mills.[27]

A leasing document of 1175 survives in which the Templars
leased casal Nurith from Mount Thabor for an annual rent of
20 besants.[28] This casal had been in the possession of Mount
Thabor since at least July 1103.[29] Although we have, as usual,
almost no record of Templar properties in the Principality of
Galilee, this leasing agreement shows that the Order did take
positive steps to acquire properties in the area. It is also noticeable
that the map of Frankish properties around the Templar castles of
Saphet and Le Chastellez is completely blank, with the exception
of villages mentioned only in non-Christian sources. This would
seem to indicate tentatively that the Templar properties in the
north of the principality were extensive. This is perhaps what one
would expect, given the very active process undertaken by the
Hospitallers in acquiring estates around Belvoir.

Raymond III confirmed the sale of three casalia to the
Hospitallers in May 1179. These properties were the villages
of Einchalem, Eincanephis, and Azatil. The casalia were sold
by Walter, Viscount of Tiberias, to the Hospitallers for the sum
of 1,000 besants. They are described as being 'in territorio
Neapol[itano]' in the margin of the charter. The properties do *not*
seem to have been in the territory of Nablus, however, at least
not as we now envisage it. Eincanephis is north-west of La Feve,
Einchalem is close to Petit Gerin (Zarin), and Azatil is just north
of Grand Gerin (Jenin). All thus appear to be in the Principality
of Galilee.[30]

[26] *Cart. gén. Hosp.*, No. 422; *Reg. Hier.*, No. 492.
[27] *Cart. gén. Hosp.*, No. 459; *Reg. Hier.*, No. 522.
[28] *Cart. gén. Hosp.*, ii. 907, No. 17; *Reg. Hier. Add.*, No. 535a.
[29] *Cart. gén. Hosp.*, No. 2832; *Reg. Hier.*, No. 39.
[30] *Cart. gén. Hosp.*, iv, No. 563 *bis*; *Reg. Hier.*, No. 583.

In 1180 King Baldwin IV gave the Hospitallers 100 tents of Bedouin near Belvoir.[31] The Statutes of the Hospital drawn up in 1182 provide another oblique reference to the Order's possessions in Galilee. In it, the Commander of the Hospital in Tiberias is said to be obliged to send two quintals of sugar to the Hospital in Jerusalem each year: presumably, therefore, the Order had sugar cane plantations near Tiberias.[32]

A charter survives from *c.*1240 in which the Teutonic Knights promised to give a quarter of the revenues of casal Arabia to the Hospitallers, until the sum of 5,000 besants had been paid off, the amount for which the casal had been mortgaged to the Hospitallers. The site was certainly under Frankish domination at this date, for we are told that if the casal was occupied by Saracens the Teutonic Knights would not have to continue making payments to the Hospitallers. As Arabia is sited to the north-north-east of Sephorie, the casal, like Sephorie itself, may have been in Frankish hands since 1229.[33] In December 1241 the Teutonic Knights acquired the rights to casal Corsy, sited on the eastern side of the Sea of Galilee, though it is doubtful whether this territory was in Christian hands at the time.[34]

On 1 April 1255 the Hospitallers were given Mount Thabor by the Pope, and were charged with building a castle on the site (see below). In June the Hospitallers took corporal possession of the monastery and its nearby properties.[35] In the period 30 June to 2 July 1255 the Hospitallers visited the area between Nazareth and the Sea of Galilee, inspected some of these properties, and placed them under the control of various headmen. The casalia visited were Jubeil, Casta, Cafarsset, Saronia, Demie, Seiera, Lubie, Arbel, Egdis (Hecdix), and Casal Robert.[36] Ownership of these casalia was the subject of some dispute, however. In 1262 the Templars gave their possessions in casal Cafarsset (or perhaps the casal itself) to the Hospitallers as part of a wide-ranging agreement between the two Orders. Cafarsset was described as

[31] *Cart. gén. Hosp.*, No. 582; *Reg. Hier.*, No. 593.

[32] *Cart. gén. Hosp.*, No. 627; *Reg. Hier. Add.*, No. 614a.

[33] Arabia is sited at Prawer–Benvenisti Map, ref. 169/201; *Cart. gén. Hosp.*, No. 2245; *Reg. Hier.*, No. 1097.

[34] *Tab. ord. Theut.*, No. 90 and p. 124; *Reg. Hier.*, No. 1104.

[35] See Riley-Smith, *Knights of St John*, pp. 413–17.

[36] *Cart. gén. Hosp.*, No. 2747; *Reg. Hier.*, No. 1237. See Riley-Smith, *Knights of St John*, pp. 427–8.

being 'en la seignorie de Tabarie'.[37] Similarly, in February 1265 Eschiva, Princess of Galilee, was in dispute with the Hospitallers over several of these casalia and some others. It was eventually decided that Eschiva should be allowed possession of Demie, Seiera, Lubie, and Arbel (all of which had been taken into corporal possession by the Order in 1255), and four others: Beitegon, Harousse, Hordzi, and Quepsene. Ownership of the casalia must have been a moot point, however, as the princess was obliged to give the Hospitallers the substantial compensation of 200 carrucates of land for the properties.[38]

It is clear that huge tracts of land within Galilee were out of the direct control of the princes long before the collapse that followed Hattin: moreover, the rise in religious landholdings continued when parts of the principality were recovered in the thirteenth century, although, as in other seigneuries, it was only the Military Orders who benefited to any great extent.

FORTIFIED SITES

As with Caesarea, a review of each of the fortified sites in the principality provides a useful guide to the balance of influence and land ownership within the seigneury.

Petit Gerin, a village with a Frankish population, was situated on the trade route between Damascus and Acre. Its only fortification was a defensive tower: in 1183, when the village was destroyed by the Muslims, the inhabitants had already fled to better fortified sites.[39]

Le Chastellez was a castle built by the king in 1178 on the east side of the Jordan at the place known as Jacob's Ford. It took six months to build. On completion the castle had been given to the Templars and we are told that the king also gave them the surrounding region. Although the castle was lost almost immediately to the Muslims, this is further evidence that the king retained ownership, or ownership rights, over much of the land traditionally thought to belong to the Principality of Galilee on the east of the Jordan.[40]

---

[37] *Cart. gén. Hosp.*, No. 3029; *Reg. Hier.*, No. 1319.
[38] *Cart. gén. Hosp.*, No. 3116; *Reg. Hier. Add.*, No. 1336a.
[39] William of Tyre, pp. 1050–2. Ownership of the site is unknown.
[40] William of Tyre, pp. 1003–4.

Saphet seems to have been built in 1102 and was therefore probably constructed by Baldwin I or Hugh de St Omer.[41] Prior to 1168 we know it belonged to Fulk, Constable of Tiberias.[42] In 1168 we find the king and the Templars had already purchased the castle from Fulk and from this time onwards the castle seems to have been in the hands of the Templars.[43] The king can thus be seen to be directly subsidizing the involvement of the Military Orders in the principality: presumably, even at this date, secular resources were stretched to the limit. Saphet was surrendered to Saladin in the winter of 1188. It was later reoccupied and rebuilt.

Although surviving evidence about the Templars is, as usual, scarce, the Order seems to have owned extensive estates around Saphet. As we have discussed, there are almost no surviving Frankish place-names nearby, possibly, as at Château Pélérin, a result of the loss of Templar records. Significantly the Order also seems to have had an administrative structure for controlling properties nearby. When the rebuilt castle surrendered to Baybars in 1266 the main negotiator for the Templars was an administrative officer, a Syrian Christian (who subsequently proved treacherous) called Leon le Casalier.[44] The granting to the Order of Le Chastellez (sited close to Saphet, to the east), together with its surrounding lands, probably implies a royal recognition of Templar presence and influence in the area: as the Order would have been the most immediate beneficiary of enhanced security in the region, it must have seemed appropriate to place Le Chastellez in their care.

Buria was a village with a Frankish population and a small tower of limited defensive value. In 1182 the Muslims launched a night raid on the village. The inhabitants fled to the tower but after only four hours' action it looked as though it was going to collapse and the Franks surrendered. Five hundred prisoners were taken and many Frankish dead were left in the fields. The poor performance of the tower shows the wisdom of the inhabitants of Petit Gerin in abandoning their village altogether:

---

[41] See Deschamps, *La Défense*, ii. 119–20, for a full discussion of Arab sources on this subject. For the rebuilding of Saphet, see Huygens, *De Constructione castri Saphet*, and Pringle, 'Reconstructing the Castle of Safad'.   [42] *Reg. Hier.*, No. 447.
[43] Ibid.   [44] 'Les Gestes des Chiprois', pp. 764–5.

doubtless the settlers at Buria would have fled to Mount Thabor if they had had time.[45]

The monastery of Mount Thabor was partly fortified in the twelfth century: in 1183 a Muslim force sent by Saladin was unable to capture it, though it was later fortified by the Muslims in the thirteenth century. On 1 April 1255, the monastery was given to the Hospitallers by the Pope. A castle was built by the Order and a castellan appointed by 1259.[46] The castle at Mount Thabor was an important one, with a garrison of 40 knights (compared with a garrison of 60 knights at Crac des Chevaliers in the same period).[47]

The castle of Forbelet belonged to the Hospitallers.[48] We only hear of the castle after their acquisition of Belvoir and it thus seems likely that it was constructed by the Order to protect and administer the extensive estates it was building up in the area.

La Feve was a Templar castle which seems to have been an administrative depot for the Order's local estates: in 1188 the Hospitallers captured two caravans transporting arms and provisions taken from the Templars at La Feve.[49] The site was described in 1172 as 'a castle of no small size in whose grounds they [the Templars] have made a large cistern with a wheeled machine'.[50] The Hospitallers had claims to the property through their acquisition of Mount Thabor[51] but renounced them in 1262 in return for the Templars' renunciation of rights elsewhere.[52]

Grand Gerin was a fortified town which owed the service of 25 sergeants.[53] Grand Gerin seems to have been held in secular hands for most of the twelfth century for we find a 'Mahengotus, dominus de Gerin' appearing as a senior vassal of the Principality of Galilee in 1154.[54]

In 1182 a razzia was launched against Grand Gerin[55] and in 1183 a Muslim detachment pillaged the town.[56] More raids were

---

[45] William of Tyre, pp. 1026–8; Abu-Shamah; iv. 217–8; Ibn al-Athir, 'Kamil', i. 651–2.

[46] For the assault of 1183 see William of Tyre, pp. 1050–2. For the castellan of Mount Thabor, see *Cart. gén. Hosp.*, Nos. 2934–6.

[47] *Cart. gén. Hosp.*, Nos. 2726–7.

[48] Ernoul, ed. Mas-Latrie, p. 61.

[49] Abu-Shamah, iv. 344–5.

[50] 'Theodorich', p. 64.

[51] *Reg. Hier.*, No. 1230.

[52] *Reg. Hier.*, No. 1318.

[53] John of Ibelin, p. 427.

[54] *Reg. Hier.*, No. 297.

[55] Ibn al-Athir, 'Kamil', i. 652–3.

[56] Abu-Shamah, iv. 246.

co-ordinated by Saladin in 1184 and Gerin was dismantled, together with its fortifications.[57] In the face of enemy action the town appears to have been completely indefensible: presumably the fortifications were sufficient to deter bandits but little else.

The Cave de Sueth (Habis Jaldak) was probably in Frankish hands from before 1109.[58] In 1113 Prince Joscelyn agreed to give Castle 'Thamanin' to the Muslims (location now unknown) in return for which he received peaceful possession of the Cave de Sueth and half the Terre de Sueth. The treaty was soon renounced, however.[59] When the fortress was besieged by Nur-ad-Din in 1158 it was King Baldwin III who came to its aid, and it was he who placed men in the castle and reprovisioned it.

The Cave de Sueth was under the control of Fulk of Tiberias when it fell to the Muslims in 1182, but as it was the king who reprovisioned and selected the garrison on its recapture later that year it is not clear whether Fulk held it in fief from the Prince of Galilee or from the king, whose father had been part-purchaser of Saphet from Fulk prior to 1168 and may have given him the Cave de Sueth as compensation. The Cave de Sueth seems to have fallen permanently into Muslim hands *before* 1187.

Qasr Berdaouil (Castle Baldwin) was probably built by Baldwin I in 1105 and was captured and demolished by the Muslims soon afterwards.

The major *castle of Belvoir*, or at least the site of the castle, belonged to Ivo Velos prior to 1168, by which time we find it in the possession of the Hospitallers. The castle held out against Saladin for a year after Hattin and on its return to Frankish hands was once again in the possession of the Hospitallers. It remained so until its final loss in 1247.

CONCLUSIONS

The evidence indicates that the power of the secular lords of the principality collapsed at a much earlier date than has generally

[57] Ibid. 256; Baha'-ad-Din, tr. Wilson, p. 97.

[58] In 1109 Baldwin I concluded a treaty with the Muslims in which the Terre de Sueth was divided between them and the Franks. Qalanisi, ed. Gibb. p. 92; Abou'l-Mehacen, p. 491; Abou'l-Modaffer, p. 541. The treaty broke down in late 1111 or early 1112, when the Frankish garrison of the Cave de Sueth (Habis Jaldak) was killed and the fortress taken; Qalanisi, ed. Gibb. p. 121; Ibn al-Athir, 'Kamil', i. 286; Abou'l-Modaffer, p. 544.

[59] Qalanisi, ed. Gibb, pp. 133–4.

been supposed. Far from gradually losing their power and influence in the thirteenth century, the process had already taken place by 1170 and the Princes of Galilee had little power over the principality (as it is now envisaged) thereafter. The defence of Galilee was, of course, a crucial issue. An examination of the ownership of the major fortifications of the principality produces surprising results. *Belvoir* was in the hands of the Hospitallers from *c*.1168 onwards: before then it does not seem to have been a major fortification. *Forbelet* was a Hospitaller castle, probably built after their acquisition of Belvoir, while *La Feve* was a Templar stronghold. *Mount Thabor* was in the hands of the Benedictines and was later an important Hospitaller castle. *Saphet* was in the hands of Fulk of Tiberias prior to 1168, at which time it was bought by the king and the Templars and entrusted into the care of the latter. *Le Chastellez* was another Templar castle, built by the king and the Order. Ownership of the *Cave de Sueth* is unknown, but it was possibly held by Fulk of Tiberias from the crown. Similarly, *Qasr Berdaouil* was probably a royal castle. It seems, therefore, that, with the exception of Tiberias itself, all major fortifications were outside the direct control of the Princes of Galilee. Even Tiberias was not amongst the strongest fortifications in Galilee, falling relatively easily in 1187 and proving indefensible in the 1240s. Moreover, this situation was apparent even *before* Hattin: from 1168 onwards all castles except Tiberias were out of the hands of the Princes of Galilee. Defence of the region was thus largely in the hands of the king and the Military Orders long before Hattin: and in a feudal society in an almost perpetual state of war an inability to fulfil military functions was inevitably accompanied by loss of power and influence in other spheres.

The shouldering of defence burdens by other institutions was accompanied by the separation of large portions of the principality from the effective control of the prince: landed estates and other revenues were needed to provide an inducement for the shouldering of such burdens and to provide the resources necessary for their continued fulfilment.

We know that this occurred in at least three cases (Belvoir, Saphet, and Le Chastellez) in the Principality of Galilee. The case for which most firm evidence exists is, as one might expect, that of the Hospitallers. The Order acquired Belvoir for an almost nominal sum and proceeded rapidly to build up extensive estates in the area. These estates were so large that a second castle (the smaller fortification of Forbelet) was built or acquired further west in order to protect and administer them. The Templars held Saphet in the north, and were given Le Chastellez and its lands upon completion. Therefore, it seems extremely likely that they had extensive estates in the north of the principality.

The king was also involved in the defence of Galilee, not always, one suspects, entirely voluntarily. The king had to pay the lion's share of the purchase price of Saphet, even though it was to be entrusted to the Templars. Presumably the local secular authorities had indicated that they could no longer shoulder the expenses involved and the king was forced to intervene to ensure the security of the region. We have also seen that a large proportion, if not the majority, of security operations in the trans-Jordanian region were controlled by the king. Inevitably this meant that large elements of royal domain land were retained in the Principality of Galilee on both sides of the Jordan.

We are thus presented with a situation whereby the Principality of Galilee was becoming more fragmented and less easily controlled by the prince. After 1168 we find that two large sections of the principality (one in the north, owned by the Templars, and one in the south, owned by the Hospitallers) had become, in practice if not in theory, semi-independent marches, each responsible for its own section of border security. In addition, royal presence in the trans-Jordan must inevitably have reduced revenues from the fertile Terre de Sueth.

One is left with the question of why the local secular authorities were unable to find the resources necessary to shoulder military burdens. The first point to make must be that under *any* circumstances these burdens would have been heavy. In addition, however, there are two major factors which we can identify as greatly exacerbating these difficulties. The first of these was the presence of religious institutions, other than the Military Orders, in the principality. We know that Mount Thabor owned extensive estates throughout the Principality of Galilee. Even after the effective collapse of the monastery in 1255 the properties were given into the hands of another religious institution, the Hospitallers. These estates must have been a drain on the overall structure of the principality, reducing the level of resources available for supporting essential military forces. The presence of other religious bodies only made matters worse: the combined estates of the Holy Sepulchre, the monastery of Josaphat, and various bishoprics, for example, also made substantial inroads on the amount of land available for distribution as secular fiefs.

The second major factor was the gradual dismemberment of the principality in the twelfth century. Haifa, which was originally promised to Tancred, was made into an independent seigneury. As we have seen, Toron was detached from the Principality of Galilee, as was Chastel Neuf. Nazareth was made into an independent religious seigneury and the conquered territory of Dera was not, as one might have expected, added to the principality. These actions (which, taken together, affect an enormous area) were part of a general policy of reducing the power of the more influential vassals. As in other lordships, however, this policy, while certainly making political sense for the king, ran the risk of leaving secular authorities under-resourced to meet their military responsibilities. The evidence would suggest that this, in combination with the other factors discussed above, was precisely what had happened in the Principality of Galilee by the 1160s.

The Principality of Galilee and the Lordship of Caesarea exemplify a more general decay of seigneurial power that has not been commented upon by historians of the kingdom: the same process can be traced in most of the other lordships. Indeed, smaller seigneuries were probably even harder hit since they were more heavily dependent on fiefs held in the royal domain: their seigneurial centres may have been too small for their needs even when they were in full possession of them. Each loss of territory must have been a progressively harder blow to their lords. In short, contrary to accepted opinion, the evidence points towards the seigneuries of the Latin Kingdom having become increasingly weak in the twelfth century and possessing only the smallest fraction of their original power in the thirteenth century.

6

Seigneurial Resources III:
The Examples of Sidon and Arsur

THE lordships of the Latin Kingdom were, as we have seen, militarily and financially much less powerful than has hitherto been assumed. Two lordships have always been identified as weak, however, because their poverty forced their lords to sell them to the Military Orders.[1] This assertion, while true on one level, hides a deeper irony: that it was only the success of the Lords of Sidon and Arsur in retaining control of extensive portions of their land that made the sale of the seigneuries an attractive proposition to a Military Order. In the case of other lordships, such as Caesarea, the landed assets available to the seigneury were no longer sufficient to justify the extra military expenses that a take-over of the lordship would have entailed: potential purchasers were therefore not forthcoming.

One thus has the paradoxical situation that the strength of Sidon in particular, throughout most of the Latin Kingdom's history, has led to modern perceptions of it being one of the weakest seigneuries, while the truly weak lordships, which had suffered substantial internal dissolution even in the twelfth century, are now perceived to be amongst the most stable.

SIDON

Compared to other lordships of similar size, the number of grants and sales made to the Church within the Lordship of Sidon were remarkably small: it seems to have been this prudence which accounted for the relative stability of landholdings in the seigneury.

Sidon was captured in December 1110 by King Baldwin I,

---

[1] e.g. Riley-Smith, *Feudal Nobility*, p. 30.

with the naval assistance of King Sigurd of Norway.[2] The capture of the city without Italian aid saved the king from the necessity of giving away large sections of the town and surrounding lands as happened later, for instance, at Tyre. He did give the Venetians a small gift after the capture of the town (but this seems to have been little more than a celebratory gesture and was not even sited in the Seigneury of Sidon): in 1123 Patriarch Gormund confirmed that the Venetians should have in Acre '. . . another part of the same street having one wooden house, and two of stone, which were formerly reed huts, the same which King Baldwin of Jerusalem originally gave to blessed Mark and to Doge Ordolafo and his successors in consideration of the acquisition of Sidon . . .'.[3] Despite containing a port, we know of no landholdings within the Lordship of Sidon by the Italian or French merchant communities.

The Church did own lands in the seigneury, but relatively few compared to other lordships. Eustace Grenier was the first and most generous of the Lords of Sidon: he could afford to be, being Lord of Caesarea, Sidon, and, through his wife, Jericho.[4] In 1115 he gave the Brothers of Josaphat casal Capharabra, described as being in the territory of Sidon, together with a house in Sidon itself.[5] He also gave them a *mahomeria* and a garden sited just outside the town.[6] We also know that in the same period a certain 'Engerannus Luvet', a vassal of the lordship, had given Josaphat an unspecified casal.[7]

There is evidence in a papal confirmation of 1158 of the properties of St Mary of the Latins that the Church had two casalia in the city of Sidon.[8] In 1162 Lord Gerard of Sidon gave rights to the Hospitallers in the lordship. References to Sidon and

---

[2] William of Tyre, pp. 517–19; Albert of Aix, pp. 675, 678—9; Ibn al-Athir, 'Kamil', i. 275–6; Qalanisi, ed. Gibb, p. 107. Fulcher of Chartres, p. 548, also specifically mentions that the rural inhabitants of the area agreed to stay and continue to cultivate the land under Frankish rule.

[3] William of Tyre, pp. 577–81; *Reg. Hier.*, No. 102.

[4] For Jericho see William of Tyre, p. 519. At the time of which William wrote, the property was worth 5,000 gold pieces.

[5] *Chartes de Josaphat*, ed. Delaborde, No. 6; *Reg. Hier.*, No. 80.

[6] *Chartes de Josaphat*, ed. Kohler, No. 12; *Reg. Hier. Add.*, No. 114b.

[7] *Chartes de Josaphat*, ed. Kohler, No. 12; *Reg. Hier. Add.*, No. 114b. The generosity of Eustace and his vassals to Josaphat is at least partly explained by the fact that the first Archbishop of Caesarea (another of Eustace's fiefs) was also the first Abbot of Josaphat.

[8] *Reg. Hier.*, No. 331; see also 'Papst-Kaiser', p. 46.

Beaufort in a papal confirmation of 1153 show that the Order already held unspecified rights or properties in or around these two places by that date.[9] Gerard now gave the brothers the right to have two gates in the town of Sidon, a place outside ('une place en dehors pres des aires . . .'), and all the forewall from the Tower of Baldwin to the Tower of the Sea.[10] This charter is unfortunately available only in rubric form. It is clear that the Hospitallers were being given an element of military responsibility for Sidon, but the exact extent of this is unclear: a previous document of the same kind, for instance, which would look very similar in rubric form, stipulated that the fortifications in the care of the Military Order should be returned to secular hands in time of war.[11]

In 1164 Gerard made a small grant to the monks of Josaphat: all the olive trees which were to be found on the lands which the Brothers owned near to Sidon.[12] In 1174 we find King Amalric giving the Hospitallers an annual rent of 230 besants to be taken annually from a house which he had in Nablus, in return for the casal and river of Damor, sited in the Lordship of Sidon, which was in the possession of the Hospitallers.[13] These are the only religious holdings that we know of in the Lordship of Sidon, prior to the battle of Hattin; in other words, four casalia (Capharabra and an unnamed casal owned by Josaphat, and two unnamed casalia owned by St Mary of the Latins), and four smaller grants.

We know that the Church owned the equivalent of approximately 55.3 casalia in Caesarea by 1187, a lordship about 1,200 square kilometres in size. This can be expressed as one casal owned by the Church for every 21.7 square kilometres. Sidon, on the other hand, (including the Schuf) was a substantially larger seigneury, comprising approximately 1,800 square kilometres. Using the same methodology employed in analysing the data for Caesarea (assuming, for statistical purposes, that a smaller grant of land comprised 20 per cent of a casal) we know that 4.8 casalia were in the hands of the Church in 1187 or one casal owned by the Church for every 375 square kilometres. Even given the

[9] *Cart. gén. Hosp.*, No. 217; *Reg. Hier. Add.*, No. 280b.

[10] *Cart. gén. Hosp.*, No. 302; *Reg. Hier. Add.*, No. 376b.

[11] *Cart. gén. Hosp.*, No. 2160; *Reg. Hier. Add.*, No. 1076a; see *Tab. ord. Theut.*, No. 40; *Reg. Hier.*, No. 810.

[12] *Chartes de Josaphat*, ed. Kohler, No. 36; *Reg. Hier. Add.*, No. 393c.

[13] *Cart. gén. Hosp.*, No. 454; *Reg. Hier. Add.*, No. 517a.

inaccuracies inherent in such a comparison (such as variations in the size of individual casalia) it is clear that the Church in the twelfth century had extremely limited holdings in Sidon, relative to those in other seigneuries.[14]

In 1228, after the recovery of Sidon, Balian, Lord of Sidon (c.1210–1240), granted the Teutonic Knights lands and gardens in the lordship. In the description of the position of these gifts we are given insights into land ownership around the town:

Divisiones vero iardini predicti tales sunt: . . . ab occidente habens viam rectam, que transit inter iardinos et inter terram domini Rauli Ianuensis; . . . contra aquilonem habens partem vie et olivas domini Guillelmi de Lye. Divisiones autem supradicte vinee tales sunt: . . . ab occidente viam rectam, que vadit inter iardinos contra flumen de ipsa civitate Sydonis; contra meridiem habens olivas domus Templi; contra aquilonem habens olivas domini Brixi. Divisiones vero terre supradicte tales sunt: . . . contra aquilonem habet campum, qui tangit iardinum domini Egidii; . . .

The garden given to the brothers was also described as 'que dicitur iardinus comitisse'.[15]

This tells us much about land ownership in the area immediately around Sidon. Prior to the grant to the Teutonic Knights we see that: the Lord of Sidon owned lands and gardens; a Lord Raul owned lands; Lord William de Lye owned an olive grove, as did the Templars; the Lord 'Brixi' also owned an olive grove; the Lord Giles owned a garden and the countess had previously owned a garden. So there were seven property owners, of which only one was a religious institution.

A papal pancart of c.1238 confirmed that the church of 'S Mariae et Omnium Sanctorum Acconensi' owned 'ex dono nobilis viri Baliani, Domini Sidonien domos et curtes sitas in civitate Sidonien . . . .'.[16] It is surely no coincidence that all of Balian's known gifts to religious institutions consisted of urban or suburban properties, in or around Sidon. Even when making gifts it appears that he was making a conscious effort to encourage the repopulation of the town of Sidon after the disasters of the preceding decades by donations that would, in the long term, add to the strength of the seigneury rather than detract from it.

---

[14] Benvenisti, *The Crusaders in the Holy Land*, p. 15.

[15] *Tab. ord. Theut.*, No. 62; *Reg. Hier.*, No. 986; see also *Tab. ord. Theut.*, p. 126.

[16] *Italia Sacra*, vii. 39–40; *Reg. Hier.*, No. 1085.

These are the only religious holdings that we know of in the lordship before its financial problems in the 1250s. It is quite remarkable that in such a large lordship so few properties had left secular hands by the mid-thirteenth century.

Under Lord Julian of Sidon the seigneury collapsed and it is his actions that have created the impression of weakness. In 1249 Sidon was sacked by a Damascene army.[17] By 1253 St Louis had managed to rebuild the two castles of Sidon but had not had time to complete the city walls: in that year the Muslims attacked again, and although Simon de Montbeliard, the garrison, and a small number of citizens were able to take refuge in the Castle of the Sea, 2,000 people were killed in the unwalled town.[18] St Louis returned to Sidon in July 1253 and undertook yet more repairs.[19] In these circumstances it is not surprising that Julian was suffering from acute financial problems, and the process of dissolution within the lordship began. The final straw came in 1260 when Sidon was overrun by the Mongols.[20] Before leaving, the Mongols destroyed the city walls yet again: it must have been obvious to everyone that the town of Sidon, given the resources available, was indefensible.

Even in these straits, however, Lord Julian (often denigrated as a spendthrift) took care to keep his seigneurial centre as intact as possible. In August 1254 he sold an estate to the Hospitallers for the sum of 24,000 besants. It is significant that the estate (Casal Robert) was situated in the Principality of Galilee.[21] By 1256 Julian's financial needs were even more pressing and he sold extensive properties to the Teutonic Knights: even here, however, it is noticeable that he sold only the semi-independent (and administratively distinct) Schuf to the Order. The Lordship of Sidon was retained until the last possible moment. The end of Julian's attempts to sustain the lordship came in 1260 when he found himself completely unable to repair the damage done to the walls of Sidon by the Mongols. He sold (or possibly leased) the whole Lordship of Sidon and Beaufort to the Templars.[22]

The *Estoire de Eracles, Gestes des Chiprois*, and 'Annales de

---

[17] Jemal ad-Din, in Michaud, *Bibliothèque des Croisades*, iv. 453.
[18] John of Joinville, pp. 302–3.
[19] Ibid. 318–20. *Eracles*, pp. 440–1.
[20] 'Les Gestes des Chiprois', pp. 751–2; *Eracles*, pp. 444–5.
[21] *Cart. gén. Hosp.*, No. 2688; *Reg. Hier.*, No. 1217.
[22] *Eracles*, p. 445; 'Les Gestes des Chiprois, p. 752; 'Annales de Terre Sainte', p. 449.

Terre Sainte' all say that Sidon was sold. Philip of Novara says it was leased, however. There were also some previous negotiations with the Hospitallers.[23] The suggestion in Philip of Novara that the lordship was leased rather than sold raises interesting questions and perhaps sheds new light on the later responsibilities of Julian and his sons. The status of the lordship after 1260 is superficially clear: it had passed from the hands of the Lords of Sidon to the Templars. The sale of the lordship created problems for all concerned, however. The Templars were now in possession of a lordship in which the Hospitallers held properties. The Orders rationalized this situation soon after the Templars took over Sidon, by an agreement whereby, in return for concessions elsewhere, the Hospitallers were persuaded to renounce all their rights and properties in Damor, Sidon, and Beaufort.[24]

Julian's problems were more intransigent. The sale had been made during a regency, but Henry of Antioch–Lusignan made sure that the alienation did not go uncontested. Julian was only able to end the dispute by promising that he would continue to provide the full military contingent of the fief (i.e. 40 knights) and agreeing that his sons would continue to provide the service in return for money fiefs.[25]

Julian's son, Balian II, succeeded to the title of Lord of Sidon when Julian became a religious and received a money fief of 7,000 besants a year. Julian's second son, John, also received a money fief of 4,000 besants per annum from the king. It looks as though the king was attempting to make Julian and his heirs fulfil the obligations of Lord of Sidon, even though they were no longer in direct control of the fief.[26]

Moreover, two charters of 1261, a year *after* the sale of the lordship, seem to indicate that Julian was seeking to emphasize that he was still Lord of Sidon. In a form of words not used before, he twice refers to John de la Tor (at the head of the witness list) as 'Johan de la Tor, conestable de ma dite seignorie de Seete'. These charters also indicate, by the presence of the

[23] *Cart. gén. Hosp.*, No. 3029; Philip of Novara, 'Livre', pp. 530–1.

[24] *Cart. gén. Hosp.*, Nos. 3026, 3028, 3029; *Reg. Hier.*, Nos. 1318, 1319; *Reg. Hier. Add.*, No. 1317c.

[25] *Eracles*, p. 445; Philip of Novara, 'Livre', pp. 530–1.

[26] Philip of Novara, 'Livre', p. 531.

Constable and 'Johan Harneis, mareschal', that elements of the lordship's administration were retained after the lordship passed into the hands of the Templars. The title of Lord of Sidon only lapsed in 1276, with the death of Balian II.[27]

All this evidence points towards a *lease* rather than an outright sale: this would account for the fact that the king felt able to insist that the military obligations of the lordship should continue to be fulfilled and explain why Julian referred to himself as Lord of Sidon (with his own administrative officers) after 1260.

The gradual dissolution of the lordship in the 1250s, culminating in the agreement with the Templars in 1260, has been used as evidence for the hypothesis that Sidon was one of the few truly weak lordships. What has never been commented upon, however, is the fact that this same documentation is clear proof that *until* 1256 Sidon (including the Schuf) was in fact one of the strongest seigneuries: after all, one can only dispose of what one still possesses. Ironically, most lordships were so emaciated by this time that extensive sales were no longer possible: the resources available for sale had long since been disposed of.

The extent of secular landholdings is nowhere more apparent than in the semi-independent Schuf (though it was by now in the possession of the Lords of Sidon). Because of the relatively full documentation that accompanied the gradual sale of the Schuf to the Teutonic Knights we are able to compile a list of the properties that comprised the fief:

Properties retained by Julian of Sidon, Lord of Schuf:
　　39 named properties (casalia or gastinae);[28]
　　4 named gastinae (claimed);[29]
　　An unspecified number of other properties.[30]

Fief of John of Schuf:
　　3 gastinae near Sidon;[31]
　　2 gardens;[32]
　　1 house in Sidon;[33]
　　Unspecified land near Sidon;[34]
　　45 named casalia;[35]
　　22 other gastinae (at least).[36]

---

[27] *Tab. ord. Theut.*, Nos. 117–18; *Reg. Hier.*, Nos. 1300–1.
[28] *Reg. Hier.*, Nos. 1253, 1254.　　[29] Ibid. 1253.　　[30] Ibid.
[31] Ibid. 1252.　　[32] Ibid. 1252, 1256.　　[33] Ibid. 1252.
[34] Ibid.　　[35] Ibid. 1256, 1300.　　[36] Ibid.

Fief of John de la Tor:
 1 casal.[37]

We see that at least 114 properties (excluding unspecified lands, gardens, etc.) were in secular hands in the Schuf alone. Of religious holdings we know only that the Templars were contesting possession of four gastinae claimed by Julian of Sidon.[38] Such a high concentration of properties in secular hands outside the royal domain is unprecedented: no documentary evidence has survived showing a greater degree of secular landholding in *any* lordship in *any* period of the Latin Kingdom's history. That the Lords of Sidon (and Schuf) and their vassals had been able to retain such a large number of properties until 1256 (long after most other seigneuries had been effectively emaciated) is truly remarkable.

A document of 1257 (or 1258) shows that a similar situation existed within the Lordship of Sidon proper. In selling several properties to the Hospitallers, Lord Julian gives us valuable information about the distribution of landholdings in Sidon. Julian sold the casalia of Daraya, Haanouf, and Maroenie to the Order, together with their gastinae of Bothma, Ecfareisson, Karbet el Ezairac, Ecfardebess, Bedagon el Hammem, and Toreille el Sefargelis.[39]

La Maroenie (sited to the south-east of Sidon in the Valley of Essomar) was described as follows: 'devers sollail levant a un cazal de sire Guillaume Meingot, lequel a nom Zefta, et devers midi a un cazal del Evesque, lequel a nom Teffahata, et devers sollail couchant a la Daordie el Hadidi, et devers boire (a) la Messeigeha'.

The locale around Haanouf and Daraye (very close to each other in the valley of el-Karroub, and sited to the north-east of Sidon) was described as follows:

Et les autres deus casaus, c'est asavoir Haanouf et Daraye, sieent en la clym el Karroub; et joint Ahanouf devers sollail levant a un casal de sire Johan de Fenion, qui est apele le Geleilie, et devers midi a deus casaus,

---

[37] *Reg. Hier.*, No. 1265.
[38] *Tab. ord. Theut.*, No. 108; *Reg. Hier.*, No. 1253; 'ce sont le[s] gastines, de qui la question est dou Temple et de nous, qui sont sur le damer, des quels ce sont les nons: la Delhemie, la Lehedie, le Mechaiera, Margekeneiroh'.
[39] *Cart. gén. Hosp.*, No. 2852; *Reg. Hier.*, No. 1257.

qui sunt de sire Balian de Mimarz, qui sunt apelez le Zahrorie et
Bequifs, et devers sollail levant a Oedi el Hammem, et devers midi au
devant dit cazal Hanouf et a Esshym, et devers sollail cochant au
borgem qui est de sire Gervaise Amoros, et devers boire joint al avant dit
Oedi el Hammem et a la terre de sire Johan Pisan.

There is a clear distinction made in listing properties: those
owned by Lord Julian are mentioned by name only, while those
held by others have their ownership specified. Thus, we can
compile two lists of land ownership in two valleys of the Lordship
of Sidon immediately prior to 1257:

Valley of Essomar:
  Casal Maroenie, owned by Lord Julian
  Casal Zefta, owned by William Meingot[40]
  Casal Teffahata, owned by the Bishop of Sidon
  Casal Daordie el Hadidi, owned by Lord Julian
  Casal Messeigeha, owned by Lord Julian

Valley of el Karroub:
  Casal Haanouf, owned by Lord Julian
  Casal Daraya, owned by Lord Julian
  Casal Geleilie, owned by John de Fenion
  Casal Zahrorie, owned by Balian de Mimars
  Casal Bequifs, owned by Balian de Mimars
  Wadi el Hammem, owned by Lord Julian
  Casal Esshym, owned by Lord Julian
  A 'borgem' (borgesie?) owned by Gervaise Amoros
  Land, owned by John the Pisan

In addition there were six gastinae in the two valleys dependent
on Maroenie, Haanouf, and Daraye, all owned by Lord Julian:

  Gastina Bothma
  Gastina Ecfareisson
  Gastina Karbet el Ezairac
  Gastina Ecfardebess
  Gastina Bedagon el Hammem
  Gastina Toreille el Sefargelis

Of these twenty properties we know that thirteen were owned by
Lord Julian, six by his vassals, and only one (Teffahata) by the

---

[40] The Meingot family were long established in the Lordship of Sidon and had been
vassals at least from the 1120s onwards.

Church. Once again, compared to other lordships such as Caesarea, the state of secular landholdings in Sidon, up to 1256 at least, appears to be very healthy indeed. In this context it is interesting to note that it was only in 1257 that an *iqta* was granted by al-Mu'zz Aybak (1250–7, the first Bahri Mamluk sultan of Egypt) to Sa'd ad-Din Khidr, brother of Hajji II, giving him several villages outside the Gharb, in the Schuf, Wadi at-Taym, and Iqlim al-Kharrub.[41]

An examination of the fortifications of the lordship also indicates that, far from being one of the weakest seigneuries, Sidon was possibly the *only* major lordship where the lords maintained a dominant role throughout the twelfth century and beyond.

BELHACEM

The cave fortress of Belhacem probably came into Frankish possession in 1128.[42] It was also mentioned in a thirteenth century text: 'Item, episcopatum Sidonensem, castrum quod Belfet dicitur, et Cavam Belciassem, et protenditur haec terra per dietam et plus.' It thus seems that a small Muslim cave fortress was taken and utilized by the crusaders. It is likely that the crusader presence in the fort dates from 1128, and that ownership of the fortification was in the hands of the Lord of Sidon.[43]

BEAUFORT

Beaufort came into Frankish hands in 1139[44] but, as we have seen, there is no evidence that King Fulk gave the castle to the Lords of Sidon: it is only in witness lists of the Lordship of Sidon from 1158 onwards (i.e. long after Fulk's death) that we find the name 'de Belfort' appearing.[45] This would seem to indicate that the castle was in the hands of the Lords of Sidon by this time. By the time to which John of Ibelin's lists refer, the castle was an important, and integral, part of the Lordship of Sidon. John

---

[41] Salibi, *Maronite Historians*, p. 208. Shidyaq enumerated the following villages of the Schuf: al-Ma'asir al-Fawqaniyya, Ba'dharan, 'Ayn Matur, Batlun, 'Ayn Uzay, Kafarnabrakh, Brih, and Gharifa.   [42] William of Tyre, p. 619.
[43] *Cod. dip. geros.*, i. 466; 'Recherches', ed. Rey, p. 19.
[44] Deschamps, *La Défense*, ii. 178.
[45] See chapter 3, section 3, under The Lordship of Sidon.

referred to 'Le seignor de Seete et de Biaufor', and 'La baronie de Seete, de qui Biaufort et Cesaire et Bessan sont . . .' Moreover, the knights' service owed by Sidon and Beaufort was given as a joint figure: 'De Seet et de Biaufort, XL. chevaliers.' Beaufort was thus acquired by Gerard sometime between 1139 and 1158 (probably between 1143 and 1158, given Fulk's policy towards the higher nobility).[46] Beaufort only left the hands of the Lords of Sidon in 1260, when the seigneury was sold, or leased, to the Templars.[47]

CAVE DE TYRON

Cave castles played an important part in the defence of the north of the Lordship of Sidon. As we have seen, Belhacem was a cave fortress, as was the major fortification in the north, the Cave de Tyron. In December 1133 the Muslims captured it.[48] The Franks must have recaptured the castle sometime between 1133 and 1165, for in the latter year the Muslims took the fortress once again:

About the same time Shirkuh, so often mentioned, a man bent on destroying the Christians, seized a fortress belonging to the Christians sited in the territory of Sidon suddenly and without warning. The place was known as the Cave de Tyron and was considered impregnable. It is said that the capture was accomplished by bribing the custodians. That the fortress had fallen into the enemy's hands through collusion with its guardians was quite apparent, for as soon as it was surrendered all those within escaped to the enemy's country, with the exception of their chief. By a lucky chance he was caught and came to a miserable end at Sidon, where he was hanged.[49]

The ownership of the castle at the time of its capture is not explicitly stated, but there are strong hints that it belonged to the Lord of Sidon. The fortress is described as being 'in territorio Sydoniensi situm', while the garrison's commander was taken and hanged at Sidon, rather than at a royal court.[50] It was in the

[46] John of Ibelin, pp. 420, 422.
[47] *Eracles*, p. 445; 'Les Gestes des Chiprois', p. 752; 'Annales de Terre Sainte', p. 449; Philip of Novara, 'Livre', pp. 530–1.
[48] Qalanisi, ed. Gibb, p. 224; Ibn al-Athir, 'Kamil', i. 401; Abou'l Feda, p. 21.
[49] William of Tyre, pp. 877–9.
[50] The desertion to the Muslims *en masse* may imply that a large proportion of the garrison were of native Christian stock. William of Tyre seems in no doubt as to the guilt

hands of Lord Julian of Sidon when it was finally sold to the Teutonic Knights in 1256.[51]

One thus sees that all the fortresses of the lordship and most of its lands were (when in Frankish possession) in secular hands until 1256, when the dissolution of the seigneury began.

ARSUR

Like Sidon, the Lordship of Arsur has been singled out as one of the few truly weak lordships, purely on the basis of its sale to the Hospitallers. All the evidence indicates that, unlike most other

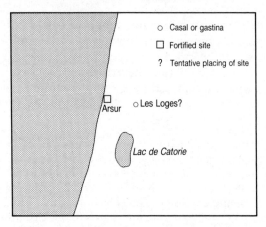

7. Arsur

lordships, however, the Lords of Arsur were able to retain the lands of the seigneury and its only fortified point (the walled town and citadel of Arsur) in their own hands: when it came to be sold, the lordship was still a relatively compact and unified whole.

It seems that the lordship was created in the early 1160s. We first come across a Lord of Arsur in 1163, when a certain

of the garrison in 'betraying' the castle to the enemy, but it is possible that they were merely persuaded to surrender in what they may have perceived to have been an impossible situation. Also in 1165 William tells us that another 'impregnable cave' sited beyond the Jordan was surrendered to the Muslims by the Templars: William of Tyre, p. 879. The twelve members of the Templar garrison, William claims, were hanged by the furious king. The almost simultaneous collapse of two cave fortresses may say more about the 'impregnability' of such places than about the treachery of their garrisons.

[51] *Tab. ord. Theut.*, No. 110; *Reg. Hier.*, No. 1255.

'Johannes de Arsur' appeared towards the top of a witness list.[52] In 1168 John of Arsur appeared as 'dominus Johannes de Azoto' on a charter of the Prince of Galilee, making plain his status as lord.[53]

The only religious landholding that one can definitely ascribe to the Lordship of Arsur proper is an unknown casal which the Hospitallers possessed 'in terra de Azoto' prior to 1110.[54] Even the vassals of the lordship did not own much of the surrounding land. We find a 'Johannes de Logia' witnessing a charter for the Lord of Arsur in 1241, so it seems likely that he held Les Loges from Lord John.[55] This was a substantial fief: in 1269 it was thought capable of producing an annual rent of 700 besants.[56] By this time, however, Les Loges was in the hands of the Lord of Arsur, so the 'de Logia' family had presumably died out in the meantime. This deduction is reinforced by the absence of the 'de Logia' family from witness lists in 1255 and 1261.[57]

More evidence is provided by the unique document of sale by which Lord Balian of Arsur transferred the seigneury to the Hospitallers in 1261.[58] In it, Balian listed all the landed holdings of his vassals within the seigneury. The vassals of the lordship proper (vassals with holdings entirely outside the lordship do not seem to have been included) consisted of six knights and twenty-one sergeantries:

---

[52] 'Les Archives', ed. Delaville, p. 99; *Reg. Hier.*, No. 379.

[53] *Cart. gén. Hosp.*, No. 398; *Reg. Hier.*, No. 448.

[54] The casal had been given to the Order by Anselm de Turre David; *Cart. gén. Hosp.*, No. 20; *Reg. Hier.*, No. 57. This gift was confirmed in 1154 by King Baldwin III; *Cart. gén. Hosp.*, No. 225; *Reg. Hier.*, No. 293. The Hospitallers also owned Tres Pontes but it is uncertain which lordship the property belonged to. A gift to the Order of mills, the whole island of Tres Pontes, and 10 carrucates of land was confirmed by Count Hugh of Jaffa in 1133. *Cart. gén. Hosp.*, No. 97; *Reg. Hier.*, No. 147. The gift was confirmed by the Pope in 1153. *Cart. gén. Hosp.*, No. 217; *Reg. Hier. Add.*, No. 280b. In 1241 the Hospitallers were in possession of half the mills. The remainder, together with the adjacent island, were purchased from John III, Lord of Arsur (c.1234–c.1258), for 3,000 besants. *Cart. gén. Hosp.*, Nos. 2274, 2277; *Reg. Hier.*, No. 1100; As Tres Pontes is sited between the County of Jaffa and the Lordship of Arsur, the administrative position of the property is in doubt. The sale by Lord John was perhaps not unrelated to the castle-building which he was undertaking at this time, for in 'Les Gestes des Chiprois' we read: 'En l'an de MCCXLI, Johan de Ybelin, fis dou seignor de Baruth, comensa a fermer le chasteau d'Arsuf.' 'Les Gestes des Chiprois', p. 728.

[55] *Reg. Hier.*, No. 1100.

[56] *Cart. gén. Hosp.*, No. 3323; *Reg. Hier.*, No. 1370.

[57] *Reg. Hier.*, Nos. 1241, 1302.

[58] *Cart. gén. Hosp.*, No. 2985; *Reg. Hier.* No. 1302.

Knights:
Johan de Cauquelie
Dimenche d'Arsur
Johan de Margat
Odde de Selouquie
Johan d'Arsur
Johan de Giberin 'a CCC L besanz et II charrues de terre'

Sergeants:
Raou de Merlo
Gui d'Arsur 'a XXV besanz et le durgemanage, et demi disme
    de VII casaus'
maistre Pierre le Charpentier la feme de Gervaise
le fie d'Estiene Vescont
Adam 'a XXIIII besanz et une livreisons et estoveirs, et restor a
    une beste, et l'escrivanage de la terre por le service d'un
    escrivain'
le fie de Brehin
Ihane por le fie de Jacob
les heirs d'Antoine Chapelet 'ont C besanz, et II livreisons et
    estoveirs a III chevaucheures, et restor de II, et une maison
    en la ville, et une piece de terre devant la ville'
'si com il est en son prevelege, maistre Alain en sa vie a C
    besanz, et a ses heirs L besanz'
maistre Pierre de Biauvais
Guillelme le Boutillier
Bertheleme l'Escrivain
Johan l'Escrivain
maistre Robert
les heirs de Vassal le Quec
Bertran le Quec
prestre Linart 'a XL besanz . . . et le lac de Catorie, ensi con
    les devises sont en son prevelege'
Phelippe dou Juge
le fie de Guillelme le Mareschau
le fie de Johan de Soraguiau

It is clear that very few of the vassals held land within the
lordship and even when they did, the amounts held were
relatively small: Johan de Giberin (Bethgibelin?) had two
carrucates, the heirs of Antoine Chapelet had a house in Arsur

and a piece of land outside, and 'prestre Linart' held the lake of Catorie (under certain conditions which are no longer known to us). In addition, Guy held the half-tithes on seven of the lordship's casalia for his service as dragoman. By contrast, the fact that Balian's dragoman held the half-tithes on seven casalia shows that at least seven properties were held by the Lord of Arsur.

The document also raises interesting questions about the office of the scribanage. Adam was given 24 besants, some other benefits, and 'l'escrivanage de la terre por le service d'un escrivain'. The 'scribanage of the land' seems to have entailed traditional benefits, for these are not explicitly listed. In return for the receipt of these traditional benefits, however, Adam was to provide the service of an 'escrivain'.

Riley-Smith rightly points out that there is a distinction between the scribanage and scribes: 'Among them are to be found a group differentiated from the rest by their title of scribanus as opposed to scriba or escrivain . . .' and 'It may be that the scribanus differed from the scriba in that he held his office by feudal tenure . . .'[59] Might it not also be possible that the holder of the scribanage was the chief scribe? Scribes were financial officers responsible for collecting taxes, and evidence exists for their presence in most lordships (we know of twenty-five office holders). There is also evidence that a substantial number were of native stock. With the scribanage, however, we know of only six office holders and on the list of the vassals of Arsur, Adam, holder of the scribanage, is clearly superior to Berthelme l'Escrivain and Johan l'Escrivain.

From the list it seems that Adam held a sergeantry *and* the scribanage (which is specifically related to the service he owes as an escrivain). With Berthelme and Johan, however, we find that they hold only sergeantries worth 40 besants each and various other benefits. The rights of scribanage, on the other hand, were much more valuable: the scribanage of the lands of Geoffrey le Tor was exchanged for lands later sold for 1,600 besants,[60] and the scribanage of a single village (Bethduras) was sold for 250 besants in 1176.[61] Clearly Adam was the social and financial

[59] *Feudal Nobility*, pp. 55–8.
[60] *Tab. ord. Theut.*, No. 16; *Cart. gén. Hosp.*, No. 1996.
[61] *Cart. gén. Hosp.*, Nos. 516–18.

superior of Berthelme and Johan, yet all three are described as being an 'escrivain'.

It seems likely in this case that the holder of the scribanage was the chief scribe, responsible for the other scribes in the lordship. This would certainly account for the high financial value of the scribanage (my interpretation would make the holder a key official in the lordship) as well as the fact that the scribanage, in every case, seems to have covered the *entire* lordship (if the scribanage was merely a perquisite there is no reason why it would have had to cover an entire administrative area). It would also explain why there were so many more scribes than holders of the scribanage.

The Hospitallers began the process of improving Arsur's fortifications almost as soon as they took over the lordship, in particular walling the suburb which had developed to the east of the town. The Order maintained a considerable garrison in Arsur but, after a siege lasting 40 days, were forced to relinquish the town and take refuge in the citadel, together with the civil population. After three days the barbican near the south gate collapsed and the commander of the garrison surrendered on the condition that the survivors be allowed to leave unharmed. Baybars agreed but broke his promise once the citadel was occupied: the garrison was led off into slavery.[62]

It thus seems that the Lords of Arsur held a much higher proportion of the lands of the seigneury than was the case in most other lordships of the Latin Kingdom, and only disposed of the lordship when it became apparent that their most strenuous efforts would not prevail against the growing Muslim threat. Their wisdom in doing this is confirmed when one considers that a substantial Hospitaller garrison was unable to hold the town for more than five years.

The scale of Hospitaller casualties indicates the commitment they had made to the defence of the lordship. Eighty or ninety Brothers were killed and about 180 taken into slavery (figures that may include liegemen, such as the knights of Arsur, and mercenaries). The extent of Christian losses at Arsur was recognized by Pope Clement IV who, in a letter of July 1265, asked the King of Armenia to help the Order because

---

[62] 'Les Gestes des Chiprois', pp. 758–9; 'Annales de Terre Sainte', p. 452; *Eracles*, p. 450; al-Maqrizi, tr. Quatremere, i: 2. 8–10; Abu-Shamah, v. 205.

'. . . Caesaream violenter optinuit et Azotum, effuso sanguine Christi militum, et nonnullis ex eis, quod est multis morte lugubrius, captivatis . . .'.[63]

It seems, ironically, that the two lordships which were bought wholesale by the Military Orders were in fact, up to that point, the strongest. It was only when the military situation became hopeless that Sidon and Arsur were sold and it seems extremely likely that their lords found ready purchasers precisely because of their strength: Sidon and Arsur were probably the only two seigneuries where enough of the lordship survived in secular hands to make purchase *en bloc* an attractive proposition for a Military Order.

[63] *Cart. gén. Hosp.*, No. 3173.

7

Conclusions

WHEN I started this study I rather expected to be arguing that the power of the lordships of the Latin Kingdom had in fact been underestimated in the past and that underneath their constitutional conflict with the monarchy in the thirteenth century there must have been a basis of economic and political strength.

I am now convinced that this was not the case. Far from discovering a source of seigneurial strength, it appears that even those historians who have argued that the lordships were weak have in fact been *understating* the case. I would now argue that the constitutional conflict of the thirteenth century was an over-reaction to a century of relative impotence and only possible because of an effective secular power vacuum. The exaggerated emphasis the nobility placed on their rights and privileges was the rather pedantic reaction of a class which had long been deprived of real power: it had developed a school of jurists because other, more practical, forms of political expression had been denied to it. The constitutional conflict in the thirteenth century was *not* the resurgence of a powerful and politically independent seigneurial framework: even against a monarchy that was extraordinarily weak, or absent altogether, seigneurial resources (with the possible exception of the Lordship of Sidon) were so slight that it must have been personal fiefs held in Cyprus and money fiefs in Acre, rather than the lordships of the Latin Kingdom, that allowed the nobility to continue their struggle.

We have seen that the monarchy possessed the means, and the political will, to manipulate the lordships when it felt it necessary. The reversion of lordships to the crown was one of the main opportunities for carrying out this manipulation, but it was the political and structural exploitation of seigneurial reversion, rather than just the material gains it produced, from which the monarchy derived its most important benefits. While the lordship was in the hands of the king he could change its form, its military potential, and ultimately the degree of power which any future lord of the seigneury would be able to wield.

Ironically, it was the king's power to create new lordships which provided him with one of his most important ways of controlling the nobility. By creating small seigneuries (particularly on the eastern borders of the kingdom and around Ascalon, often at the expense of larger ones) the monarchy was able to impose a greater level of royal control in the kingdom: smaller seigneuries presented no threat to the monarchy and could, in some cases, even be made dependent on an administrative centre of the royal domain rather than being accorded the full status of a major lordship.

The retention of lands in the royal domain was another means of exercising control, the effect of which was to ensure that a higher proportion of the kingdom's resources was under direct royal control at any given time. Similarly, the deliberate imposition of limitations on the extent of the seigneuries was another way to increase royal resources at the expense of potentially troublesome vassals.

In addition to the creation, reversion, and retention of seigneuries, the king had several other means of control at his disposal. The dispersal of properties held by the lord of one seigneury within the boundaries of other lordships was an effective way of diminishing the political and military independence of the nobility. A totally disproportionate level of such property dispersal is accounted for by the smaller lordships. It seems that in creating these lordships the Kings of Jerusalem took pains to ensure that the properties belonging to their lords were spread throughout the kingdom. Even more direct constraints on the ability of lords to take unilateral political action could be imposed by ensuring that a substantial proportion of the fiefs held by the lords were dependent on the royal domain. In some instances the links between the smaller lordships and the crown were so close that several (Scandaleon, Haifa, and Blanchegarde) were made directly dependent on the royal domain at Acre.

The monarchy clearly had many ways of ensuring that the lordships could be manipulated. In the face of such pressure, all the evidence points towards the seigneuries being economically unable to resist. As we have seen, even some of the most substantial lordships, such as Caesarea and the Principality of

Galilee, were by no means as strong as the extent of their administrative boundaries would suggest. The combination of gifts and acquisitions accruing to the Military Orders and other religious institutions, coupled with royal manipulation of their economic structure (such as the retention of royal lands within a seigneury) meant that the lords owned less and less of their lordships. It appears that Sidon and Arsur, the lordships that have been singled out as examples of seigneurial weakness, were, until their sale or lease to the Military Orders, those which were economically soundest: the vast majority of seigneuries were mere shadows of their former selves by the thirteenth century, and had been becoming progressively weaker since the mid-twelfth century.

It seems, overall, that the monarchy was better equipped to manipulate the seigneurial structure of the kingdom than has previously been thought: and that the seigneuries were even less well able, in terms of material resources, to resist.

References

For a full bibliography of crusading literature the reader is advised to refer to Hans Eberhard Mayer, *Bibliographie zur Geschichte der Kreuzzuge* (Hanover, 1960), which lists works up to 1958, and Mayer, 'Literaturbericht über die Geschichte der Kreuzzuge', in *Historische Zeitschrift*, 3 (1969), pp. 641–736, for publications from 1958 to 1967.

DOCUMENTS AND COLLECTIONS OF MATERIALS

'Actes passés en 1271, 1274, et 1279 à l'Aias (Petite Arménie) et à Beyrouth par devant des notaires genois', ed. C. Desimoni, AOL 1 (1881).

Les Archives, la Bibliothèque et le trésor de l'ordre de Saint-Jean de Jérusalem à Malte, ed. J. Delaville Le Roulx (Bibliothèque des Écoles françaises d'Athènes et de Rome, i. 32; Paris, 1883).

Cartulaire de l'église du Saint-Sépulcre de Jérusalem, ed. E. de Rozière (Collection des documents inédits sur l'histoire de France, i. 5; Paris, 1849).

Le Cartulaire du Chapitre du Saint-Sépulcre de Jérusalem, ed. G. Bresc-Bautier (Paris, 1984).

Cartulaire général de l'ordre des Hospitaliers de St-Jean de Jérusalem (1100–1310), ed. J. Delaville Le Roulx, 4 vols. (Paris, 1894–1906).

'Chartes de l'abbaye de Notre-Dame de la vallée de Josaphat en Terre Sainte (1108–1291): Analyse et extraits', ed. C. Kohler, ROL 7 (1899).

Chartes de la Terre Sainte provenant de l'abbaye de Notre Dame de Josaphat, ed. H. F. Delaborde (Bibliothèque des Écoles françaises d'Athènes et de Rome i. 19; Paris, 1880).

'Chartes de Terre Sainte', ed. J. Delaville Le Roulx, ROL 11 (1905–8).

'Chartes du Mont-Thabor', ed. J. Delaville Le Roulx, *Cart. gén. Hosp.* ii.

Codice diplomatico del sacro militare ordine gerosolimitano oggi di Malta, ed. S. Paoli, 2 vols. (Lucca, 1733–7).

'Un diplome inédit d'Amaury I, roi de Jérusalem, en faveur de l'abbaye du Temple-Notre-Seigneur (1166)', ed. F. Chalandon, ROL 8 (1900–1).

'Documents inédits concernant l'Orient latin et les croisades (XIIᵉ–XIVᵉ siècle)', ed. C. Kohler, ROL 7 (1899).

'Fragment d'un cartulaire de l'ordre de Saint-Lazare, en Terre Sainte', ed. A. de Marsy, *AOL* 2 (1884).

Historia diplomatica Frederici secundi, ed. J. L. de Huillard-Breholles, 6 pts. in 12 vols. (Paris, 1852–61).

'Inventaire de pièces de Terre Sainte de l'ordre de l'Hopital', ed. J. Delaville Le Roulx, *ROL* 3 (1895).

Italia Sacra, ed. F. Ughelli, 10 vols. (Venice, 1721).

JAMES OF VITRY, *Lettres*, ed. R. B. C. Huygens (Leyden, 1960).

'Papst-, Kaiser- und Normannenurkunden aus Unteritalien', ed. W. Holtzmann, *QFIAB* 35 (1955).

'Quatre pièces relatives à l'ordre teutonique en Orient', *AOL* 2 (1884).

'Quatre titres des propriétés des Genois à Acre et à Tyr', ed. C. Desimoni, *AOL* 2 (1884).

Recherches géographiques et historiques sur la domination des latins en Orient, ed. E. G. Rey (Paris, 1877).

Regesta regni Hierosolymitani 1097–1291, comp. R. Rohricht (Innsbruck, 1893). *Additamentum* (1904).

'Sankt Samuel auf dem Freudenberge und sein Besitz nach einem unbekannten Diplom Konig Balduins V', ed. H. E. Mayer, *QFIAB* 44 (1964).

Tabulae ordinis Theutonici, ed. E. Strehlke (Berlin, 1869).

'Titres de l'hôpital des bretons d'Acre', ed. J. Delaville Le Roulx, *AOL* 1 (1881).

Urkunden zur alteren Handels- und Staatsgeschichte der Republik Venedig mit besonderer Beziehung auf Byzanz und die Levante, ed. G. L. F. Tafel and G. M. Thomas (Fontes rerum Austriacarum; sec. 2. 12–14), 3 vols. (Vienna, 1856–7).

LEGAL TEXTS AND NARRATIVE SOURCES

ABOU'L-FEDA, 'Résumé de l'histoire des croisades tiré des Annales d'Abou'l-Feda', ed. and tr. in *RHC or.*, i.

ABOU'L-MEHACEN, 'Extraits du Nodjoum ez-Zahireh', extracts ed. and tr. in *RHC or.*, iii.

ABOU'L-MODAFFER YOUSSOF, 'Extraits du Mirat ez-Zaman', extracts ed. and tr. in *RHC or.*, iii.

ABU-SHAMAH, 'Kitab al-raudatain fi akhbar al-daulatain', extracts ed. and tr. in *RHC or.*, iv–v.

AL-'AINI, 'Iqd al-juman fi tarikh ahl al-zaman', extracts ed. and tr. in *RHC or.*, ii.

—— 'Le Collier de Perles', extracts ed. and tr. in *RHC or.*, ii. 1.

ALBERT OF AIX, 'Historia Hierosolymitana', *RHC oc.*, iv.

AL-MAQRIZI, *Histoire des sultans mamlouks de l'Égypte*, extracts tr. M. E. Quatremere, 4 pts. in 2 vols. (Paris, 1837–45).

—— *History of Egypt*, tr. Blochet *ROL*, 8–10 (Paris, 1900–2).

AMADI, FRANCESCO, *Chroniques de Chypre d'Amadi et de Strambaldi*, ed. R. de Mas-Latrie, 2 vols. (Paris, 1891–3).

'Annales de Terre Sainte', ed. R. Rohricht and G. Raynaud, *AOL* 2 (1884).

BAHA'-AD-DIN, *Kitab al-nawadir al-sultaniya wa'l-mahasin al-yusufiya*, tr. C. W. Wilson (London, 1897).

'De Expugnatione Terrae Sanctae per Saladinum Libellus', *Radulphi de Coggeshall Chronicon Anglicanum*, ed. J. Stevenson (Rolls Series, 62; London 1875).

EKKEHARD OF AURA, 'Hierosolymita', *RHC oc.*, v.

ERNOUL, *Chronique d'Ernoul et de Bernard le Trésorier*, ed. L. de Mas-Latrie (Paris, 1871).

—— *La Continuation de Guillaume de Tyr (1184–1197)*, ed. M. R. Morgan (Paris, 1982).

L'Estoire de Eracles empereur et la conqueste de la Terre d'Outremer, *RHC oc.*, i–ii.

FULCHER OF CHARTRES, *Historia Hierosolymitana*, ed. H. Hagenmeyer (Heidelburg, 1913).

Gesta Francorum et Aliorum Hierosolimitanorum, ed. R. Hill (London, 1962).

'Les Gestes des Chiprois', *RHC arm.*, ii.

'Historia Nicaena vel Antiochena', *RHC oc.*, v.

HUYGENS, R. B. C., *De Constructione castri Saphet* (Amsterdam, Oxford, New York, 1981).

IBN AL-ATHIR, 'Kamil al-tawarikh', extracts ed. and tr. in *RHC or.*, i–ii.

—— 'Histoire des Atabecs de Mosul', ed. and tr. in *RHC or.*, ii. 2.

IBN AL-FURAT, *Tarikh al-Duwal wa'l Muluk*, extracts, ed. and tr. U. and M. C. Lyons, *Ayyubids, Mamlukes and Crusaders* (Historical Introduction and Notes by J. S. C. Riley-Smith, 2 vols.; Cambridge, 1971).

IBN AL-QALANISI, *Dhail tarikh Dimashq*, extracts tr. H. A. R. Gibb (University of London Historical Series, 5; London, 1932).

IBN JUBAIR, 'Extrait du Voyage d'Ibn Dojbeir', extracts ed. and tr. in *RHC or.*, iii.

JAMES OF VITRY, 'Historia orientalis seu Hierosolymitana', ed. J. Bongars, in *Gesta Dei per Francos*, i. (Hannau, 1611).

JOHN OF IBELIN, 'Livre des assises de la haute cour', *RHC Lois*, i.

JOHN OF JOINVILLE, *Histoire de saint Louis*, ed. N. de Wailly (Paris, 1874).

LAMBERT OF ARDRES, 'Historia Comitum Ghisnensium', *Monumenta Germaniae Historica Scriptorum*, xxiv (Hanover, 1879).

'Les Lignages d'Outremer', *RHC Lois*, ii.

LYONS, U. and M. C., and RILEY-SMITH, J. S. C., eds., *Ayyubids*,

Mamlukes and Crusaders (Historical Introduction and Notes by J. S. C. Riley-Smith, 2 vols., Cambridge, 1971).

MICHAUD, J. F., *Bibliothèque des croisades*, ii, *Extraits des historiens arabes*, tr. M. Reinaud, 2 vols. (Paris, 1822).

PARIS, MATTHEW, *Chronica maiora*, ed. H. R. Luard (Rolls Series, 57; 7 vols. London, 1872–83).

PHILIP OF NOVARA, 'Memoirs': see 'Les Gestes des Chiprois'.

—— 'Livre de forme de plait', *RHC Lois*, i.

RALPH OF CAEN, 'Gesta Tancredi in Expeditione Hierosolymitana', *RHC oc.*, iii.

Recueil des historiens des croisades (Paris, 1841–1906): *Documents arméniens*, 2 vols. (1869–1906); *Historiens occidentaux*, 5 vols. (1844–95); *Historiens orientaux*, 5 vols. (1872–1902).

Roger de Wendover, ed. H. Howlett (Rolls Series, 84, 3 vols.; London 1886–9).

Roger of Howden, ed. W. Stubbs (Rolls Series, 51, 4 vols.; London 1868–71).

ROTHELIN, 'Continuation de Guillaume de Tyr de 1229 à 1261, dite du manuscrit de Rothelin', *RHC oc.*, ii.

SALIBI, K. S., *Maronite Historians of Medieval Lebanon* (Beirut, 1959). 'Table chronologique de Hethoum', *RHC arm.*, i.

'Theodorich's Description of the Holy Places', *Palestine Pilgrim Texts Society*, 5 (London, 1896).

WILLIAM OF NEWBOROUGH, *Chronicles of the Reigns of Stephen, Henry II and Richard I*, ed. R. Howlett (Rolls Series, 82; London 1884).

WILLIAM OF TYRE, *Historia rerum in partibus transmarinis gestarum*, ed. R. B. C. Huygens (Tvrnholti, 1986).

SECONDARY WORKS

BENVENISTI, M., *The Crusaders in the Holy Land* (Jerusalem, 1970).

CAHEN, C., 'La féodalité et les institutions politiques de l'Orient latin', in *Oriente e occidente nel medio evo* (Accademia nazionale dei Lincei, Fondazione 'Alessandro Volta', XII Convengo 'Volta'; Rome, 1957).

CONDER, C. R., and KITCHENER, H. H., *Survey of Western Palestine: Memoirs of the Topography, Orography, Hydrography and Archaeology*, 3 vols. (London, 1881–3).

DESCHAMPS, P., *Les Châteaux des croises en Terre Sainte*, ii. *La Défense du royaume de Jérusalem* (Haut Commissariat de la République française en Syrie et au Liban, Service des Antiquités et Beaux-Arts, Bibliothèque archéologique et historique, 34; Paris, 1939).

DU CANGE, C. du FRESNE, *Les Familles d'outre-mer*, ed. E. G. Rey

(Collection des documents inédits sur l'histoire de France, 18; Paris, 1869).

DUSSAUD, R., *Topographie historique de la Syrie antique et médiévale* (Paris, 1927).

EDBURY, P., 'John of Ibelin's Title to the County of Jaffa and Ascalon', *EHR* 98 (1983), 115–133.

FAVREAU, M. L., 'Die Kreuzfahrerherrschaft Scandalion (Iskanderune)' *ZDPV* 93 (1977), 12–29.

GROUSSET, R., *Histoire des croisades et du royaume franc de Jérusalem*, 3 vols. (Paris, 1934–6).

HAGENMEYER, H., 'Chronologie de l'histoire du royaume de Jérusalem: Regne de Baudouin I (1101–1118)', *ROL* 9 (1902), *ROL* 10 (1903–4), *ROL* 11 (1905–8), *ROL* 12 (1911).

—— 'Chronologie de la première croisade', *ROL* 6 (1898), *ROL* 7 (1900), *ROL* 8 (1900–1).

HAMILTON, B., *The Latin Church in the Crusader States* (London, 1980).

HILSCH, P., 'Der Deutsche Ritterorden im sudlichen Libanon', *ZDPV* 96 (1980), 174–89.

HOLT, P. M., 'Baybars' Treaty with the Lady of Beirut in 667–1269', in P. W. Edbury (ed.) *Crusade and Settlement* (Cardiff, 1985).

MAS-LATRIE, L. de, 'Les Seigneurs du Crac de Montreal', *Archivio Veneto*, vol. 25 (1883).

MAYER, H. E., 'Studies in the History of Queen Melisende of Jerusalem', *Dumbarton Oaks Papers*, 26 (Washington, 1972).

—— 'Carving up Crusaders: The Early Ibelins and Ramlas', in B. Z. Kedar, H. E. Mayer, R. C. Smail (eds.), *Outremer* (Jerusalem, 1982).

—— 'Die Herrschaftsbildung in Hebron', *ZDPV* 101 (1985), 64–81.

—— 'The Origins of the County of Jaffa', *Israel Exploration Journal*, 35 (1985), 35–45.

—— 'Ibelin versus Ibelin', *Proceedings of the American Philosophical Society*, 122 (1978).

—— 'The Double County of Jaffa and Ascalon', in P. Edbury (ed.) *Crusade and Settlement* (Cardiff, 1985).

—— 'John of Jaffa, his Opponents and his Fiefs', *Proceedings of the American Philosophical Society*, 128 (1984).

—— 'The Origins of the Lordships of Ramla and Lydda', *Speculum*, 60 (1985), 537–52.

—— 'Die Seigneurie de Joscelin und der Deutsche Orden', J. Fleckenstein and M. Hellmann (eds.), *Die geistlichen Ritterorden Europas* (Sigmaringen, 1980).

MOELLER, C., 'Les Flamands du Ternois au royaume latin de Jérusalem', in *Mélanges Paul Fredericq* (Bruxelles, 1904).

LA MONTE, J. L., *Feudal Monarchy in the Latin Kingdom of Jerusalem, 1100–1291* (Monographs of the Mediaeval Academy of America, 4; Cambridge, Mass., 1932).

—— 'John d'Ibelin: The Old Lord of Beirut, 1177–1236', *Byzantion*, 12 (1937), 417–58.

—— 'The Lords of Sidon in the Twelfth and Thirteenth Centuries', *Byzantion*, 17 (1944/5), 183–211.

—— 'The Lords of Caesarea in the Period of the Crusades', *Speculum*, 22 (1947), 145–61.

—— and DOWNS, N., 'The Lords of Bethsan in the Kingdoms of Jerusalem and Cyprus', *Medievalia et Humanistica*, 6 (1950), 57–75.

NICKERSON, M. E., 'The Seigneury of Beirut in the Twelfth Century and the Brisebarre Family of Beirut-Blanchegarde', *Byzantion*, 19 (1949), 141–85.

PRAWER, J., *Crusader Institutions* (Oxford, 1980).

—— and BENVENISTI, M., 'Crusader Palestine', Sheet 12/IX of the *Atlas of Israel* (Jerusalem, 1960).

PRINGLE, D., 'Excavations at Al-Burj Al-Ahmar', Society for the Study of the Crusades and the Latin East, Bulletin 4 (1984).

—— 'Reconstructing the Castle of Safad', *Palestine Exploration Quarterly*, 117 (1985).

—— *The Red Tower (Al-Burj al-Ahmar): Settlement in the Plain of Sharon at the Time of the Crusaders and Mamluks 1099–1516* (London, 1986).

REY, E., 'Les seigneurs de Mont-Real et de la Terre d'outre le Jourdain', *ROL* 4 (1896).

—— 'Les Seigneurs de Baruth', *ROL* 4 (1896).

—— *Les Colonies franques de Syrie au XIIeme et XIIIeme siècles* (Paris, 1883).

RICHARD, J., *Le Royaume latin de Jérusalem* (Paris, 1953).

—— 'Les Listes des seigneuries dans "Le Livre de Jean d'Ibelin": recherches sur l'Assebebe et Mimars', *RHDFE*, 4. 32 (1954).

RILEY-SMITH, J. S. C., *The Knights of St John in Jerusalem and Cyprus, c.1050–1310* (London, 1967).

—— 'The Motives of the Earliest Crusaders and the Settlement of Latin Palestine, 1095–1100', *English Historical Review*, 98 (1983), 721–36.

—— *The Feudal Nobility and the Kingdom of Jerusalem, 1174–1277* (London, 1973).

Index